JOURNAL FOR THE STUDY OF THE OLD TESTAMENT
SUPPLEMENT SERIES
167

JSOT Press
Sheffield

Second Zechariah and the
Deuteronomic School

Raymond F. Person

Journal for the Study of the Old Testament
Supplement Series 167

Published by JSOT Press
JSOT Press is an imprint of
Sheffield Academic Press Ltd
343 Fulwood Road
Sheffield S10 3BP
England

Typeset by Sheffield Academic Press
and
Printed on acid-free paper in Great Britain
by Biddles Ltd
Guildford

British Library Cataloguing in Publication Data

Person, Raymond Franklin
    Second Zechariah and the Deuteronomic
    School.—(JSOT Supplement Series, ISSN
    0309-0787; No. 167
    I. Title II. Series
    224

ISBN 1-85075-455-1

CONTENTS

ACKNOWLEDGMENTS

This work, a revision of my PhD dissertation, marks the end of my many years as a full-time student in institutions of higher education. During this time, I have received tremendous support from numerous people too many to mention, including family and friends, professors and peers: in Memphis, Tennessee, where I grew up; in Enid, Oklahoma, where I attended Phillips University and Phillips Graduate Seminary; in Göttingen, Germany, where I studied for seven months; in Durham, North Carolina, where I attended Duke University; and in Pittsboro, North Carolina, where I wrote this work. To all of the people in these and other places who have touched my life, I say 'thanks'.

I especially want to thank the members of my dissertation committee–Eric M. Meyers, my advisor, James L. Crenshaw, Melvin K.H. Peters, Carol L. Meyers, and Wesley A. Kort. A special thanks also goes to S. Elizabeth Kelly, my wife, who has supported me through the hardest of times. In addition, I thank Stacy M. Adams and Thomas A. Lavery, two students at Ohio Northern University, for their careful preparation of the indexes.

ABBREVIATIONS

AB	Anchor Bible
AOAT	Alter Orient und Altes Testament
ATANT	Abhandlungen zur Theologie des Alten und Neuen Testaments
ATD	Das Alte Testament Deutsch
ATDan	Acta theologica danica
AUSS	*Andrews University Seminary Studies*
BETL	Bibliotheca ephemeridum theologicarum lovaniensium
BHS	*Biblia hebraica stuttgartensia*
Bib	*Biblica*
BIOSCS	Bullentin of the International Society of Septuagint and Cognate Studies
BWANT	Beiträge zur Wissenschaft vom Alten und Neuen Testament
BZ	*Biblische Zeitschrift*
BZAW	Beihefte zur *ZAW*
CBC	Cambridge Bible Commentary
CBQ	*Catholic Biblical Quarterly*
ConBOT	Coniectanea biblica, Old Testament
EvT	*Evangelische Theologie*
FOTL	The Forms of the Old Testament Literature
FRLANT	Forschungen zur Religion und Literatur des Alten und Neuen Testaments
GTA	Göttingen Theologishe Arbeiten
GTJ	*Grace Theological Journal*
HAR	*Hebrew Annual Review*
HSM	Harvard Semitic Monographs
HTR	*Harvard Theological Review*
HUCA	*Hebrew Union College Annual*
IBC	Interpretation: A Bible Commentary for Teaching and Preaching
IBS	*Irish Biblical Studies*
ICC	International Critical Commentary
IEJ	*Israel Exploration Journal*
Int	*Interpretation*
JAOS	*Journal of the American Oriental Society*
JBL	*Journal of Biblical Literature*
JEA	*Journal of Egyptian Archaeology*

JETS	*Journal of the Evangelical Theological Society*
JNES	*Journal of Near Eastern Studies*
JNSL	*Journal of Northwest Semitic Languages*
JQR	*Jewish Quarterly Review*
JSOT	*Journal for the Study of the Old Testament*
JSOTSup	*Journal for the Study of the Old Testament* Supplement Series
NCB	New Century Bible
NICOT	New International Commentary on the Old Testament
NovTSup	*Novum Testamentum* Supplements
OBO	Orbis biblicus et orientalis
Or	*Orientalia* (Rome)
OTL	Old Testament Library
OTS	*Oudtestamentische Studiën*
PEQ	*Palestine Exploration Quarterly*
PTMS	Pittsburgh Theological Monograph Series
RB	*Revue biblique*
RHPR	*Revue d'historie et de philosophie religieuses*
SB	Sources bibliques
SBLDS	SBL Dissertation Series
SBT	Studies in Biblical Theology
ScrHier	Scripta Hierosolymitana
TDOT	G.J. Botterweck and H. Ringgren (eds.), *Theological Dictionary of the Old Testament*
ThWAT	G.J. Botterweck and H. Ringgren (eds.), *Theologisches Wörterbuch zum Alten Testament*
TZ	*Theologische Zeitschrift*
VT	*Vetus Testamentum*
WBC	Word Biblical Commentary
WMANT	Wissenschaftliche Monographien zum Alten und Neuen Testament
ZAW	*Zeitschrift für die alttestamentliche Wissenschaft*
§	Identifier for examples of Deuteronomic language in II Zech (see Chapter 3)
†	Identifier for examples of Deuteronomic influence in II Zech (see Chapter 4)
‡	Identifier for examples of marked Deuteronomic influence in II Zech (see Chapter 4)

INTRODUCTION

The contention of this work is that the Deuteronomic school[1] was responsible for the canonical form of Zech with the addition of II Zech (chs. 9–14) to I Zech (chs. 1–8). This contention builds upon presuppositions drawn from previous research in both Zech studies and studies of Deuteronomic literature (DtrH, Jer).

The first group of presuppositions concerns Zech and includes the following: (1) the division of Zech into I Zech and II Zech, (2) the production of II Zech after I Zech sometime between 520 BCE and 458 BCE, and (3) the single redaction of II Zech. Thus, II Zech post-dated I Zech and was produced by one individual or group. The second group of presuppositions concerns the Deuteronomic school and its literature and includes the following: (1) both DtrH and Jer are Deuteronomic productions that underwent more than one redaction within the Deuteronomic school; (2) the evidence of multiple Deuteronomic redactions suggests a school of redactors rather than one individual; and (3) the Deuteronomic school produced works of different genres. Thus, the Deuteronomists produced works of different genres, some of which underwent various revisions. As will be argued fully below,[2] this redactional activity seems to have spanned at least the exilic and post-exilic periods.

As just noted, Jer is considered to be the result of Deuteronomic redaction. This hypothesis was first developed by J. Philip Hyatt and

---

1. In this work, the Deuteronomic school is understood to be a scribal guild which was active in the exilic and post-exilic periods (and possibly the pre-exilic period) and which reinterpreted earlier material (e.g. proto-Deut, Jeremianic poetry) within their particular theological and literary tradition. This position is developed more fully below, especially in Part I, where evidence for the post-exilic activity of the school is given, and Part III, which sketches the social setting and theology of the school in its post-exilic setting.

2. See Part I.

has been refined by numerous commentators.³ The methodology used by proponents of this hypothesis concerns the presence of phraseology and themes within the redactional prose in Jer that have parallels in DtrH. Below, this methodology and the aforementioned presuppositions concerning Zech and Deuteronomic literature combine to suggest the following conclusion: II Zech is a product of the Deuteronomic school, somewhat analogous to the Deuteronomic prose in Jer. II Zech thus greatly enhances our knowledge of the Deuteronomic school and its redactional activities in the post-exilic period.

Presuppositions

Since this work rests on the results of previous scholarship, these presuppositions require further examination.

The Redactional Division of the Book of Zechariah

The differences in content, style and vocabulary between I Zech and II Zech have been noticed since the sixteenth century.⁴ The differences

3.   J.P. Hyatt, 'Jeremiah and Deuteronomy', in *A Prophet to the Nations* (ed. L.G. Perdue and B.W. Kovacs; Winona Lake, IN: Eisenbrauns, 1984), pp. 113-27; J.P. Hyatt, 'The Deuteronomic Edition of Jeremiah', in *A Prophet to the Nations* (ed. Perdue and Kovacs), pp. 247-67; cf. R.P. Carroll, *Jeremiah* (OTL; Philadelphia: Westminster Press, 1986), pp. 38-50; S. Herrmann, *Die prophetischen Heilser-wartungen im Alten Testament* (BWANT, 5.5; Stuttgart: W. Kohlhammer, 1965), pp. 159-241; W. McKane, *A Critical and Exegetical Commentary on Jeremiah*, I (ICC; Edinburgh: T. & T. Clark, 1986), pp. xlvii-lxxxiii; E.W. Nicholson, *Preaching to the Exiles* (New York: Schocken Books, 1970), pp. 34-37; W. Thiel, *Die deutero-nomische Redaktion von Jeremia 1–25* (WMANT, 41; Neukirchen: Neukirchener Verlag, 1973); W. Thiel, *Die deuteronomische Redaktion von Jeremia 26–45* (WMANT, 52; Neukirchen: Neukirchener Verlag, 1981); E. Tov, 'The Literary History of the Book of Jeremiah in the Light of its Textual History', in *Empirical Models for Biblical Criticism* (ed. J.H. Tigay; Philadelphia: University of Pennsylvania Press, 1985), p. 232; M. Weinfeld, *Deuteronomy and the Deuteronomic School* (Oxford: Clarendon Press, 1972), pp. 27-32.

4.   For the most thorough discussion of these differences, see H.G. Mitchell, J.M.P. Smith and J.A. Bewer, *Haggai, Zechariah, Malachi and Jonah* (ICC; Edinburgh: T. & T. Clark, 1912), pp. 233-44. For reviews of scholarship, see T. Chary, *Aggée–Zacharie, Malachie* (SB; Paris: Libraire Lecoffre, 1969), pp. 127-28; Mitchell, *Haggai, Zechariah*, pp. 244-59; B. Otzen, *Studien über Deutero-sacharja* (ATDan, 6; Copenhagen: Prostant apud Munksgaard, 1964), pp. 11-34; M. Saebø, *Sacharja 9–14: Untersuchungen von Text und Form* (WMANT, 34;

in content include the following: (1) The prophet Zechariah is mentioned by name in I Zech (1.1, 7; 7.1, 8), but not in II Zech. (2) I Zech includes date formulae (1.1, 7; 7.1); II Zech has none. (3) In I Zech, Joshua ben Jehozadak (3.1, 3, 6, 8, 9; 6.11) and Zerubbabel (4.6, 7, 9, 10) play important roles as leaders; in II Zech, no particular leader is named. (4) The restoration of the temple is central to I Zech; in II Zech, the temple is assumed to have been rebuilt and no longer receives emphasis. (5) I Zech primarily concerns the province Yehud; the purview of II Zech is more universal. The stylistic differences include three elements: (1) In I Zech, visions are important; in II Zech, no visions are found. (2) I Zech refers to 'the former prophets' (1.4; 7.7, 12), but II Zech is much more heavily influenced by earlier prophetic material and draws upon a wider spectrum of earlier material.[5] In addition, even though it is heavily dependent on earlier prophets, II Zech does not demonstrate the influence of Hag,[6] thereby bringing into question the authenticity of II Zech, since Zechariah and Haggai were presumably contemporary prophets with similar goals and views. (3) Whereas I Zech is closer to classical prophecy, II Zech is closer to apocalyptic literature.[7] The differences in vocabulary include characteristic phraseology of I Zech not found in II Zech and vice versa.[8] Because of these differences, the division of Zech is widely accepted.

Until recently, the division of Zech was based solely upon these differences. This division, however, has now received support from

Neukirchen: Neukirchener Verlag, 1969), pp. 14-20.

5. On the relationship of II Zech to earlier biblical material, see M. Delcor, 'Les sources du Deutéro-Zacharie et ses procédés d'emprunt', *RB* 59 (1952), pp. 385-411; R.A. Mason, 'Some Examples of Inner Biblical Exegesis in Zech IX–XIV', *Studia Evangelica* 7 (1982), pp. 343-54; and R.A. Mason, 'The Use of Earlier Biblical Material in Zechariah 9–14: A Study of Inner Biblical Exegesis' (PhD dissertation, University of London, 1973).

6. The most comprehensive work to date on inner-biblical exegesis in II Zech is Mason's dissertation, 'Use of Earlier Biblical Material in Zechariah 9–14'. In this work, there is only one reference to Haggai (p. 93).

7. See R. North, 'Prophecy to Apocalyptic via Zechariah', in *Congress Volume, Uppsala 1971* (ed. H. Nyberg *et al.*; VTSup, 17; Leiden: E.J. Brill, 1972), pp. 47-71.

8. For a list of these differences, see Mitchell, *Haggai, Zechariah*, pp. 236, 322.

the use of statistical linguistics in studies by Yehuda Radday and his colleagues and by David Petersen and Stephen Portnoy.[9]

The Achaemenid Date of II Zech

Although there has been wide agreement on the division of Zech, there has been no unanimity about the dating of II Zech. Suggested dates range from the eighth to the second century BCE.[10] Until recently, most suggestions for the date have been based upon the commentator's understanding of supposed allusions to historical events. For example, since Wilhelm Rudolph understood יון חניכי ('die Kämpen Griechen-lands'—his reconstructed Hebrew text for Zech 9.13) to refer to the time of Alexander the Great, he assigned Zech 11.4–13.9 to the Hellenistic period.[11] However, recent studies have suggested the futility of relating II Zech to historical events for the purpose of dating because II Zech differs from earlier prophetic material. This point has been argued most forcefully by Paul Hanson and Rex Mason. Hanson, for example, described the methodological flaws in trying to relate II Zech to political history in his discussion of Zech 9:

> [T]he genre of the composition has been perceived incorrectly, and thus an inappropriate method of interpretation has been applied; in short, a Divine Warrior Hymn has been mistaken for a poetic report of an histori-cal event, that is to say, cosmic war has become confused with mundane war.[12]

9.   Y.T. Radday and D. Wickman, 'The Unity of Zechariah Examined in the Light of Statisical Linguistics', *ZAW* 87 (1975), pp. 30-55; Y.T. Radday and M.A. Pollatschek, 'Vocabulary Richness in Post-Exilic Prophetic Books', *ZAW* 92 (1980), pp. 333-46. Cf. S.L. Portnoy and D.L. Petersen, 'Biblical Texts and Statistical Analysis: Zechariah and Beyond', *JBL* 103 (1984), pp. 11-21. Portnoy and Petersen strongly criticized the method used by Radday and his colleagues and concluded that II Zech requires subdivision (chs. 9–11 = II Zech; chs. 12–14 = III Zech). However, Yadday and his colleagues, on the one hand, and Portnoy and Petersen, on the other, are in agreement concerning the division of Zech into I Zech and II Zech.

10.   A.E. Hill, 'Dating Second Zechariah: A Linguistic Re-examination', *HAR* 6 (1982), p. 106.

11.   W. Rudolph, *Haggai–Sacharja 1-8–Sacharja 9-14–Malaechi* (KAT, XIII/4; Gütersloh: Gütersloh Verlagshaus Gerd Mohn, 1976), pp. 183-84, 187-88.

12.   P.D. Hanson, 'Zechariah 9 and the Recapitulation of an Ancient Ritual Pattern', *JBL* 92 (1973), pp. 37-38. See also North, 'Prophecy to Apocalyptic via Zechariah', pp. 70-71.

Mason, likewise, asserted that 'the traditional questions of date, historical context and authorship are not the most helpful ones to ask first of these chapters'.[13] His conclusion is based upon his work on inner-biblical exegesis in II Zech, which suggests that II Zech refers more often to earlier biblical material than to contemporary historical events. Taken together, the critiques of Hanson and Mason strongly suggest that II Zech, which has apocalyptic interests and which uses earlier biblical material, does not regularly refer to historical events. Rather, II Zech refers to earlier traditions in light of expectations concerning the future.

Since relating II Zech to historical events is not helpful in determining its date, what other methods can be used? As early as 1881, Bernhard Stade utilized inner-biblical exegesis as a means for proposing a late date for II Zech (306–278 BCE).[14] Following Stade's lead, many other commentators—including Matthias Delcor (third century BCE), Rex Mason (300 BCE), and H.G. Mitchell (333–217 BCE)[15]—have argued that II Zech's dependence on earlier biblical material requires a late date for II Zech. This argument finds its strongest support in Mason's observation that II Zech reinterprets I Zech and must, therefore, be dated later.[16] Today, based upon the observation of literary dependence of II Zech on earlier biblical material, there is a growing consensus that II Zech postdates I Zech.

Although the use of inner-biblical exegesis is leading to a consensus that II Zech postdates I Zech, disagreement concerning the date of II Zech has continued to focus upon what commentators understood to be historical references in II Zech. For example, Delcor's argument for a date in the third century BCE rested upon his understanding of allusions to Alexander the Great in Zech 9.1-8.[17] Such argumentation

13. 'Some Examples', p. 343. See also 'Use of Earlier Biblical Material in Zechariah 9–14', p. 2.

14. B. Stade, 'Deuterosacharja. Eine kritische Studie', *ZAW* 1 (1881), pp. 1-96; 2 (1882), pp. 151-72, 275-309. See the discussion of Stade's influence on Zech studies in Mitchell, *Haggai, Zechariah*, pp. 250-59; Otzen, *Studien über Deuterosacharja*, pp. 26-34.

15. Delcor, 'Sources', pp. 402-406; Mason, 'Use of Earlier Biblical Material in Zechariah 9–14', p. 310; Mitchell, *Haggai, Zechariah*, pp. 250-59.

16. R.A. Mason, 'The Relation of Zech. 9–14 to Proto-Zechariah', *ZAW* 88 (1976), pp. 227-39.

17. M. Delcor, 'Les allusions a Alexandre le Grand dans Zach 9.1-8', *VT* 1 (1951), pp. 110-24. See also 'Sources', pp. 402-406.

for the date of II Zech does not properly recognize the genre of II Zech, for II Zech refers more to eschatological time and earlier biblical material than historical events. Another method is therefore required. Such a method may be statistical linguistics, which Andrew Hill has applied to the question of the date of II Zech.[18] Adapting Robert Polzin's typological, linguistic approach,[19] Hill compared grammatical and syntactic features of II Zech to those of other late Hebrew literature and concluded that the date of II Zech is sometime between Hag–Zech 1–8 (520 BCE) and Ezra (458 BCE).[20] The validity of his dating of II Zech is assumed in this work.

The Unity of II Zech[21]

Until recently, many scholars dated II Zech according to their interpretation of assumed historical references in the text. Some of these same scholars translated these assumptions into what they understood to be evidence of various collections within II Zech. For example, Benedikt Otzen identified four collections on the basis of allusions he found to historical events.[22] (1) Zech 9–10 from the time of Josiah; (2) Zech 11 immediately before the destruction of Jerusalem; (3) Zech 12–13 from the early exilic period; and (4) Zech 14 from the late post-exilic period. Similarly, H.G. Mitchell understood Zech 9–14 as being composed in four stages.[23] (1) Zech 9.1-10 was an independent oracle 'soon after the battle of Issus'; (2) Zech 9.11–11.3 dates from the time of Ptolemy III; (3) the 'pessimistic' Zech 11.4-17; 13.7-9 was written 'soon after the battle of Raphia'; and (4) the 'optimistic' Zech 12.1-13.6; 14.1-21 dates from about the same time as Zech 11.4-17; 13.7-9. Likewise, Douglas Jones argued for three divisions—Zech 9–11; 12–13; 14—with the first coming from a prophet in Damascus and the

18. 'Dating Second Zechariah'.

19. R. Polzin, *Late Biblical Hebrew* (HSM, 12; Missoula, MT: Scholars Press, 1976).

20. 'Dating Second Zechariah', p. 130. P.D. Hanson (*The Dawn of Apocalyptic* [Philadelphia: Fortress Press, 1979], pp. 286-87, 400) dated II Zech between 475 BCE and 425 BCE, on the basis of his reconstruction of the development of apocalyptic eschatology.

21. For a review of scholarship concerning this issue, see especially Chary, *Aggée–Zacharie, Malachie*, pp. 131-34.

22. *Studien über Deuterosacharja*, p. 212.

23. *Haggai, Zechariah*, pp. 258-59.

others from two Judaean prophets.[24] Such arguments do not take adequate account of the literary character of II Zech and, therefore, have been rejected in relationship to the date of II Zech. Such arguments also should not be used to address the question of the unity of II Zech and are likewise rejected.

Another part of the argument against the unity of II Zech concerns the superscription משא דבר יהוה, which occurs only three times in the Hebrew Bible (Zech 9.1; 12.1; Mal 1.1). Because this superscription suggests a literary division between Zech 1–8; 9–11 and 12–14, some commentators have referred to three source divisions as, respectively, I Zech, II Zech and III Zech.[25] However, this superscription is possibly a later addition which divided an originally unified work (II Zech) when Mal, another collection of prophetic material, was appended. Hence, the occurrence of this superscription does not, by itself, suggest a division of II Zech.

The most recent argument for divisions within Zech 9–14 is that of Stephen Portnoy and David Petersen.[26] They combine two approaches: critical biblical exegesis and statistical linguistics. Within his argument from the area of biblical exegesis, Petersen[27] made three types of observations—on content, form and tradition history—which he understood as suggesting the division of Zech 12–14 from Zech 9–11: Concerning content, he claimed that Zech 9–11 differs from Zech 12–14 in that Zech 9–11 refers to the 'shepherds, a metaphoric reference to the community's leaders', whereas in Zech 12–14 'there is only a vague reference to such community functionaries'.[28] Concerning form, he made three observations: (1) Zechariah 9–11 adapt forms that are

24. D.R. Jones, *Haggai, Zechariah, Malachi* (Torch Commentary; London: SCM Press, 1962), pp. 117-20, 170-71. See also D.R. Jones, 'A Fresh Interpretation of Zechariah IX–XI', *VT* 12 (1962), pp. 241-59.

25. E.R. Achtemeier, *Nahum–Malachi* (IBC; Atlanta: John Knox, 1986) p. 107; Chary, *Aggée–Zacharie, Malachie*, pp. 138-39; B.S. Childs, *Introduction to the Old Testament as Scripture* (Philadelphia: Fortress Press, 1979), pp. 479-81. Achtemeier, Chary and Childs limited their division of II Zech to Zech 9–11 and Zech 12–14. However, those who have more complicated divisions of II Zech also used this observation as a part of their argument. See also those works listed in nn. 22-24 above.

26. 'Zechariah and Beyond'.

27. Since Portnoy is a statistican, I assume that the comments concerning the results of critical methods in biblical studies represent Petersen's own work.

28. Portnoy and Petersen, 'Zechariah and Beyond', p. 18.

found elsewhere in prophetic literature (i.e. divine warrior hymns, taunt song, commissioning narrative), whereas Zech 12–14 'defy simple form-critical classification'.[29] (2) In contrast to Zech 9–11, Zech 12–14 use the phrase 'on that day' as a structural device. (3) Zech 9–11 are 'essentially poetry' in contrast to Zech 12–14, which are 'essentially prose'.[30] Concerning tradition history, he distinguished Zech 9–11 from Zech 12–14 in that the former is an example of 'early apocalyptic' and the latter, 'middle and late apocalyptic'.[31]

With the assistance of Portnoy (a statistican), Petersen supported his arguments from critical exegetical methods with the results of their statistical analysis. They concluded that there are three distinct divisions in Zech: 1–8, 9–11 and 12–14. Thus, they argued that the combined results of Petersen's exegesis and their statistical analysis suggest that Zech 9–11 and Zech 12–14 are distinct units from different authors.

Although their effort to integrate exegetical methods with statistical linguistics is commendable, some criticisms of the application of their integrated method, both of Petersen's conclusions from his exegetical work and of the data base for their statistical analysis, are in order. First, Petersen's exegetical conclusions based on content, form and tradition history will be examined. Concerning content, he strove to maintain a difference between the portrayal of leadership between Zech 9–11 and Zech 12–14; however, that difference is weak. What significant difference is there between a 'metaphoric reference' to leadership in Zech 9–11 and a 'vague reference' to leadership in Zech 12–14? In my judgment, the 'metaphoric reference' of 'shepherd' in Zech 9–11 also appears to be 'vague'. Also, this 'metaphoric reference' reoccurs in Zech 12–14 (13.7). Therefore, his argument based upon content for the division of II Zech is rejected. Concerning form, he presented three observations which he understood to suggest the division of II Zech: (1) Formal differences between Zech 9–11 and Zech 12–14 suggest different authors. This argument improperly assumes that an author is unlikely to change forms when the content suggests such a change. Although he allowed for formal variety in

29. Portnoy and Petersen, 'Zechariah and Beyond', p. 19.

30. Portnoy and Petersen, 'Zechariah and Beyond', p. 20.

31. Portnoy and Petersen, 'Zechariah and Beyond', p. 20. Here, Petersen's argument is quite similar to that of O. Plöger, *Theocracy and Eschatology* (Oxford: Blackwell, 1968), pp. 78-96.

Zech 9–11, he disallowed formal differences between Zech 9–11 and
Zech 12–14. Could it not be that the same author both adapted known
prophetic forms and created new forms as the change in his themes
required? Are there not other passages in prophetic literature that
'defy simple form-critical classification'? (2) The phrase 'on that day'
is concentrated in Zech 12–14.[32] However, it is also found in Zech
9–11.[33] Also, since the phrase 'on that day' has eschatological connota-
tions, one would expect it to be concentrated in the material emphasizing eschatological themes (i.e. Zech 12–14). Therefore, the same
author may have heightened his use of the formula 'on that day' when
he began his discussion of the future day of Yahweh. (3) Zech 9–11
are 'essentially poetry'. But, this contradicts studies of statistical
linguistics concerning prose particles. J. Hoftijzer analysized the prose
particle את in Zech 9–14 and concluded that Zech 10–14 were prose
and Zech 9 was poetry.[34] Therefore, Petersen's argument is circular
in that he assumed[35] Zech 9–11 to be poetry and then contrasted this
'poetry' to the prose in Zech 12–14. Concerning tradition history,
Petersen's distinction between Zech 9–11 as 'early apocalyptic' and
Zech 12–14 as 'middle and late apocalyptic' is not the only interpretation that can be given to this material. For example, consider
Robert North's position:

> At first sight his disconnectedness seems…to postulate a distinct Third or
> Fourth Zechariah. Yet various types of artful structuring have been seen
> by experts to unite all of Zc ix–xiv and thereby give it also a kinship with
> the erudite structures of Apocalyptic.[36]

In summary, Petersen's exegesis of II Zech is circular and, therefore,
does not necessarily support the statistical analysis done with Portnoy.

Petersen's determination of Zech 9–11 as poetry contradicts studies
of prose particles. If Zech 9 is poetry and Zech 10–11 are prose, then

32. Zech 12.3, 4, 6, 8 (2×), 9, 11; 13.1, 2, 4; 14.4, 6, 8, 9, 13, 20, 2 1.

33. Zech 9.6; 11.11. On this phrase, see §19 below.

34. J. Hoftijzer, 'Remarks concerning the Use of the Particle את in Classical
Hebrew', *OTS* 14 (1965), pp. 76-77. Hill ('Dating Second Zechariah', p. 107)
followed Hoftijzer's analysis. See also E.M. Meyers, 'Messianism in First and
Second Zechariah and the "End" of Biblical Prophecy', in *Dwight Young Festschrift*
(Winona Lake, IN: Eisenbrauns: forthcoming), pp. 8-9, 22 n. 20.

35. Petersen provides no reasons for classifying Zech 9–11 as poetry in this
article.

36. 'Prophecy to Apocalyptic via Zechariah', p. 71.

the data base that Portnoy and Petersen used is seriously skewed. In other words, if Zech 9 is a poetic source (used by the redactor of Zech 9–11), it should be removed from the statistical base for Zech 9–11 so as to enable a comparison of the prose of Zech 10–11 to that of Zech 12–14.[37] If, as suggested by Portnoy and Petersen, this is such an 'exacerbated' problem when comparing Zech 1–8 to Zech 9–14,[38] it would be further exacerbated when comparing the smaller units of Zech 9–11 and Zech 12–14. Therefore, the data base for their statistical analysis depended upon Petersen's questionable determination that all of Zech 9–11 was poetry from the hand of a different author than the prose of Zech 12–14. Since their statistical analysis has serious methodological problems concerning their data base, their conclusions concerning the division of II Zech are rejected.

The arguments against the unity of II Zech have just been questioned on methodological grounds. But, what is the validity of the arguments for the unity of II Zech? In the following paragraphs, arguments for the unity of II Zech will be reviewed.

Paul Lamarche argued for the unity of Zech 9–14 on the basis of a literary analysis. He presented an elaborate chiastic pattern for the structure of Zech 9–14,[39] which he assumed proved the literary unity of II Zech. Although his literary analysis was artful, it did not necessarily suggest the unity of Zech 9–14, for such a literary analysis can show literary unity for literature known to have come from various individuals.[40] In other words, such literary analysis can demonstrate the present *literary* unity of a work, whether unified or composite, but it *cannot* demonstrate that such a literary unity was necessarily the result of *one individual*. Therefore, Lamarche's analysis cannot stand alone as evidence of the unity of II Zech.

The type of work which, in my opinion, best demonstrates the unity

37. In his statistical analysis, Hill ('Dating Second Zechariah', p. 107) likewise argued that the poetry in Zech 9 must be removed from the data base for Zech 9–11 for purposes of comparison.

38. Portnoy and Petersen, 'Zechariah and Beyond', p. 15.

39. *Zacharie IX–XIV* (Paris: Gabala, 1961), pp. 112-13.

    A. Lacocque ('Zacharie 9–14', in *Commentaire de l'ancien Testament*, XIc [Neuchatel: Delachaux & Niestlé, 1981], p. 131) assumed Lamarche's conclusion.

40. E.g. R.W. Pierce, 'Literary Connectors and a Haggai/Zechariah/Malachi Corpus', *JETS* 27 (1984), pp. 277-88; R. Polzin, *Moses and the Deuteronomist* (New York: Seabury, 1980); D.A. Schneider, 'The Unity of the Book of the Twelve' (PhD dissertation, Yale University, 1979).

of II Zech is the work on inner-biblical exegesis in II Zech. Delcor observed that the different sections of II Zech are similar in that they all are heavily dependent on earlier biblical material, especially the following prophetic works in order of their importance: Ezek, Jer, II Isa and III Isa.[41] Because of this similarity, he concluded that 'an attentive examination shows that the thought, preoccupations, expressions are substantially the same';[42] therefore, II Zech is the work of one author.

Building upon the work of Delcor, Mason reached similar conclusions in his 1973 dissertation.[43] (1) Like Delcor, he pointed to various parallels between the different sections of II Zech and previous prophetic literature, especially II Isa, III Isa, Jer and Ezek. He later wrote:

> the literary dependence...is found in all sections of chs. 9–14...Again this suggests that...they must have been edited, used and presented by those who shared a similar outlook.[44]

(2) His work also showed a continuity from I Zech to II Zech concerning the following themes: 'the prominence of the Zion tradition; the divine cleansing of the community; universalism; the appeal to the earlier prophets; and the provision of leadership as a sign of new age'.[45] Because of these two observations, he concluded that 'we seem to have here the work of a prophet or traditio-circle who revered the words of the great prophets, and who saw in them predictions which were to be filled in the later events of their own day'.[46]

41. 'Sources', p. 411.

42. 'Sources', p. 411. My translation.

43. 'Uses of Earlier Biblical Material in Zechariah 9–14'. Mason's two articles ('Some Examples'; 'Relation of Zech 9–14 to Proto-Zechariah') are based upon his unpublished dissertation. When possible, I refer to Mason's articles, which are more available to the reader.

44. *The Book of Haggai, Zechariah, and Malachi* (CBC; Cambridge: Cambridge University Press, 1977), p. 81.

45. 'Relation of Zech 9–14 to Proto-Zechariah', p. 238.

46. 'Some Examples', p. 353. See also *Haggai, Zechariah, and Malachi*, p. 79; 'Uses of Earlier Biblical Material in Zechariah 9–14', pp. 297-98. Mason used 'traditio-circle' because he concluded that Zech 14 is a somewhat later work by someone within the same tradition circle as Zech 9–13. This conclusion is based upon what Mason saw as a more schismatic outlook in Zech 14 than in Zech 9–13 ('Uses of Earlier Biblical Material in Zechariah 9–14', p. 298). Since, as even Mason acknowledged, this difference was simply one of degree, it is possible that one redactor built up to such a view at the end of his work.

Below, I develop further the conclusions of Delcor and Mason, who suggest that the consistent dependence of II Zech on earlier biblical material suggests that II Zech is unified—that is, the work of one individual. This development builds upon the observation that not only did the redactor of II Zech borrow heavily from prophetic literature, but that II Zech is especially influenced by Deuteronomic literature, including Deuteronomic phraseology. Such a heavy influence suggests that II Zech is the product of a Deuteronomist. Therefore, I likewise argue for the unity of II Zech.

The Unity of the Deuteronomic History and its Multiple Redactions[47]
Since the primary contention of this work is that II Zech is the result of a Deuteronomic redaction, it is necessary to discuss my understanding of the Deuteronomic school and its literature.

Martin Noth's 1943 work on DtrH[48] set the stage for later discussions of this material. He argued that Deut–Kgs was the unified work of an exilic historian. This historian, the 'Deuteronomist', edited various sources into a unified narrative that began with Moses in Egypt (Deut) and ended with the exile (Kgs). The thesis that Deut–Kgs demonstrates a unity because of a common redactional process has been widely assumed since Noth's work.

In relationship to Noth's thesis concerning the redaction history of DtrH, three schools can be identified.[49] (1) The unity school is comprised of those who, following Noth, still maintain that DtrH is the product of one individual, one redaction.[50] (2) The dual-redaction

47. For a recent survey of scholarship on DtrH, see P.R. Ackroyd, 'The Historical Literature', in *The Hebrew Bible and its Modern Interpreters* (ed. D.A. Knight and G.M. Tucker; SBLBMI, 1; Philadelphia: Fortress Press; Chico, CA: Scholars Press, 1985), pp. 297-323. For my more detailed discussion, see below, Chapter 1.

48. *Überlieferungsgeschichtliche Studien* (Tübingen: Niemeyer, 1943). English translation of the first part concerning DtrH: *Deuteronomistic History* (JSOTSup, 15; Sheffield: JSOT Press, 1981).

49. Some scholars do not fall into any of the schools discussed below. E.g. M. Rose, *Deuteronomist und Jahwist* (ATANT, 67; Zürich: Theologischer Verlag, 1981); J. Van Seters, *In Search of History* (New Haven: Yale University Press, 1988); H. Weippert, 'Die "deuteronomistischen" Beurteilungen der Könige von Israel und Juda und das Problem der Redaktion der Königsbücher', *Bib* 53 (1972), pp. 301-39.

50. E.g. H.-D. Hoffmann, *Reform und Reformen* (ATANT, 66; Zürich: Theologischer Verlag, 1980), pp. 316-20; B.O. Long, *I Kings with an Introduction*

school has as its founder Frank Cross.[51] He identified two redactions of DtrH. The first redaction (Dtr[1]) occurred during the reign of Josiah and emphasized the sin of the northern kingdom and the eternal covenant with David. The second redaction (Dtr[2]) occurred during the exile and emphasized the disobedience to Yahweh's word through the prophets and the need of repentance for the basis of any future restoration. Cross has had many supporters, especially among his Harvard students and other American scholars.[52] (3) The trito-redaction school comes from the combined effort of the Göttingen scholar Rudolph Smend and his student, Walter Dietrich.[53] They argued for three redactions of DtrH with a different perspective by each redactor—a history writer (DtrG), a prophetic redactor, (DtrP) and a nomistic redactor (DtrN). They also have found many supporters, especially among Smend's students and other European scholars.[54]

to Historical Literature (FOTL, 9; Grand Rapids: Eerdmans, 1984), pp. 31-32; Polzin, *Moses*, p. 72; R. Polzin, *Samuel and the Deuteronomist* (San Francisco: Harper & Row, 1989), pp. 9-11, 64, 72.

51. 'The Themes of the Book of Kings and the Structure of the Deuteronomic History', in *Canaanite Myth and Hebrew Epic* (Cambridge: Cambridge University Press, 1973), pp. 274-89.

52. E.g. B.C. Birch, *The Rise of the Israelite Monarchy* (SBLDS, 27; Missoula, MT: Scholars Press, 1976); R. E. Friedman, *The Exile and Biblical Narrative* (HSM, 22; Chico, CA: Scholars Press, 1981), pp. 1-43; B. Halpern, *The First Historians* (San Francisco: Harper & Row, 1988); A.D.H. Mayes, *The Story of Israel between Settlement and Exile* (London: SCM Press, 1983); P.K. McCarter, *I Samuel* (AB, 8; Garden City, NY: Doubleday, 1980); R.D. Nelson, *The Double Redaction of the Deuteronomistic History* (JSOTSup, 18; Sheffield: JSOT Press, 1981).

53. R. Smend, 'Das Gesetz und die Völker. Ein Betrag zur deuteronomistischen Redaktionsgeschichte', in *Probleme biblischer Theologie* (ed. H.W. Wolff; Munich: Chr. Kaiser Verlag, 1971), pp. 494-509; R. Smend, *Die Entstehung des Alten Testaments* (Stuttgart: W. Kohlhammer, 1981), pp. 110-25. Cf. W. Dietrich, *Prophetie und Geschichte* (FRLANT, 108; Göttingen: Vandenhoeck & Ruprecht, 1972); W. Dietrich, *David, Saul und die Propheten* (BWANT, 7.2; Stuttgart: W. Kohlhammer, 1987).

54. E.g. G. Hentschel, *1 Könige* (Neue Echter Bibel; Würzburg: Echter Verlag, 1984), pp. 7-9; T.N.D. Mettinger, *The Dethronement of Sabaoth* (trans. F.H. Cryer; ConBOT, 18; Lund: CWK Gleerup, 1982), p. 38; J.A. Soggin, *Judges* (OTL; Philadelphia: Westminster Press, 1981), p. xi; H. Spieckermann, *Juda unter Assur in der Sargonidzeit* (FRLANT, 129; Göttingen: Vandenhoeck & Ruprecht, 1982); T. Veijola, *Die ewige Dynastie* (Helsinki: Academia Scientarium Fennica, 1975); E. Würthwein, *Die Bücher der Könige: 1 Könige 1–16* (ATD, 11.1; Göttingen:

These three schools accept Noth's basic thesis that there is a literary unity that justifies the identification of Deut–Kgs as DtrH; that view is also is assumed here. Like the dual-redaction and the trito-redaction school (and against the unity school), the contention that DtrH underwent at least two Deuteronomic redactions is argued below. However, the formulation of this contention as presented in this work differs significantly from the specific formulations of both the dual-redaction and the trito-redaction school. The evidence presented below[55] suggests that there was, at least, an exilic and a post-exilic redaction of DtrH, but it contradicts both the dual-redaction and trito-redaction school's approach in two ways. (1) Neither one of these redactions can be conveniently identified with the postulated redactions as understood by either school—that is, they do not correspond to either Dtr^1 or Dtr^2, on the one hand, or DtrH, DtrP or DtrN, on the other. (2) The dual-redaction school's argument for a pre-exilic redaction and the trito-redaction school's argument for two exilic redactions require further study—that is, the evidence given below neither rejects nor confirms the possibility of three or more Deuteronomic redactions. Rather, it simply suggests that there were *at least* two, an exilic and a post-exilic redaction.

The Deuteronomic Redaction of the Book of Jeremiah[56]
DtrH and II Zech differ generically in that DtrH is historigraphy and Zech is a prophetic collection; therefore, the comparison of II Zech to other Deuteronomic literature that is generically closer would be more relevant to the present study. Such a comparison can be made when Jer is considered Deuteronomic literature. Therefore, below I discuss the secondary literature concerning the argument for the Deuteronomic redaction of Jer.

Building upon previous work,[57] J. Philip Hyatt first proposed in

Vandenhoeck & Ruprecht, 1977); E. Würthwein, *Die Bücher der Köinge: 1 Könige 17–2 Könige 25* (ATD, 11.2; Göttingen: Vandenhoeck & Ruprecht, 1984).

55. See Chapter 1.

56. For recent surveys on Jer studies, see S. Herrmann, *Jeremia: Der Prophet und das Buch* (ErFor, 271; Darmstadt: Wissenschaftliche Buchgesellschaft, 1990), pp. 53-181; L.G. Perdue, 'Jeremiah in Modern Research: Approaches and Issues', in *A Prophet to the Nations* (ed. L.G. Perdue and B.W. Kovacs; Winona Lake, IN: Eisenbrauns, 1984), pp. 1-31.

57. In his most developed presentation of this understanding ('Deuteronomic

1942[58] that some form of Jer was edited by a Deuteronomic redactor. His understanding of the redaction of Jer followed the then generally accepted view of the four 'sources' of Jer: Jeremianic poetry ('source A'), Baruch's biography ('source B'), Deuteronomic prose sermons ('source C') and miscellaneous poetry and prose ('source D').[59] His innovation was that he understood the evidence for the source of Deuteronomic prose sermons ('source C') to imply not simply a source, but a Deuteronomic redaction. Thus, his overall view of Jer is as follows: A Deuteronomic redactor used Jeremianic poetry ('source A') and Baruch's biography ('source B') as sources which he reinterpreted with the addition of his own material, the prose sermons (formerly, 'source C'); therefore, the Deuteronomic redaction of Jer, according to Hyatt, is limited to Jer 1–45. In the post-exilic period, another redactor ('post-D[euteronomic]') added non-Jeremianic material ('source D').

In his 1942 article concerning the relationship of the prophet Jeremiah to Deut, Hyatt suggested that 'one of the main purposes of these editors...was to attempt to show that Jeremiah did approve of the Deuteronomic reforms'.[60] The types of evidence he presented include the following:[61] (1) 'dates in the Book of Jeremiah intended to make Jeremiah begin his public career before the time of the Deuteronomic reforms'; (2) 'passages inserted in Jeremiah to emphasize the existence of pre-Deuteronomic sins during the prophet's early career'; (3) 'Jer. 11.1-8 written to prove that Jeremiah was an active supporter of the Deuteronomic reforms'; (4) 'passages designed to explain the Exile and its misfortunes as due to disobedience of Yahweh and worship of foreign gods'; (5) 'passages which definitely predict restoration from Exile and future prosperity'; and (6) 'legalistic passages inserted to

Edition of Jeremiah', pp. 248-51), Hyatt briefly discussed the work of the following commentators who had recognized Deuteronomic influence in Jer: B. Duhm, C.H. Cornill, A.S. Peake, P. Volz, S. Mowinckel, G. Hölscher, H. May, R.H. Pfeiffer and W. Rudolph.

58. 'Jeremiah and Deuteronomy', pp. 121-26.

59. S. Mowinckel, *Zur Komposition des Buches Jeremia* (Kristiania: Jacob Dybwad, 1914). A contemporary commentator who maintains this view is John Bright (*Jeremiah* [AB, 21; Garden City, NY: Doubleday, 1965]).

60. 'Jeremiah and Deuteronomy', p. 121. See also, 'Deuteronomic Edition of Jeremiah', p. 264.

61. 'Jeremiah and Deuteronomy', pp. 121-26. The following quotes come from Hyatt's section headings.

prove that Jeremiah knew the laws of Deuteronomy'.

Hyatt's most developed presentation was his 1951 article, 'The Deuteronomic Edition of Jeremiah',[62] where he provided a list of Deuteronomic phraseology in the prose sermons of Jer. He then discussed each literary unit in Jer wherein he found evidence of Deuteronomic redaction and concluded with a list of what he considered to be post-Deuteronomic additions because of their post-exilic date—that is, after the presumed time of the Deuteronomic school.

Although his thesis continues to attract some dissenters,[63] Hyatt's work has influenced numerous Jer scholars, most notably W. Thiel, Ernest Nicholson, Emanuel Tov, William McKane, Robert Carroll and Ronald Clements. In the following paragraphs, these Jeremiah scholars and their development of Hyatt's thesis concerning the Deuteronomic redaction of Jer will be briefly discussed.

Building upon the work of Hyatt and Herrmann,[64] Thiel wrote a dissertation intitled 'Die deuteronomistische Redaktion des Büches Jeremia' (1970).[65] His understanding of the Deuteronomic redaction of Jer is quite similar to that of Hyatt in two ways: (1) His argument is also basically a redefinition of 'source C' into a Deuteronomic redaction. (2) Like Hyatt, he also limits Deuteronomic redaction to Jer 1–45 to which post-Deuteronomic material was added.

In *Preaching to the Exiles* (1970), Nicholson accepted Hyatt's thesis

62. See also the brief discussion in Hyatt's introduction to his commentary, 'The Book of Jeremiah', *IB*, V, pp. 788-90.

63. E.g. J. Bright, 'The Date of the Prose Sermons of Jeremiah', in *A Prophet to the Nations* (ed. L.G. Perdue and B.W. Kovacs; Winona Lake, IN: Eisenbrauns, 1984); W.L. Holladay, 'A Fresh Look at "Source B" and "Source C" in Jeremiah', in *A Prophet to the Nations* (ed. Perdue and Kovacs), pp. 213-28; J. Unterman, *From Repentance to Redemption* (JSOTSup, 54; Sheffield: JSOT Press, 1981); H. Weippert, *Die Prosareden des Jeremiasbuches* (BZAW, 132; Berlin: Walter de Gruyter, 1973). For a critique of Bright's criticism in defense of the Deuteronomic redaction of Jer, see Nicholson, *Preaching*, pp. 28-32. For a critique of Weippert's criticism in defense of the Deuteronomic redaction of Jer, see McKane, *Jeremiah*, I, pp. xli-xlvii; W. McKane, 'Relations between Poetry and Prose in the Book of Jeremiah with Special Reference to Jeremiah iii 6-11 and xii 14-17', in *A Prophet to the Nations* (ed. Perdue and Kovacs), pp. 269-84.

64. *Prophetischen Heilserwartungen*, pp. 159-241.

65. His dissertation has been published in two volumes: *Redaktion von Jeremia 1–25* (1973) and *Redaktion von Jeremia 26–45* (1981). Only the second volume underwent significant revision from his dissertation.

of the Deuteronomic redaction of Jer but developed it further with regard to the so-called Baruch's biography ('source B').[66] He argued that this 'biographical' material was primarily theological in purpose, thereby diminishing the distinction previously made between the 'theological' prose sermons ('source C') and the 'biographical' narratives ('source B'). He also noted Deuteronomic phraseology in these 'biographies'. Therefore, he concluded that the distinction between these so-called 'sources' should be rejected and that the 'biographical' material, like the prose sermons, was from the hand of a Deuteronomic redactor.

Tov's work on Jer[67] is best known for his development of the thesis that LXX-Jer preserves an earlier redaction of Jer than does MT-Jer. However, he not only accepted the thesis of the Deuteronomic redaction of Jer but went on to revise it in relationship to his text-critical work, concluding that both LXX-Jer and MT-Jer were products of Deuteronomic redaction.[68]

In three recent commentaries on Jer, the thesis of the Deuteronomic redaction of Jer is accepted. In his 1986 commentary,[69] McKane proposed the idea of a 'rolling corpus' for the composition of Jer, which included Deuteronomic redaction. Both Carroll, in his 1986 commentary,[70] and Clements, in his 1989 commentary,[71] accepted Nicholson's reformulation of the Deuteronomic redaction of Jer in that they likewise argued that the prose sermons ('source C') and the 'biographical'

---

66. *Preaching*, pp. 34-37. See also, E.W. Nicholson, *The Book of the Prophet Jeremiah: Chapters 1–25* (CBC; Cambridge: Cambridge University Press, 1973), pp. 10-16.

67. In three very similar articles, E. Tov presents his argument. These three articles are, in order of their publication: 'L'incidence de la critique textuelle sur la critique littéraire dans le livre de Jérémie', *RB* 79 (1972), pp. 189-99; 'Some Aspects of the Textual and Literary History of the Book of Jeremiah', in *Le livre de Jérémie* (ed. P.-M. Bogaert; BETL, 54; Leuven: Leuven University Press, 1981), pp. 15-67; and 'Literary History'. For further discussion of the relationship of LXX-Jer and MT-Jer, see below, Chapter 2.

68. 'L'incidence', p. 199, my translation. See also 'Aspects', p. 164; 'Literary History', p. 232.

69. *Jeremiah*, I, pp. xlvii-lxxxiii. See also 'Relations between Poetry and Prose in the Book of Jeremiah'.

70. *Jeremiah*, pp. 38-50. See also R. Carroll, *From Chaos to Covenant* (New York: Crossroad, 1981).

71. *Jeremiah* (IBC; Atlanta: John Knox, 1988), pp. 10-12.

material ('source B') are both products of Deuteronomic redaction.

I assume that the present book of Jer is basically a Deuteronomic collection. This position does not deny the possibility of some later additions. However, much of what has been considered post-Deuteronomic was identified as such based upon the assumption that the Deuteronomic redaction of Jer was produced in the exilic period. Since this assumption is refuted below,[72] the argument that post-exilic material is necessarily post-Deuteronomic is rejected; therefore, the possibility that such post-exilic material may be Deuteronomic requires re-examination. However, even if this post-exilic material were included, this material may not have come from the hand of a Deuteronomic redactor but may represent another source used by a Deuteronomic redactor (such as the oracles against the nations in Jer 46–51). As noted above, Tov's text-critical work re-enforces this position in that both LXX-Jer and the later MT-Jer are products of the Deuteronomic school.

For the present study, it is more relevant to compare Zech to the Deuteronomic redaction of Jer than to DtrH. This heightened relevance is not only because Jer and Zech are closer due to their common prophetic genre, but also because my contention of the Deuteronomic redaction of Zech depends upon my adaptation of the method used in the argument of the Deuteronomic redaction of Jer and its application to Zech.[73] With the application of this methodology, Jer and Zech are shown to be closely related in three ways: (1) the use of Deuteronomic language in the redactional material, (2) their common redactional setting (i.e. Achaemenid Yehud),[74] and (3) their shared theology.[75]

The 'Deuteronomist'/'Historian' versus the 'Deuteronomic School'
Noth's identification of one 'Deuteronomist' who was responsible for DtrH continues to have it supporters.[76] However, the previous two

72. Chapter 2.
73. See below Part II.
74. See below Chapter 7.
75. See below Chapter 8.
76. E.g. Polzin, *Moses and the Deuteronomist*; Van Seters, *In Search of History*. Although they both followed Noth's thesis, Polzin and Van Seters differ greatly. Polzin understood that DtrH is entirely the work of the 'Deuteronomist'. In contrast, Van Seters rejected the existence of a Deuteronomic school in favor of only one 'Deuteronomist'; however, he argued that DtrH has undergone extensive post-Deuteronomic redaction.

observations—the multiple redactions of DtrH and Jer—suggest that no one individual was responsible for both DtrH and the Deuteronomic redaction of Jer. The evidence for multiple Deuteronomic redactions of both DtrH and Jer indicates that various individuals, members of the 'Deuteronomic school', were responsible for their production. Here, the term 'school' refers primarily to a guild-like organization. Within this structure, however, instruction may have occurred; therefore, the use of 'school' to refer to a guild does not preclude that instruction occurred within the Deuteronomic school. In fact, I postulate two different possible settings for education in relationship to the Deuteronomic school: (1) the training of scribes within its own structure and (2) the teaching of the authoritative religious literature to a wider, popular audience.[77]

The training of scribes in the Deuteronomic school would have involved the study and copying of authoritative texts. Those scribes who were the most accomplished would have moved up in the guild hierarchy until they received the status wherein they could leave their own imprint on the authoritative literature, thus becoming composers and redactors.[78] Such a process would have promoted a conservative transmission of distinctive Deuteronomic characteristics (e.g. themes, phraseology) in that all Deuteronomic redactors would have firstly learned their scribal craft from copying texts that contain such characteristics and secondly achieved their status within a guild structure which existed primarily for the preservation of these authoritative texts. This conservativism would not, however, have completely denied all creativity, for different Deuteronomic redactors dealt with various authoritative traditions and literary genres within different periods of the Deuteronomic school's history.[79]

77. On the social setting of the Deuteronomic school, see below, Chapter 7.

78. This understanding of accomplished scribes becoming composers and redactors is consistent with other literature of the ancient Near East. See below, Chapter 7.

79. This view is somewhat similar to that of Weinfeld, *Deuteronomy and the Deuteronomic School*, p. 4: 'The fact that the Deuteronomist and the editor of the prose sermons in Jeremiah used idioms and expressions not found in the book of Deuteronomy proper points to a continuous ideological and literary development within the deuteronomic circle and attests to the dynamism of the school. Indeed, an examination of the linguistic and ideaological fabric of the deuteronomic movement shows that its development progressed from Deuteronomy through deuteronomic historiography to the prose sermons in the book of Jeremiah.'

The Deuteronomic School's Redaction of Various Genres

The redactional activity of the Deuteronomic school included a substantial variety of literary forms. First, the Deuteronomic school utilized various genres within the different books it redacted. For example, Moshe Weinfeld has discussed the forms of different orations (valedictory address, prophetic oration, liturgical oration, military oration) in DtrH as well as the relationship between Deut and the forms of vassal treaties and law codes.[80] Second, the books that the Deuteronomic school redacted can themselves be distinquished according to their overall form and content: law (Deut), history (Josh–Kgs) and prophecy (Jer).[81] Therefore, no one literary form can be called *the* primary literary form of the Deuteronomic school,[82] because the Deuteronomic school was responsible for the production of various literary forms, including possibly II Zech.

The Problems of Source and Redaction in II Zech

Since the Deuteronomic school's redactional activity spanned time and included multiple redactions of various genres, the possibility of the Deuteronomic redaction of Zech must be seriously considered. Before beginning this consideration, a review of various understandings of the problem of the source and redaction of II Zech may prove helpful.

---

80. *Deuteronomy and the Deuteronomic School*, pp. 10-178.

81. Weinfeld, *Deuteronomy and the Deuteronomic School*, p. 8.

82. Noth explained the general lack of references to the Latter Prophets in DtrH (the Former Prophets) as the consequence of the historian not being aware of these works (*Deuteronomistic History*, p. 86). Noth's explanation has generally been rejected and replaced with the argument that the Deuteronomic school had a 'supplementary' collection of the Latter Prophets and, therefore, avoided unnecessary duplication (e.g. J. Blenkinsopp, *Prophecy and Canon* [Center of the Study of Judaism and Christainity in Antiquity, 3; Notre Dame, IN: University of Notre Dame Press, 1977], pp. 98, 102; R.E. Clements, *Prophecy and Tradition* [Atlanta: John Knox, 1975], pp. 47-48). Although I am in basic agreement with this understanding, I prefer to avoid the terminology of 'supplementarity' because it necessarily implies that one genre is primary and the other secondary. Rather, I prefer to describe the relationship between the Former Prophets and the Latter Prophets within a Deuteronomic canon as 'complementary'. For a review of scholarship concerning the relationship between the 'Former Prophets' and the 'Latter Prophets', see C.T. Begg, 'A Bible Mystery: The Absence of Jeremiah in the Deuteronomistic History', *IBS* 7 (1985), pp. 139-64.

In many works on II Zech, the issue of who is responsible for the material in and the redaction of II Zech is avoided by the use of such general terminology as 'the prophet' or 'II Zech'. Also, most of the discussion concerning these questions has centered on the date of the material and its redaction rather than determining more about what was the social location of the individual or group responsible for this material. However, there have been some attempts to locate II Zech within a social setting. Below, I will discuss these attempts, emphasizing those which also date II Zech to the post-exilic period.

By far the most influential observations concerning II Zech have been the observations that II Zech reinterprets earlier prophetic material. Delcor concluded that II Zech is heavily influenced by earlier prophetic collections with the most influential being, in order of their importance, Ezek, Jer, II Isa and III Isa.[83] Lamarche argued for a close connection between II Zech and the Suffering Servant in II Isa.[84] Mason concluded that II Zech is a reinterpretation of I Zech with heavy influences of earlier prophetic works, especially II Isa, Jer and Ezek.[85] André Lacocque noted that II Zech was influenced by previous prophets, especially Jer, Ezek, Joel, III Isa.[86] The dependence of II Zech upon earlier prophets surpasses that of other prophets, both in quantity and quality. Other prophets are understood to have been influenced by earlier prophets;[87] however, this influence is limited to specific passages or to the prophet's overall theology. In contrast, II Zech appears to be influenced by some earlier biblical literature in almost every verse and this influence includes obvious allusions to earlier prophetic works (e.g. Zech 11.1-3 // Jer 25.34-38[88]) as well as direct quotation (e.g. Zech 13.5 // Amos 7.14). Therefore, II Zech is unique in its heavy dependence on a variety of earlier prophetic collections.

83. Delcor, 'Sources', p. 411.

84. Lamarche, *Zacharie IX–XIV*, pp. 124-47.

85. Mason, 'Some Examples' and 'Use of Earlier Biblical Materials in Zechariah 9–14'.

86. My translation of Lacocque, 'Zacharie 9–14', p. 139.

87. For example, see W.L. Holladay, 'The Background of Jeremiah's Self-Understanding: Moses, Samuel, and Psalm 22', in *A Prophet to the Nations* (ed. Perdue and Kovacs), pp. 313-24.

88. Delcor, 'Sources', p. 387; Jones, *Haggai, Zechariah, Malachi*, pp. 148-49; Lacocque, 'Zacharie 9–14', p. 170; Mason, 'Use of Earlier Biblical Material in Zechariah 9–14', p. 107. Also, see below §20, §21.

Although the unique quality of II Zech's heavy dependence on earlier biblical material is now generally accepted, this observation has not necessarily led commentators to re-examine the question of whether or not the individual responsible for II Zech was a prophet. In fact, those commentators who continue to call the individual behind II Zech a 'prophet' include those who have argued for II Zech's dependence on earlier biblical material, such as Jones and Mason.[89] However, the observation of II Zech's dependence on earlier prophetic collections has led a few commentators to conclude that the individual behind II Zech was not a prophet. For example, North claimed that

> Second-Zechariah does not 'act like a prophet' in the sense of making independent and original oracles of his own. Instead he seems concerned with gathering up expectations of the earlier prophets and interpreting them or showing them how they are to be fulfilled.[90]

North's conclusion is supported by recent sociological and anthropological models of prophecy—that is, although a prophet is certainly influenced by his tradition, the prophet's message is presumed to come independently within the process of intermediation between the deity and humanity.[91] Hence, II Zech with his heavy dependence on earlier prophetic literature, in North's words, 'does not act like a prophet', but acts more like a redactor. Paul Redditt also suggested that II Zech was not a prophet; however, his suggestion stemmed not only from II Zech's dependence on earlier prophets but also on the condemnation of contemporary prophets.[92]

89. Jones, 'Fresh Interpretation of Zechariah IX–XI'; *Haggai, Zechariah, Malachi*, pp. 117-20. Cf. Mason, *Haggai, Zechariah, and Malachi*, p. 76; 'Some Examples', p. 353; 'Use of Earlier Biblical Material in Zechariah 9–14', p. 35. Although Mason calls the individual responsible for II Zech a 'prophet' in these instances, his use is inconsistent, for he also refers to a 'traditio-circle'. See below n. 95.

90. 'Prophecy to Apocalyptic via Zechariah', p. 51. Similarly, R.C. Dentan ('Zechariah 9–14', *IB*, VI, p. 1109): 'Our author clearly does not regard himself as a prophet...While he imitates the style of the great prophets of former days, he is not an ecstatic, but a writer and a self-conscious literary artist.'

91. M. Buss, 'An Anthropological Perspective upon Prophetic Call Narratives', *Semeia* 21 (1981), pp. 9-30; T.W. Overholt, 'The Ghost Dance of 1890 and the Nature of the Prophetic Process', *Ethnohistory* 21 (1974), pp. 37-63; and R.R. Wilson, *Prophecy and Society in Ancient Israel* (Philadelphia: Fortress Press, 1980).

92. Israel's Shepherds: Hope and Pessimism in Zechariah 9–14' *CBQ* 51 (1989), pp. 639-40.

This observation of II Zech's heigthened dependence upon earlier biblical literature is not the only characteristic of II Zech that may suggest that the individual behind II Zech is not a prophet. The prosaic character of II Zech (excluding Zech 9)[93] perhaps suggests that this individual was not a prophet, but a redactor who made use of prophetic themes and formulas within his/her prose.

When the individual responsible for II Zech is no longer considered a prophet, the emphasis upon the community behind II Zech becomes stronger, as is evident in the work of Hanson. In *The Dawn of Apocalyptic*, he postulated a conflict in the post-exilic period between two ideological groups: a hierocratic group and a visionary group. The hierocratic group consisted of Zadokite priests and their collaborators (including the prophets Haggai and Zechariah); the visionary group, 'disciples of Second Isaiah' and Levitical priests. This conflict primarily concerned the pragmatic restoration of the pre-exilic Zadokite cult, on the one hand, and the vision of Yahweh's miraculous restoration of a new sacral order, on the other hand. Based upon his understanding of this rift, Hanson located II Zech within the visionary group, thereby connecting II Zech with III Isa and contrasting it with I Zech.[94]

A discussion of the community responsible for II Zech is also found in Mason's work. His remarks concerning this 'traditio-circle'[95] included two analogies for the relationship between I Zech and

93. Zech 10–14 even contrasts with the 'oracular prose'/'elevated prose' of Hag and I Zech. For a discussion of this 'elevated prose' in Hag and I Zech, see C.L. Meyers and E.M. Meyers, *Haggai, Zechariah 1–8* (AB, 25B; Garden City, NY: Doubleday, 1987), pp. lxiii-lxvii.

94. Hanson, *Dawn of Apocalyptic*, pp. 283-84.

95. Mason's label for the individual(s) responsible for II Zech is inconsistent, sometimes denoting an individual ('prophet': *Haggai, Zechariah and Malachi*, p. 76; 'Some Examples', p. 353; 'Use of Earlier Biblical Material in Zechariah 9–14', p. 35; 'author': *Haggai, Zechariah and Malachi*, pp. 77-78) and at other times denoting a group (*Haggai, Zechariah and Malachi*, pp. 79-82; 'Relation of Zech 9–14 to Proto-Zechariah', p. 238; 'Some Examples', p. 353; 'Use of Earlier Biblical Material in Zechariah 9–14', pp. 35, 133, 299). Also, his terminology for the group to which II Zech belonged varies: 'tradition', 'traditio-circle', 'group', 'school' and 'circle'. Such inconsistency may suggest that Mason understands the individual responsible for II Zech as a prophet who belonged to a Zecharianic school of prophets (see especially 'Relation of Zech 9–14 to Proto-Zechariah', p. 238; 'Use of Earlier Biblical Material in Zechariah 9–14', p. 133).

II Zech. First, he used the analogy of II Zech coming from a 'Zechariah "school"' much as II Isa came from an 'Isaiah "school"'.[96] Second, he suggested that II Zech had some connection to the 'Jeremiah/ Deuteronomist tradition' as illustrated in the following quotations:

> [It is] also possible that he is setting his own prophetic word deliberately in the spirit of the Jeremiah/Deuteronomist tradition from which he draws.[97]

> The Jeremiah/Deuteronomist tradition…appears to be re-interpreted and re-applied.[98]

> Some striking similarity of thought, in particular to that of the circles amongst whom the words and traditions of Jeremiah received expansion, can be detected.[99]

In other words, in this analogy he used the relationship between the historical Jeremiah and the Deuteronomic prose in Jer to describe the relationship between I Zech and II Zech.

The thesis of the present work builds upon Mason's analogy between I Zech and II Zech, on the one hand, and Jeremianic poetry and Deuteronomic prose in Jer, on the other. In fact, I take this analogy as having a basis not only in the comparison of these two prophetic books, but upon a connection of source and redaction—that is, the Deuteronomic school may have redacted both Jer and Zech. Analogous to the Deuteronomic reinterpretation of Jeremianic poetry in the prose sections of Jer, II Zech is possibly the product of a Deuteronomic redactor who reinterpreted I Zech in light of other prophetic material, new historical circumstances, and expectations of the future.

My thesis of the Deuteronomic redaction of Zech will be presented below in three parts. In Part I, the prevailing view that the Deuteronomic school ceased during the exilic period is rejected on the basis of text-critical and thematic evidence in DtrH (Chapter 1) and the Deuteronomic redaction of Jer (Chapter 2). Thus, Part I demonstrates the possibility of the Deuteronomic redaction of a post-exilic book such as Zech. Part II consists of four chapters concerning II Zech, its

96. 'Relation of Zech 9–14 to Proto-Zechariah', p. 238; 'Use of Earlier Biblical Material in Zechariah 9–14', p. 133.

97. 'Use of Earlier Biblical Material in Zechariah 9–14', pp. 96-97.

98. 'Use of Earlier Biblical Material in Zechariah 9–14', p. 96.

99. 'Use of Earlier Biblical Material in Zechariah 9–14', p. 131.

Deuteronomic origin, and its place within the book of Zech. Three different types of evidence for the possible Deuteronomic production of the prose in II Zech are given: (1) Deuteronomic phraseology (Chapter 3), (2) the significant influence of various Deuteronomic passages (Chapter 4), and (3) the reinterpretation of Deuteronomic themes and imagery (Chapter 5). Chapter 6 summarizes these three types of evidence and suggests that the addition of II Zech to I Zech brought about the Deuteronomic redaction of Zech. Part III buttresses the thesis of the Deuteronomic redaction of Zech by explicating further its implications concerning the probable social setting of the Deuteronomic school in the post-exilic period (Chapter 7) and Deuteronomic theology in this setting (Chapter 8).

Part I

DEUTERONOMIC REDACTION IN THE POST-EXILIC PERIOD

The majority of scholars limit the Deuteronomic school to the pre-exilic and/or exilic periods. However, in this part, text-critical and thematic evidence suggesting that the redactional work of the Deuteronomic school continued well into the post-exilic period will be presented. This presentation begins in Chapter 1 with a discussion of this evidence as it relates to the Deuteronomic History (DtrH) and continues in Chapter 2 concerning the Deuteronomic redaction of Jer. The conclusions concerning the post-exilic redactions of DtrH and of the Deuteronomic redaction of Jer are reached independently; however, together they present a strong argument for Deuteronomic redactional activity in the post-exilic period.

Chapter 1

THE DEUTERONOMIC HISTORY

Discussions concerning the date of redactional activity in DtrH generally emphasize DtrH's origin—either the origin of the sources used by the Deuteronomic redactors or the first Deuteronomic redaction—rather than focusing upon the latter stages of redactional activity. Therefore, discussions concerning the date of redactional activity in DtrH have not been successful in determining these latter stages. Before proceeding with the evidence for the post-exilic setting of these latter stages, I will review the arguments made by the majority of scholars for an exilic setting for the final redaction of DtrH.

The work of Noth set the stage for present discussions of DtrH, including the generally accepted date of DtrH to the exilic period.

> [The Deuteronomic historian] wrote in the middle of the 6th century BCE when the history of the Israelite people was at an end; for the later history of the post-exilic community was a completely different matter—both its internal and external conditions were different—and it was the Chronicler who first thought of explaining it as a linear continuation of the earlier history of the nation.[1]

Noth's argument for an exilic date of DtrH can be summed up in the following way: Since the period discussed in DtrH ends with the exile and does not include a discussion of the return, the work of the Deuteronomic historian must be exilic.

Noth's argument has been readily accepted by the majority of scholars who limited Deuteronomic redactional activity to the pre-exilic and/or exilic periods. This majority comprises two different schools of thought:[2] those scholars who argued for the 'unity' of DtrH

---

1. Noth, *Deuteronomic History*, p. 79.
2. Some scholars do not fall into any of the schools discussed below. M. Brettler, 'Ideology, History and Theology in 2 Kings XVIII 7-23', *VT* 39 (1989), pp. 268-82; Rose, *Deuteronomist und Jahwist*; Van Seters, *In Search of History*; and

(i.e. only one redaction) and those scholars who argued for a dual redaction of DtrH.

Most interpreters who have continued to argue for the unity of DtrH simply accepted Noth's exilic date for the redaction of DtrH. For example, Burke Long defended an exilic date by simply stating that 'whatever their theories about the redaction and compositional history, most scholars agree that in its present form the books of Kings (and the Dtr History of which they are a part) originated in the exile'.[3] Therefore, those scholars who have maintained DtrH's unity have generally accepted Noth's exilic date without providing any additional support.

Cross, many of his students, and some others have argued for a dual redaction of DtrH,[4] but their rejection of Noth's understanding of the unity of DtrH has not affected their argument for the dating of the final redaction of DtrH. Cross explained the 'failure of... a dominant theme of God's coming restoration', a theme he expected in every exilic text, 'by moving the primary Deuteronomistic history from the setting of the Exile'.[5] In other words, Cross assumed that Noth was correct in locating the final redaction of DtrH in the exilic period, but he found it odd that there was not a strong theme of restoration in this exilic work. Therefore, he argued that if the majority of DtrH comes from the Josianic period, one can easily explain this 'failure'. To this 'primary Deuteronomistic history' (Dtr[1]), which ended in the Josianic period, an exilic Deuteronomistic redactor (Dtr[2]) 'updated the history by adding a chronicle of events subsequent to Josiah's reign'.[6] Again, the argument for the exilic redaction of DtrH was simply the

Weippert, '"Deuteronomistischen" Beurteilungen'. However, Noth's influence also continues strongly in their work—see especially Brettler's discussion of his last redactional level as exilic ('Ideology', pp. 281-82) and Van Seters's exilic date for his 'Deuteronomistic Historian' (*In Search of History*, pp. 230, 359).

3. Long, *I Kings*, p. 32. Similarly, Hoffmann, *Reform und Reformen*, p. 316-20; H.A. Kenik, *Design for Kingship* (SBLDS, 69; Chico, CA: Scholars Press, 1983), pp. 1-26; Polzin, *Moses*, p. 72; Polzin, *Samuel*, pp. 9-11, 64, 72.

4. Cf. Cross, 'Themes and Structure'; e.g. Birch, *Rise of the Israelite Monarchy*; Friedman, *Exile and Biblical Narrative*, pp. 1-43; Halpern, *First Historians*; J.D. Levenson, 'The Last Four Verses in Kings', *JBL* 103 (1984), pp. 353-61; Mayes, *Story of Israel*; McCarter, *I Samuel*; S.L. McKenzie, 'The Prophetic History and the Redaction of Kings', *HAR* 9 (1985), pp. 203-20; Nelson, *Double Redaction*.

5. Cross, 'Themes and Structure', p. 289.

6. Cross, 'Themes and Structure', p. 287.

following: the redaction process begins where the historical narrative stops and ends shortly thereafter.

In contrast to the two schools discussed above, the Göttingen school[7] has somewhat challenged the generally held view of an exilic setting for DtrH. Smend first proposed two post-587 redactions.[8] Later,[9] he accepted some of the revisions made by his student, Dietrich,[10] who argued for three redactions after 587 BCE. With this revision, the general framework for the Göttingen school took form: a history writer (DtrG), a prophetic redactor (DtrP), and a nomistic redactor (DtrN). Although they also assumed Noth's exilic date for DtrH, the logic of the Göttingen school is just the opposite of Cross and others who argue for a dual redaction. Whereas Cross revised Noth's thesis by positing a second, *earlier* redaction, the Göttingen school revised Noth's thesis by positing two *later* redactions; however, in both cases they assumed Noth's exilic date as the beginning point for their argument.[11]

Some scholars, however, have not assumed Noth's exilic date of DtrH.[12] They did not necessarily challenge the logic of Noth's exilic date—they simply presented their argument for post-exilic redaction

---

7. E.g., Smend, *Entstehung*, pp. 110-25; Dietrich, *Prophetie und Geschichte*; Dietrich, *David, Saul und die Propheten*; Spieckermann, *Juda unter Assur*; Veijola, *Dynastie*; Würthwein, *1 Könige 1–16*; Würthwein, *1 Könige 17–2 Kön 25*.

8. 'Gesetz und die Völker'.

9. Smend, *Entstehung*, pp. 110-25.

10. Dietrich, *Prophetie und Geschichte*.

11. When he first proposed three redactions (*Prophetie und Geschichte*), Dietrich argued that all three were exilic. Smend rejected this dating scheme because of the brevity of the exilic period and dated the last redactor (DtrN) to the post-exilic period (*Entstehung*, pp. 110-25). In his more recent work (*David, Saul und die Propheten*, p. 152), Dietrich has accepted Smend's revision of DtrN as post-exilic.

12. A.G. Auld, 'Prophets through the Looking Glass: Between Writings and Moses', *JSOT* 27 (1983), p. 15; A.G. Auld, 'Prophets through the Looking Glass: A Response to Robert Carroll and Hugh Williamson', *JSOT* 27 (1983), p. 44; Carroll, *Jeremiah*, p. 65-82; R.F. Person, Jr, 'II Kings 24,18–25,30 and Jeremiah 52: A Text-Critical Case Study in the Redaction History of the Deuteronomistic History', *ZAW* 105 (1993), forthcoming; A. Rofé, 'Joshua 20: Historico-Literary Criticism Illustrated', in *Empirical Models for Biblical Criticism* (ed. J.H. Tigay; Philadelphia: University of Pennsylvania Press, 1985), p. 145; A. Rofé, 'The Vineyard at Naboth: The Origin and Message of the Story', *VT* 38 (1988), p. 103; Tov, 'Aspects'; Tov, 'Literary History'; Tov, 'L'incidence'.

by the Deuteronomic school. However, two of these scholars have directly challenged the Nothian argument. Carroll claimed,[13]

> it should not be assumed that Deuteronomistic circles operated for a brief period and then disappeared; nor should the possibility of a much later (i.e., fifth-century) date for Deuteronomistic activity be ruled out a priori …The termination of the history with an episode from c. 560 (II Kings 25.27-30; cf. Jer 52.31-34) does not necessarily date the history to the mid-sixth century. It may simply represent a positive ending of the story of the kings of Israel and Judah with a detail from the life of the last living Judean king.

A. Graeme Auld sarcastically wrote,[14]

> The fact that Kings ends with the fate of Judah's last king tells us no more about the date of composition (generally believed exilic) than the fact that the Pentateuch ends with the death of Moses.

In summary, Noth's exilic date of DtrH was based completely upon the following argument: the narrative of DtrH ends in the exilic period; therefore, DtrH must be exilic. This argument is an argument for a *terminus a quo* used for a *terminus ante quem* as well. The arguments made by the three major schools of scholars discussed above began with the assumption of Noth's exilic date without further argumentation. However, Noth's exilic date has not gone unchallenged; therefore, a re-evaluation of all stages of the redactional history and their settings is necessary, including a re-evaluation of the evidence presented by all of the discussants. Such a broad re-evaluation cannot be attempted in this work. However, in the following section I will provide some preliminary evidence for dating the final redaction of DtrH in the postexilic period on the basis of two methodological approaches: text-critical studies and a reassessment of some thematic concerns.

Text Critical Studies of DtrH and their Implications

The general view concerning the relationship between text (i.e. 'lower') criticism and literary (i.e. 'higher') criticism has traditionally been strictly sequential—that is, text criticism establishes *the* text to

---

13. *Jeremiah*, p. 67.
14. 'Response to Carroll and Williamson', p. 44.

which one applies literary criticism. This view is exemplified in the following statement:

> In dealing with these portions of the Bible, we distinguish between their literary and textual history. The former is concerned primarily with the creative literary activity by which earlier oral traditions were shaped into a continuous record, the extensive editorial redaction of the different written sources, and the final compilation of the available materials resulting in the appearance of the completed work. The latter is concerned with the transmission of the text and the process by which it was finally fixed.[15]

However, since the discovery of the Qumran materials, text criticism has become more than simply a tool to establish 'the text' for the literary critic. Text criticism has begun to be incorporated even more into the discussion concerning literary history, especially for those texts where the Qumran materials and the versions differ significantly from MT.

In this section, I will begin by summarizing some representative studies of the textual and literary history of DtrH in which the author clarified the correspondence between text criticism and literary criticism. I will then discuss the implications of these studies on the dating of the final Deuteronomic redaction of DtrH.

1. Orlinsky, 'Kings-Isaiah Recensions'.[16] Harry Orlinsky concluded that the textual divergence between 2 Kgs 18–20 and Isa 36–39 suggests a redaction of DtrH after that of LXX-*Vorlage* of Kings but before that of MT-Kgs. This conclusion accounts for some of the differences between MT-2 Kgs 18–20 and MT-Isa 36–39 and the closer relationship between LXX-2 Kgs 18–20 and MT-Isa 36–39 in some cases.[17]

---

15. D.N. Freedman, 'The Law and the Prophets', in *Congress Volume, Bonn 1962* (VTSup, 9; Leiden: E.J. Brill, 1963), p. 252.

16. 'The Kings–Isaiah Recensions of the Hezekiah Story', *JQR* 30 (1939–40), pp. 33-49.

For a similar conclusion, see S. Talmon, 'Case of Faulty Harmonization', *VT* 5 (1955), pp. 206-08.

17. Most recent discussions of 2 Kgs 18–20 // Isa. 36–39 have completely ignored the text critical evidence Orlinsky provided in 1939! E.g. C.T. Begg, '2 Kings 20.12-19 as an Element of the Deuteronomistic History', *CBQ* 48 (1986), pp. 27-38; B.S. Childs, *Isaiah and the Assyrian Crisis* (SBT, 3; London: SCM Press, 1967); R.E. Clements, *Isaiah and the Deliverance of Jerusalem* (JSOTSup, 13; Sheffield: JSOT Press, 1980); K.A.D. Smelik, 'Distortion of Old Testament Prophecy: The Purpose of Isaiah xxxvi and xxxvii', in *Crises and Perspectives* (ed. A.S. van der

2. Rofé, 'Joshua 20': By combining 'historico-literary criticism' and text criticism, Alexander Rofé concluded that the textual history behind the present text of Josh 20.1-7 is as follows: (a) A short version preserved in Codex Vaticanus (LXX[B]), which lacks 20.4-5 and differs significantly in 20.6, reflects knowledge of the Priestly code concerning manslaughter and refuge (Num 35.9-34). The language and themes in this short version are closely related to those of this Priestly code. (b) This short version was later redacted with the addition of 20.4-5 (found only in MT) and some rewriting of 20.6. These later revisions reflect knowledge of the Deuteronomic code concerning manslaughter and refuge (Deut 4.41-43; 19.1-13). Therefore, the version found in MT is a Deuteronomic redaction of an earlier Priestly tradition.[18]

Having established this textual history, Rofé argued that such an addition, which has knowledge of both D and P, must have been late. Such an observation is confirmed by the fact that LXX-Josh 20 does not contain the reading, which suggests that the additions were late enough that they had not made their way into the various textual traditions. Rofé suggested that these Deuteronomic additions were probably made sometime in the fourth century.[19]

Woude; OTS, 24; Leiden: E.J. Brill, 1986), pp. 71-74.

18. See similarly A. Rofé, 'The Monotheistic Argumentation in Deuteronomy 4.32-40: Contents, Composition, and Text', *VT* 35 (1985), pp. 434-45. Rofé reached a similar conclusion concerning the textual history behind Deut. 4.32-40. After arguing for the priority of the Samaritan Pentateuch and LXX of Deut. 4.33 against MT, Rofé concluded that MT-Deut. 4.33, 36, 21b, 23 are additions from a Deuteronomic redactor using both a D source and a P source.

19. 'Joshua 20', p. 145. See also A. Rofé, 'The History of the Cities of Refuge in Biblical Law', in *Studies in Bible* (ScrHier, 31; ed. S. Japhet; Jerusalem: Magnes, 1986), pp. 205-39. Here Rofé compared Exod. 21.13; Num. 35.9-34; Deut. 4.41-43; Deut. 19.1-13; and Josh. 20. From this comparison, he concluded that the second stage of the development of the cities of refuge, represented in Num. 35.25-29 and LXX-Josh. 20, is early post-exilic (late sixth or early fifth century BCE) and that the third stage, represented in MT-Josh. 20, is late post-exilic (late fifth or early fourth century BCE) ('History of the Cities of Refuge', p. 236). He placed his argument for the fourth century date of the MT additions in Josh. 20 within a larger literary and cultural context, including comparative Persian and Greek material. See also A. Rofé, 'Classes in the Prophetical Stories: Didactic Legenda and Parable', in *Studies in Prophecy* (VTSup, 26; Leiden: E.J. Brill, 1974), pp. 143-64; A. Rofé, 'The Battle of David and Goliath: Folklore, Theology, Eschatology', in *Judaic Perspectives on Ancient Israel* (ed. J. Neusner, B.A. Levine and E.S. Frerichs; Philadelphia: Fortress

3. Tov, 'Growth of the Book of Joshua'.[20] After carefully examining the variants, Tov concluded that the edition reflected in MT-Josh expanded a shorter and earlier edition that is generally reflected in LXX-Josh. Therefore, following LXX-Josh, the more original text of Josh–Judg lacked Judg 1.1–3.6. His examination of the pluses in MT-Josh led him to conclude that MT-Josh is Deuteronomic.

4. Tov, 'I Sam 16–18'[21] and Rofé, 'Battle of David and Goliath': Tov examined the textual difference between MT-1 Sam 16–18 and LXX-1 Sam 16–18 and observed that MT-1 Sam 16–18 is almost twice as long as LXX-1 Sam 16–18. After showing that the translator of LXX-1 Sam 16–18 used a literal method for his translation, Tov showed how MT-1 Sam 16–18 is a conflation of two traditions, one found in LXX-1 Sam 16–18 and the other which was an independent source used by the redactor of MT-1 Sam 16–18. Therefore, LXX-1 Sam 16–18 preserves the earlier stage of the redaction of DtrH and MT-1 Sam 16–18 manifests a later stage of development, which incorporated an independent source.[22]

Press, 1987), pp. 117-51; and Rofé, 'Vineyard at Naboth'. In these articles, Rofé concluded that three other units in DtrH (1 Kgs 12.33–13.32; 1 Sam 17; 1 Kgs 21.1-20) suggest post-exilic redaction by the Deuteronomic school. His evidence for these suggestions includes historical allusions, theological expression, late linguistic features, and allusions to various Pentateuchal sources.

20. 'The Growth of the Book of Joshua in the Light of the Evidence of the LXX Translation', in *Studies in Bible* (ed. S. Japhet; ScrHier, 31; Jerusalem: Magnes, 1986), pp. 321-39. See also A. Rofé, 'The End of the Book of Joshua according to the Septuagint', *Henoch* 4 (1982), pp. 17-32. Tov often referred to Rofé's article in agreement.

21. 'The Composition of I Samuel 16–18 in the Light of the Septuagint Version', in *Empirical Models for Biblical Criticism* (ed. J.H. Tigay; Philadelphia: University of Pennsylvania Press, 1985), pp. 97-130.

22. See also J. Lust, 'The Story of David and Goliath in Hebrew and Greek', in *The Story of David and Goliath* (ed. Dominique Barthélemy *et al.*; OBO, 73; Fribourg: Editions Universitaires Fribourg; Göttingen: Vandenhoeck & Ruprecht, 1986), pp. 5-18; McCarter, *I Samuel*, pp. 306-307; H.J. Stoebe, 'Die Goliathperikope 1 Sam. 17,1–18,5 und die Text-Form der Septuagint', *VT* 6 (1956), pp. 397-413. Against this, see D. Barthélemy, 'Trois niveaux d'analyse', in *The Story of David and Goliath* (ed. Barthélemy *et al.*), pp. 47-54; S.J. de Vries, 'David's Victory over the Philistine as Saga and Legend', *JBL* 92 (1973), pp. 23-36; D.W. Gooding, 'An Approach to the Literary and Textual Problems in the David–Goliath Story', in *The Story of David and Goliath* (ed. Barthélemy *et al.*), pp. 55-86; Rofé, 'Battle of David and Goliath', pp. 119-22. For the debate between Tov and

Rofé analyzed the David and Goliath story of MT-1 Sam 16–18 and showed that its linguistic features suggest a post-exilic date.[23] Therefore, Rofé placed the MT version of the David and Goliath story within the same period as some of the other later Deuteronomic passages in DtrH which he has identified, sometime in the fifth or fourth centuries BCE.[24]

5. Williamson, 'Death of Josiah'.[25] After noting the Chronicler's conservative use of his source in various places, Hugh Williamson argued that the textual difference between the account of Josiah's death in 2 Kgs 23.28-30 and 2 Chron 35.20-27 suggests that the source the Chronicler used was more similar to LXX-Kgs than to

Lust, on the one hand, and Barthélemy and Gooding, on the other hand, see the papers and responses in Barthélemy *et al.* (eds.), *The Story of David and Goliath*. Tov and Lust both criticized Barthélemy and Gooding for first using literary criticism and then text criticism, and argued that the sequence must be reversed (see especially Lust, 'Second Thoughts on David and Goliath', in *Story of David and Goliath* [ed. Barthélemy *et al.*], pp. 87-91).

Barthélemy's and Rofé's criticism of Tov is that, although the Greek translator was relatively literal in his translation, the Vorlage of LXX was an abridged Hebrew text. The abridgement of this Hebrew text was to remove contradictions that resulted from the conflation of two stories. Tov responded that Barthélemy's (thus, indirectly, de Vries' and Rofé's) suggestion is based upon an odd coincidence in that some ancient revisor happened to extract the material that once belonged to an independent story, thereby preserving the other independent story. Such a coincidence, according to Tov, is highly unlikely. Therefore, given the general tendency for the expansion of biblical material and the general observation that LXX of Sam reflects a shorter text than MT of Sam, Tov maintained his position for the earlier version of LXX and the conflated version of MT.

23. Rofé's analysis included some examples of late features in material common to LXX; however, most of his linguistic evidence comes from MT additions. This observation alone should have caused him to re-examine his understanding of LXX as preserving an abridgment, but he made no distinction between LXX and MT when discussing the linguistic evidence. His linguistic arguments which are not in LXX are given here in his order: (1) the plene spelling of דּוֹב in 17.37; (2) the spelling of הַקְּלָאִי with an א (17.17); (3) Hiphil infinitive absolute of ערב as a denominative verb (17.16); (4) the idiom רֹעַ לְבָבֶךָ (17.28); (5) the use of הַזֶּה with an indefinite noun (17.17); (6) the use of regular perfect verbs in the frequentive sense (17.34-35); (7) the temporal clauses in 17.55 and 17.57; (8) his understanding of חֹמֶשׁ ('Battle of David and Goliath', pp. 128-31).

24. Josh. 20; 1 Kgs 12.33–13.32; 1 Kgs 21.1-20. See n. 19 above.

25. 'The Death of Josiah and the Continuing Development of the Deuteronomic History', *VT* 32 (1982), pp. 242-48.

MT-Kgs. Therefore, his work on the Chronicler suggested different levels of redaction of DtrH, with the LXX-*Vorlage* representing the earlier redaction.[26]

6. Person, 'II Kgs 24, 18–25, 30 and Jer 52': Assuming the Deuteronomic redactor of Jer took this tradition from DtrH, I compared MT-2 Kgs 24.18–25.30; LXX-2 Kgs 24.18–25.30; MT-Jer 52; and LXX-Jer 52. From this comparison, I concluded (a) that MT-2 Kgs 24.18–25.30, LXX-2 Kgs 24.18–25.30, and MT-Jer 52 circulated longer within related scribal circles, thereby 'correcting' one another, and (b) that LXX-Jer 52 was isolated from the other three and, therefore, generally preserves the earliest form of the tradition behind the four texts. When one compares LXX-Jer 52 to the other three texts, the text-critical evidence suggests *at least* a dual redaction.

An analysis of the agreement of the later three texts against LXX-Jer 52 reveals two more conclusions: (a) This later redaction (represented by the longer texts of MT-2 Kgs 24.18–25.30; LXX-2 Kgs 24.18–25.30; MT-Jer 52) was also Deuteronomic, as evident in Deuteronomic phraseology within one of its additions.[27] (b) This same later redaction occurred in the post-exilic period, probably sometime in the fifth or fourth century. The evidence for this post-exilic dating includes the following:

1. The earliest redaction of this material cannot be before the latest events which it describes—that is, the release of the exiled king Jehoiachin in 561 BCE (2 Kgs 25.27-30 // Jer 52.31-34). The extensive reworking between the two redactions betrays a long lapse of time; therefore, it is unlikely that the later redaction would fall within the remaining

---

26. Many other studies of the relationship between Chron. and DtrH could have been used to support similar conclusions. E.g. A.G. Auld, 'The "Levitical Cities": Text and History', *ZAW* 91 (1979), pp. 194-206; W.E. Lemke, 'The Synoptic Problem in the Chronicler's History', *HTR* 58 (1965), pp. 349-63; S.L. McKenzie, *The Chronicler's Use of the Deuteronomistic History* (HSM, 33; Atlanta: Scholars Press, 1985); J.C. Trebolle, 'Redaction, Recension, and Midrash in the Books of Kings', *BIOSCS* 15 (1982), pp. 12-35. See also C.T. Begg's challenge of Williamson's conclusions ('The Death of Josiah in Chronicles: Another View', *VT* 37 [1987], pp. 1-8) and Williamson's responses to Begg's criticism ('Reliving the Death of Josiah: A Reply to C.T. Begg', *VT* 37 [1987], pp. 9-15.).

27. 2 Kgs 24.19-20 // Jer. 52.2-3. This addition is discussed further below.

period of the exile (561—538 BCE), suggesting that the later redaction must be post-exilic.

2. If MT-Jer is post-exilic, as Tov has argued,[28] then the close textual relationship of MT-Jer 52 with MT-2 Kgs 24.18–25.30 and LXX-2 Kgs 24.18–25.30 suggests that these two texts are also post-exilic.

3. Studies comparing Chron with Sam–Kgs suggest that the *Vorlage* that the Chronicler used was closer to LXX-Sam–Kgs than MT-Sam–Kgs.[29] Therefore, either the later redaction had not yet occurred or the later redaction had not yet gained the same authority and popularity as had the earlier redaction. Either of these possibilities would further support a post-exilic date for the later redaction.

4. The occurrence of 'the Jews' [היהודים] (2 Kgs 25.25 // MT-Jer 52.28, 30 // LXX-Jer lacking) suggests a post-exilic origin for the later redaction.[30]

All of these studies compare favorably with many other text-critical studies that also conclude that LXX for DtrH (often with support from Qumran, Chr, Josephus, and/or OL) generally preserves an earlier stage of the redaction process of DtrH than MT.[31] Together all of these

28. 'Aspects', pp. 166-67: 'Literary History', pp. 236-37. My arguments for the post-exilic date of MT-2 Kgs, LXX-2 Kgs and MT-Jer closely follow those of Tov concerning MT-Jer.

29. E.g. Auld, 'Levitical Cities'; Lemke, 'Synoptic Problem in the Chronicler's History'; S. L. McKenzie, '1 Kings 8: A Sample Study into the Texts of Kings Used by the Chronicler and Translated by the Old Greek' *BIOSCS* 19 (1986), pp. 15-34; Trebolle, 'Redaction, Recension, and Midrash'; Williamson, 'Death of Josiah'.

30. The singular 'Jew' (יהודי) occurs only in post-exilic literature (Zech 8.23; Est 2.5; 3.4; 5.13; 6.10; 8.7; 9.29, 31; 10.3) and MT-Jer 34.9 (lacking in LXX-Jer. 41.9).

The plural 'Jews' (יהודים) occurs only in post-exilic literature (1 Chron 4.18; Neh 1.2; 2.16; 3.33, 34; 4.6; 5.1, 8, 17; 6.6; 13.23; Est 3.6, 10, 13; 4.3, 7, 13, 14, 16; 6.13; 8.1, 3, 5, 7, 8, 9 [2×], 11, 13, 16, 17 [2×]; 9.1 [2×], 2, 3, 5, 6, 11, 12, 13, 15, 16, 18, 19, 20, 22, 23, 24 [2×], 25, 27, 28, 30; 10.3) and Deuteronomic literature, including the Deuteronomic prose sections of Jer (2 Kgs 16.6; 25.25; Jer 32.12; 38.19; 40.11, 12; 41.3; 43.9; 44.1; 52.28, 30). Some of the occurrences of the plural in the Deuteronomic prose in Jer are lacking in LXX (MT-Jer 40.12 // LXX-Jer 47; MT-Jer 52.28, 30 // LXX-Jer 52).

31. E.g. A.G. Auld, 'Judges 1 and History: A Reconsideration', *VT* 25 (1975), pp. 261-85; A.G. Auld, 'Textual and Literary Studies in the Book of Joshua', *ZAW* 90 (1978), pp. 412-17; P.-M. Bogaert, 'Les trois rédactions conservées et la forme

studies suggest that DtrH underwent, at least, a dual redaction.[32] Since
two of the text-critical studies suggest a post-exilic setting for the final
Deuteronomic redaction,[33] it is possible that the evidence for a later
redaction in the other text-critical studies should also be located within
a post-exilic setting. Such a possibility is especially supported by the
evidence that the Chronicler used a *Vorlage* closer to LXX than MT
for his material from Josh, Sam and Kgs, for the Chronicler may not
have had access to the later redaction(s).

Even though the text-critical evidence suggests at least a dual redaction of DtrH, does this *necessarily* mean that the Deuteronomic school
was responsible for the later redaction(s)? Although the answer to this
question is 'it is not necessarily so', some evidence suggests that the
Deuteronomic school was responsible for some of the later redactions.
In the following list, I provide some examples of material unique to
MT (given in italics), which the above text-critical studies have suggested are post-LXX additions. In these examples, we find language
that suggests its Deuteronomic origin.

    1. Josh 20.4-6:

> *He shall flee to one of these cities and present himself at the entrance to
> the city gate and plead his case before the elders of that city; and they
> shall admit him into the city and give him a place in which to live among
> them. Should the blood avenger pursue him, they shall not hand the
> manslayer over to him since he killed the other person without intent and
> had not been his enemy in the past. He shall live in that city until he can*

originale de l'envoi du Cantique de Moïse (Deut. 32,43)', in *Das Deuteronomium*
(ed. N. Lohfink; BETL, 68; Leuven: Leuven University Press, 1985), pp. 329-40;
S.J. de Vries, 'Three Comparisons in 1 Kings XXII 4b and its Parallel and 2 Kings
III 7b', *VT* 39 (1989), pp. 283-306; L.J. Greenspoon, *Textual Studies in the Book of
Joshua* (HSM, 28; Chico, CA: Scholars Press, 1983); J. Luyten, 'Primeval and
Eschatological Overtones in the Song of Moses', in *Das Deuteronomium* (ed.
N. Lohfink), pp. 341-47; McKenzie, *Chronicler's Use of the Deuteronomistic
History*; J.D. Shenkel, *Chronology and Recensional Development in the Greek Text
of Kings* (HSM, 1; Cambridge, MA: Harvard University Press, 1968); E.C. Ulrich,
The Qumran Text of Samuel and Josephus (HSM, 19; Missoula, MT: Scholars
Press, 1978).

    32. I use 'at least, a dual redaction' because there is no clear evidence from
these different studies suggesting that the expansive MT of each of these passages is
necessarily the result of one hand.

    33. Rofé, 'Joshua 20'; Person, 'II Kings 24,28–25,30 and Jeremiah 52'.

stand trial before the assembly until the death of the high priest who is in office at that time. Thereafter, the manslayer may go back to his home in his own town, to the town from which he fled.[34]

This is a direct quote taken from Deut 19.4-6, which also has close affinities with Deut 4.41-43.

2. Josh 1.7: 'to observe faithfully according to *all the teaching* which Moses my servant enjoined to you'.[35] The phrase 'to observe faithfully according to *all the teaching*' is frequently found in Deuteronomic literature.[36]

3. Josh 1.11: 'The land which the Lord your God gives to you *as a possession*'.[37] This phrase occurs frequently in Deuteronomic literature.[38]

4. Josh 24.17: 'For it was the Lord our God who brought us and our fathers up from the land of Egypt, *the house of bondage, and who wrought those wondrous signs before our very eyes*'.[39] Two phrases in this addition suggest Deuteronomic origin: *'the house of bondage'*[40] and *'wondrous signs'*.[41]

5. 1 Sam 18.12: 'Saul was afraid of David, *for the Lord was with him and had turned away from Saul*'.[42] The phrase *'the Lord...had turned away from Saul'* suggests a Deuteronomic origin. The metaphorical use of 'turning away' to denote apostasy has been noted before as characteristically Deuteronomic.[43] Closely related to this use

---

34. Rofé, 'Joshua 20', p. 137-39. The translation is Rofé's. See also Tov, 'Growth of the Book of Joshua', p. 335.

35. Tov, 'Growth of the Book of Joshua', p. 336. The translation is Tov's.

36. Weinfeld, *Deuteronomy and the Deuteronomic School*, p. 336.

37. Tov, 'Growth of the Book of Joshua', p. 336. The translation is Tov's.

38. Weinfeld, *Deuteronomy and the Deuteronomic School*, p. 342.

39. Tov, 'Growth of the Book of Joshua', p. 336. The translation is Tov's.

40. Weinfeld, *Deuteronomy and the Deuteronomic School*, pp. 326-27.

41. Weinfeld, *Deuteronomy and the Deuteronomic School*, p. 330.

42. Tov ('I Samuel 16–18', p. 105) concluded that this addition comes from an independent tradition, which was conflated with the earlier tradition preserved in LXX. However, he did not discuss the possibility of this later redactor being Deuteronomic. The translation is Tov's.

43. Weinfeld (*Deuteronomy and the Deuteronomic School*, p. 339) included the following phrases in his list of Deuteronomic phraseology: סור 'to turn away'; סור מן הדרך 'to turn aside from the way'; סור מאחרי יהוה 'to turn away from Yahweh'; and סור...ימין ושמאל 'to turn right or left'.

To this list, I add two other phrases that use a form of סור to describe apostasy:

is another metaphorical use of 'turning away'—the 'turning away' of Yahweh as punishment for the 'turning away' of the apostates. Although such language occurs once in the book of Hosea (Hos 9.12),[44] all other occurrences of the 'turning away' of Yahweh as punishment are within Deuteronomic literature.[45] Therefore, the metaphor of Yahweh's 'turning away' as punishment for the 'turning away' of apostates betrays a Deuteronomic origin for this later addition.

6. 2 Kgs 24.19-20 // Jer 52.2-3: '*And he did evil in the sight of Yahweh, according to all that Jehoiakim had done. For because of the anger of Yahweh it came to pass in Jerusalem and Judah that he cast them out from his presence*'.[46] Two phrases in this addition suggest Deuteronomic origin: '*he did what was evil in the sight of Yahweh*' and '*he [Yahweh] cast them out from his presence*'. The phrase 'to do what is evil in the sight of Yahweh' (עשה הרע בעיני יהוה) occurs numerous times throughout DtrH (more than 50×) and in the Deuteronomic prose of Jer (3×)[47] and this is not even taking into account the variations of this phrase such as 'to do good in the sight of Yahweh'.[48] The phrase 'to cast away from the presence of Yahweh' (השלך מעל פני יהוה) is also typically Deuteronomic.[49] Therefore, the occurrence of these

1.   לא סר מעל חמאות ירבעם 'he did not turn from the sins of Jeroboam' and its variants: 2 Kgs 3.3; 10.29,31; 13.2,6,11; 14.24; 15.9,18,24,28; 17.22.

2.   הבמות לא סרו 'the high places were not taken away': 1 Kgs 15.14; 22.44; 2 Kgs 12.4; 14.4; 15.4,35.

44. Num. 14.9: 'Their [the people of the land] protection is removed from them, and the Lord is with us'. This verse may suggest such language, but the relationship between Yahweh and the removal of the protection is not made explicit.

45. Judg 16.20; 1 Sam 16.14, 23; 18.12; 28.15, 16; 2 Sam 7.15; 2 Kgs 24.3.

46. In 'II Kings 24,18–25,30 and Jeremiah 52', I concluded that these verses found in MT-2 Kgs 24.19-20, LXX-2 Kgs 24.19-20 and MT-Jer 52 and lacking in LXX-Jer 52 are an addition to an earlier text best represented by the shorter LXX-Jer 52. The following translation is taken from MT-2 Kgs 24.19-20. The variation among MT-2 Kgs 24.19-20, LXX-2 Kgs 24.19-20 and MT-Jer 52 is so insignificant as to not affect the translation; therefore, the following translation stands equally well for these three texts. For a Hebrew synopsis of these texts, see Person, 'II Kings 24,18–25,30 and Jeremiah 52'.

47. Weinfeld (*Deuteronomy and the Deuteronomic School*, p. 339) included this phrase in his list of typical Deuteronomic phraseology.

48. Weinfeld (*Deuteronomy and the Deuteronomic School*, p. 335) also included this phrase in his list of typical Deuteronomic phraseology.

49. Weinfeld (*Deuteronomy and the Deuteronomic School*, p. 347) included this

two phrases betrays a Deuteronomic origin for this post-exilic addition.

Given the observation that Deuteronomic language and thematic concerns are found in the additional material of some of the later redactions, I see no reason to postulate another scribal group other than the Deuteronomic school for the post-exilic redaction of DtrH. Therefore, the text-critical evidence alone suggests a post-exilic setting for some redactional activity of the Deuteronomic school in DtrH.

Oddly enough, those scholars who have analyzed DtrH based solely upon MT[50] have inadvertently supported my contention that the later additions in the final redaction of DtrH—that is, the material unique to MT—are also Deuteronomic. They have done so by basing their arguments for the unity of Deuteronomic themes and language in DtrH upon the final Deuteronomic redaction (MT). In other words, these post-exilic additions in the final Deuteronomic redaction (those unique to MT) have been incorrectly treated by many as originating in the exilic period at the hand of Deuteronomic redactors. These additions have been so treated because the themes and language therein are so similar to the material in the earlier redactions (represented in textual traditions such as LXX, which have been generally ignored in redaction criticism) that these scholars could not discern a thematic or phraseological difference between what the text-critical evidence suggests came from different stages of the redaction of DtrH. In other

phrase and similar phrases which substitute different verbs (שלח, הסיר, נטש) in his list of typical Deuteronomic phraseology.

50. The following examples represent all three of the schools of thought concerning DtrH: H.J. Boecker, *Die Beurteilung der Anfänge des Königtums in den deuteronomischen Abschnitten des I. Samuelbuches* (WMANT, 31; Neukirchen: Neukirchener Verlag, 1969); R.G. Boling, 'In Those Days There was no King in Israel', in *A Light unto My Path* (ed. H. Bream, R. Heim and C. Moore; Philadelphia: Temple University Press, 1974), pp. 33-48; R.E. Clements, 'The Isaiah Narrative of 2 Kings 20.12-19 and the Date of the Deuteronomic History', in *Isac Leo Seeligman Volume* (ed. G.W. Coates and B.O. Long; Philadelphia: Fortress Press, 1977), III, pp. 209-20; Cross, 'Themes and Structure'; R.E. Friedman, 'From Egypt to Egypt: Dtr1 and Dtr2', in *Traditions in Transformation* (ed. B. Halpern and J.D. Levenson; Winona Lake, IN: Eisenbrauns, 1981), pp. 167-92; Halpern, *First Historians*; T.R. Hobbs, *2 Kings* (WBC, 18; Waco, TX: Word Books, 1985); Levenson, 'Last Four Verses in Kings'; Long, *I Kings*; Mayes, *Story of Israel*; McKenzie, 'Prophetic History and the Redaction of Kings'; Nelson, *Double Redaction*; Noth, *Deuteronomistic History*; G. Vanoni, 'Beobachtungen zur deuteronomistischen Terminologie in 2 Kön 23,25–25,30', in *Das Deuteronomium* (ed. Lohfink), pp. 357-62.

words, for the study of DtrH, the stylistic and thematic criteria for redaction criticism have proven insufficient in discerning different redactional layers evident from text criticism. This insufficiency of the stylistic and thematic criteria can be explained by noting that the language and themes of the different redactional layers are so similar that the application of these criteria could not separate out the different layers. Because of this similarity, such redaction-critical studies have fallen short and have also, inadvertently, pointed to the possibility of my thesis of post-exilic redactional activity of the Deuteronomic school.

The Theme of Restoration in DtrH and its Implications

A theme within DtrH that may suggest a post-exilic setting for the final redaction of DtrH is that of restoration following repentance. This theme is generally assumed to belong to the exilic period, thereby providing hope of the return to the exiles.[51] Although the exiles had a need for such reassurance, it was also needed by those who lived in post-exilic Yehud, who were struggling to rebuild the Temple and the community in the face of internal and external conflicts (e.g. Hag, Zech, III Isa, Chron).[52] Therefore, there is no reason to assume that restoration themes in DtrH necessarily point to an exilic rather than a post-exilic setting. The following examples of texts from DtrH contain restoration language and have been used to support the general assumption of an exilic setting of the final redaction of DtrH. As such, they provide a framework for some representative interpretations of these passages, which are based primarily upon the assumed exilic setting of DtrH. Following this review, I will make some preliminary remarks concerning how these same passages could have functioned equally well in a post-exilic setting.

51. E.g. W. Brueggemann, 'The Kerygma of the Deuteronomistic Historian', *Int* 22 (1968), pp. 387-402; H.W. Wolff, 'The Kerygma of the Deuteronomic Historical Work', in *The Vitality of Old Testament Traditions* (ed. W. Brueggeman and H.W. Wolff; Atlanta: John Knox, 1975), pp. 83-100.

52. In the 'deutero-prophetic' literature that he discussed, D.L. Petersen included as one characteristic of this literature the 'eschatological scenario' (*Late Israelite Prophecy* [SBLMS, 23; Missoula, MT: Scholars Press, 1977], p. 17). Such eschatological tendencies reassure post-exilic communities; therefore, it is equally possible that the restoration theme in DtrH also functioned in this manner. See below the section 'Eschatology' in Chapter 8.

The first three examples are taken from the book of Deuteronomy:

> When you are in distress and all these things come upon you, in the latter days you will return to Yahweh your God and you will obey his voice, for Yahweh your God is a merciful God; he will not fail you and he will not destroy you and he will not forget the covenant with your fathers which was sworn to them (Deut 4.30-31).

> And if you surely obey the voice of Yahweh your God, being careful to do all his commandments which I command you this day, Yahweh your God will set you high above all the nations of the earth. And all these blessings shall come upon you and overtake you, for you obeyed the voice of Yahweh your God (Deut 28.1-2).

> When...you remember them among all the nations where Yahweh the Lord has driven you; and when you return to Yahweh your God and obey his voice in all that I command you this day, you and your children, with all your heart and with all your soul; then Yahweh your God will reverse your captivity and have compassion upon you, and he will repent and gather you from all the peoples where Yahweh your God has scattered you (Deut 30.1-3).[53]

According to A.D.H. Mayes, these three passages come from the hand of the exilic redactor, because they generally parallel the restoration language in Second Isaiah.[54] Richard Friedman argued that these three passages belong to the exilic Dtr^2 because they reflect the theme of 'apostasy leading to exile and national dispersal, followed by repentance leading to restoration'.[55] Nicholson suggested that the 'turn again' motif in Deut 4.29-30 and Deut 30.1-6 is exilic, expressing hope to those exiled in Babylon for a future return.[56] According to Rofé, Deut 4.25-31 is exilic because these verses 'explain the punishment of exile as for the making of images and speak of repentance in exile, but not of a return to the land'.[57] Together, these representative commentators essentially argue that these three passages are exilic

---

53. Although he did not discuss whether or not Deut 30.3-4 is Deuteronomic, N. Mendecki ('Deut. 30,3-4—nachexilisch?' *BZ* 29 [1985], pp. 267-71) argued that Deut 30.3-4 is post-exilic because it betrays the influence of material in Jer, Ezek, II Isa and III Isa.

54. Mayes, *Story of Israel*, p. 39.

55. Friedman, 'From Egypt to Egypt', pp. 180-81, 183. See also Friedman, *Exile and Biblical Narrative*, pp. 19, 25.

56. Nicholson, *Preaching*, p. 76.

57. Rofé, 'Monotheistic Argumentation', p. 442.

because they attempt to explain theologically the rationale for the exile and offer the hope of restoration without the explicit report of the restoration having taken place. In other words, these commentators have assumed the argument of an exilic setting for the final redaction of DtrH and this assumption has influenced their understanding of the restoration language in these passages.

The next example is taken from the end of the book of Judges:

> And the people of Israel departed from there at that time, each to his tribe and clan, and they went out from there, each to his inheritance. In those days there was no king in Israel. Each man did what was right in his own eyes (Judg 21.24-25).

According to Robert Boling, the use of the phrase 'each man doing what is right in his own eyes' in Deut 12.8 and here in Judg 21.25 suggests what is required for Israel not only to enter the land and conquer its people (Deut 12.8), but also for Israel to 'make a new beginning' once Israel is in the land.[58] Boling assigned Judg 19.1–21.25 to the exilic redactor and suggested that the language in this passage provided hope to the exiles—that is, this passage, which narrates the conquest, was added during the exilic period to give expression to the hope of making a new beginning, a restoration.[59] Again, the implicit restoration theme is illuminated against the assumed exilic setting of the final redaction of DtrH.

The next two examples occur in the books of Kings:

> If they sin against you..., then you are angry with them, and you give them to an enemy, so that they are carried away captive to the land of the enemy, distant or near. But if they take it to heart in the land to where they have been carried and they repent and they make supplication to you in the land of their captors, saying, 'We have sinned and we have acted perversely and we are evil'. If they return to you with all their mind and with all their heart...and if they pray to you toward their land, which you gave to their fathers, the city which you have chosen, and the house which I have built for your name; then you will hear in heaven your dwelling place their prayer and their supplication, and you will maintain their cause

---

58. Boling, 'In Those Days', p. 44. A very similar line of argument for Judg 21.25 is given in W.J. Dumbrell, '"In Those Days There was no King in Israel; Every Man Did What was Right in his own Eyes". The Purpose of the Book of Judges Reconsidered', *JSOT* 25 (1983), pp. 23-33.

59. Boling, 'In Those Days', pp. 41-44. See also J.D. Martin, *The Book of Judges* (CBC; Cambridge: Cambridge University Press, 1975), pp. 225-26.

and you will forgive your people who have sinned against you and all their transgressions which they have committed against you; and you will give them compassion in the sight of their captors that they may have compassion on them (1 Kgs 8.46-50).

And in the thirty-seventh year of the exile of Jehoiachin king of Judah, in the twelfth month, on the twenty-seventh day of the month, Evil-merodach king of Babylon, in the first year of his reign, lifted up Jehoiachin king of Judah from the house of bondage; and he spoke with him kindly; and he gave him a seat above the seats of the kings who were with him in Babylon. And Jehoiachin put off his garments of bondage and he dined regularly in his presence, all the days of his life. And for his allowance, a regular allowance was given to him from the king, a portion every day, all the days of his life (2 Kgs 25.27-30).

According to Jon Levenson, 1 Kgs 8.22-53 belongs to the exilic redactor ('Dtr2') because both the theme of the foreign convert who makes a pilgrimage to Jerusalem (8.41-43) and the passage's theology of the Temple reflect 'the Exilic or the immediate post-Exilic era'.[60] Similarly, Levenson argued that 2 Kgs 25.27-30 is from the hand of the exilic redactor ('Dtr2') for the purpose of bringing 'the legacy of the promisory covenant with David into line with the new historical reality effected by the events of 587 BCE'.[61] Although he offered

---

60. 'From Temple to Synagogue: 1 Kings 8', in *Traditions in Transformation* (ed. B. Halpern; Winona Lake, IN: Eisenbrauns, 1981), p. 158. On an exilic setting for 1 Kgs 8.22-53, see also S.J. de Vries, *1 Kings* (WBC, 12; Waco, TX: Word Books, 1985), p. 126; J. Gray, *I and II Kings* (OTL; Philadelphia: Westminster Press, 1970), p. 226; G.H. Jones, *1 and 2 Kings* (2 vols.; NCB; Grand Rapids, MI: Eerdmans, 1984), I, p. 204; R.D. Nelson, *First and Second Kings* (IBC; Atlanta: John Knox, 1981), pp. 52-55; Würthwein, *1 Könige 1–16*, p. 95.

61. Levenson, 'Last Four Verses', p. 361. On an exilic setting for 2 Kgs 25.27-30, see also Halpern, *First Historians*, p. 158; S. Herrmann, *Prophetie und Wirklichkeit in der Epoche des babylonischen Exils* (Stuttgart: Calwer Verlag, 1967), pp. 12-113; Hobbs, *2 Kings*, pp. 367-69; Nelson, *First and Second Kings*, pp. 265-69; Nicholson, *Preaching*, pp. 78-79; G. von Rad, *Old Testament Theology* (2 vols.; trans. D.M.G. Stalker; New York: Harper & Row, 1962), I, pp. 334-47, esp. 343; E. Zenger, 'Die deuteronomistische Interpretation der Rehabilitierung Jojachins', *BZ* 12 (1968), p. 30. Although he argued against the understanding of 2 Kgs 25.27-30 expressing hope for a return to the Davidic monarchy, C.T. Begg ('The Significance of Jehoiachin's Release: A New Proposal', *JSOT* 36 [1986], pp. 49-56) argued that 2 Kgs 25.27-30 betrays an exilic setting with a pro-Babylonian agenda; therefore, he also assumed Noth's argument for an exilic dating.

parallels to post-exilic literature (III Isa),[62] Levenson gave no reason why these passages in Kgs are exilic rather than post-exilic. If these themes reflect 'the Exilic or the immediate post-Exilic era',[63] then why does he reject the post-exilic period as a possible setting? Since he gave no reason, we must assume his reason proceeds from his assumption of the exilic setting for the final redaction of DtrH.

We have briefly reviewed some of the interpretations concerning restoration language in DtrH and how they fit within the commentators' understanding of the redaction of DtrH. Once again, we see a general assumption at work concerning the interpretations of these passages. This assumption concerns Noth's imprecise argument for the exilic setting of the final redaction of DtrH. In other words, the assumption of an exilic setting for the final redaction of DtrH suggests that all restoration language in DtrH is *vaticinia pro eventu* (prophecy before the event) rather than *vaticinia ex eventu* (prophecy after the event).

Although it would be equally imprecise to assume that all restoration language is *vaticinia ex eventu* and, therefore, post-exilic, we must acknowledge the possibility that restoration language in DtrH may have a post-exilic setting. This acknowledgement is based upon the realization that restoration language clearly occurs in post-exilic literature. For example,

> I will strengthen the house of Judah, and the house of Joseph I will save. I will bring them back for I have compassion on them, and they will be as if I had not rejected them; for I am Yahweh their God and I will answer them (Zech 10.6).

With the possibility of both an exilic and a post-exilic setting in mind, the restoration themes in DtrH need to be re-evaluated in order to determine, if possible, the redactional setting of each passage. Such a re-evaluation should be based on the passage itself without assumptions concerning the overall redaction history of DtrH. Only following such a re-evaulation of the various passages in DtrH can one begin to elucidate the overall redaction history of DtrH.[64]

62. Levenson, '1 Kings 8', pp. 158-59.

63. Levenson, '1 Kings 8', p. 158.

64. This principle is found in Rofé's work. Rofé, 'Battle of David and Goliath', p. 124; Rofé, 'Vineyard at Naboth', p. 89. By putting this principle to work in conjunction with other methods, Rofé has detected a post-exilic setting for some restoration language in DtrH. For example, the story of David and Goliath functions within

Although such a re-evaluation is beyond the scope of this work, some preliminary remarks concerning how the restoration themes in DtrH could be understood in the context of a post-exilic setting are in order. Two themes concerning the land can be easily understood against a post-exilic setting: (1) the theme in Deut concerning the covenantal requirements upon Israel before they enter the land and (2) the theme in Judg concerning the conquest of the land, which could be lost if Yahweh's commandments are not kept. These themes can be understood as narrative forms of the admonition of what was required for the return of the exiles to Yehud and for the continuing restoration of the people of God. In other words, the post-exilic community of Yehud could be addressed in narrative through the speeches of Moses and other prominent figures in DtrH to obey Yahweh concerning what is required of them, like their ancestors, to remain and flourish in the land. The passages given above from the books of Kings could easily be viewed against the backdrop of the Second Temple (1 Kgs 8.46-50) and the post-exilic hope for the Davidides (2 Kgs 25.27-30). Nothing in the narrative of any of these passages requires an exilic, rather than a post-exilic, setting. They are equally, and possibly better, understood when they are placed within a post-exilic setting.

A disclaimer is required before proceeding further. My criticism of the above interpretations does *not* suggest that they require, in place of an exilic setting, a post-exilic setting. The assumption in favor of the final redaction of DtrH in the exilic period should be seriously questioned and, therefore, the themes of restoration need to be re-evaluated so that the possibilities of exilic *and* post-exilic settings can be taken seriously. Therefore, it may be that further research will show that some of the above passages were produced in the exilic period, while others were produced in the post-exilic period.

Summary of Chapter 1: Conclusions concerning DtrH

A majority of scholars date the final Deuteronomic redaction of DtrH to the exilic period. This date is based solely upon the following argument for a *terminus a quo* used also as a *terminus ante quem*: DtrH ends its historical narrative with the destruction of Jerusalem

the context of messianic hope of the post-exilic period. Rofé, 'Battle of David and Goliath', pp. 139-43.

and the exile; therefore, its final form is exilic. Such an argument based primarily upon the chronological framework of the narrative of DtrH is inadequate and must be rejected.

Against this majority view, I have argued that some text-critical evidence suggests that the Deuteronomic school continued into the post-exilic period. This suggestion proceeds from two observations: (1) that some of the additions in the later, expansive MT contain Deuteronomic phraseology and (2) that some of these additions heighten themes in light of a post-exilic setting and contain late linguistic features. Therefore, the intersection of text-critical studies and historical criticism has provided evidence for post-exilic redactional activity in DtrH by the Deuteronomic school. This intersection led to Rofé's conclusion that 'the widely accepted view about...the last redaction of the Deuteronomistic work in the Exilic period (mid-6th century) now needs to be reconsidered'[65] and that Deuteronomic redactional activity continued into the post-exilic period.[66]

After establishing the possibility for Deuteronomic redactional activity in the post-exilic period, the theme of restoration in DtrH was briefly reviewed. This review concluded that the general understanding of the restoration theme in DtrH begins with the assumption of the majority view for the final redaction of DtrH occurring in the exilic period—that is, the theme of restoration is *vaticinia pro eventu*, providing hope to the exiles. Although this is certainly possible in some cases, the above review rejects such *a priori* understandings of restoration language in DtrH and calls for a re-evaluation of this theme because the restoration themes in DtrH may have the same setting as restoration themes in Hag, Zech and III Isa—that is, the post-exilic period.

Before proceeding further, three disclaimers are in order. First, although I have provided evidence of post-exilic redaction in DtrH by the Deuteronomic school, the evidence does not necessarily suggest that all of the various components of DtrH were redacted anew in the post-exilic period. Since it is highly improbable that the entire DtrH would have been preserved on one scroll (or any other medium of written text in antiquity), it is possible that, even within the later periods of Deuteronomic redactional activity, these redactions were undertaken on more limited scales—that is, excluding one or more

65. 'Vineyard at Naboth', p. 103.
66. 'Joshua 20', p. 145.

scrolls. Therefore, it may have been that Deut, Sam and Kgs (or however the divisions were made by the Deuteronomic school) were redacted in the postexilic period, but that, for example, Judg reached its final form earlier. In this work, I presently refrain from offering judgment.

Secondly, the evidence given above for post-exilic redactional activity in the Deuteronomic school in DtrH suggests simply that there was Deuteronomic redactional activity in these books in the post-exilic period. It does not and cannot suggest that all of this redactional activity was from the hand of one Deuteronomic redactor. Therefore, I neither postulate a Dtr^3 (or Dtr^4 etc.) to add to the previously numbered redactors of Cross and others, nor do I identify this redactional activity with the Göttingen school's post-exilic redactor (DtrN). I simply suggest that the Deuteronomic school—that scribal group which included over a period of time the various redactors of DtrH, Jer, and any other Deuteronomic work—continued its redactional activity into the post-exilic period, hermeneutically reapplying its traditional material to new situations while essentially maintaining its thematic concerns and phraseology.

Finally, although all of the text-critical studies discussed above suggest that LXX preserves an earlier stage of the redaction of DtrH than MT, one should not be too hasty in concluding that these limited studies suggest the overall relationship between LXX and MT of DtrH. The relationship between LXX and MT must be discerned at the level of translation units in LXX rather than at the larger level of all of LXX of DtrH and, hence, may reveal conflicting conclusions for different translation units. Therefore, my generalization concerning the nature of the overall relationship between LXX and MT of DtrH is just that— a simplification that can be quite dangerous if taken too rigidly. Even though my generalization is based upon various text-critical studies scattered throughout DtrH, it remains possible that in some translation units LXX may be corrupt and inferior to MT. Text-critical work must, therefore, continue on DtrH to discern what is certainly a much more complicated relationship between MT and LXX than my own generalization represents.

Chapter 2

THE DEUTERONOMIC REDACTION OF THE BOOK OF JEREMIAH

The determination of the *terminus a quo* for the Deuteronomic redaction of Jer is relatively simple given the historical data mentioned in both MT-Jer and LXX-Jer.[1] The following historical data suggest that its composition was exilic at the earliest: (1) Deuteronomic passages in Jer recount the destruction of Jerusalem in 587 BCE, Gedaliah's governorship and death, and the flight to Egypt. If the third deportation of 582 BCE (Jer 52.30) is punishment for the murder of Gedaliah, Gedaliah's governorship lasted from 587 BCE to 582 BCE. (2) Jer 44.30 (LXX 51.30) is an addition of *vaticinia ex eventu* concerning the overthrow of Hophra, the Egyptian Pharaoh, by Amasis about the year 570 BCE. (3) Jer 22.26 is *vaticinia ex eventu* concerning the death of Jehoiachin in exile. Although the date of Jehoiachin's death is not known, we know from Jer 52.31-33 and cuneiform sources that Jehoiachin was released from prison in 561–60 BCE. Therefore, the first redaction of the present form of the book of Jeremiah is certainly exilic at the earliest.

Before proceeding further, it is important to review the work of Hyatt, who was the first to argue for a Deuteronomic redaction of Jer. Although his understanding of the scope of this Deuteronomic redaction differs with some of those who have refined his thesis (e.g. Nicholson), his argument for the exilic setting of the Deuteronomic redaction of Jer has remained widely influential among many commentators of Jer.[2] Therefore, I will summarize his arguments for this exilic setting.

After determining the *terminus a quo* of about 560 BCE, Hyatt made

1.   The following is taken from Hyatt, 'Deuteronomic Edition of Jeremiah', pp. 262-63.

2.   Unfortunately, the consequences of revising Hyatt's basic thesis in relationship to the scope of Deuteronomic redaction upon the date of the final Deuteronomic redaction have been relatively ignored, for Hyatt understood LXX-Jer to be post-exilic.

the following additional observations, which led him to conclude that the Deuteronomic redaction was exilic, around 550 BCE.[3] (1) 'the prophecies of return from exile in D are vague and general' (see Jer 32.36-41); (2) 'the attitude of D towards the Babylonians and Nebuchadnezzar is in general friendly' in contrast to the later oracles against Babylon; (3) 'the D editor of Jeremiah has his closest affinities, both in style and in substance, with the exilic D editor of Deuteronomy, Kings, Joshua, and other books edited by the D school'; and (4) 'there is no evidence of the influence of...early post-exilic writers'.

Hyatt's argument for the exilic date of the Deuteronomic redaction is reminiscent of that used for the exilic date of the final redaction of DtrH—that is, the last clear historical references in Jer are to the exilic period, and there is no specific mention of the return; therefore, the Deuteronomic redaction must be exilic. Of course, there is another element to his argument—he assumed that the final redaction of DtrH was exilic in order to emphasize that the Deuteronomic redaction of Jer occurred in the same setting.

The combined influence of Noth's dating of DtrH and Hyatt's dating of the Deuteronomic redaction of Jer has influenced numerous commentators of Jer. Such an influence is found in the work of Nicholson, Thiel, and many others.[4] As we have seen above, Noth's exilic dating of DtrH is itself questionable. However, when Noth's argument for DtrH is assumed in the study of Jer, it becomes even more problematic. Therefore, the combined influence of Noth's exilic dating of DtrH and Hyatt's exilic dating of the Deuteronomic redaction of Jer must be seriously questioned.

3.   Hyatt, 'Deuteronomic Edition of Jeremiah', pp. 263-64. The following observations are not all that Hyatt gave to support his exilic date for the Deuteronomic redaction of Jer, but are those data which are generally accepted by those who later refined his thesis (e.g. Nicholson). Hyatt's own argument was more detailed and nuanced than what is given here; therefore, his work should be consulted for a fuller understanding of the support for his dating. See also Hyatt, *Jeremiah*, pp. 788-91.

4.   E.W. Nicholson, *Deuteronomy and Tradition* (Philadelphia: Fortress Press, 1967), pp. 107-18; Nicholson, *Preaching*, p. 117; Nicholson, *Jeremiah 1–25*, pp. 10-14. Thiel, *Redaktion von Jeremia 1–25*, pp. 28-45; Thiel, *Redaktion von Jeremia 26–45*, pp. 107-112. Also, S. Böhmer, *Heimkehr und neuer Bund: Studien zu Jeremia 30–31* (GTA, 5; Göttingen: Vandenhoeck & Ruprecht, 1976), pp. 81-85; Herrmann, *Prophetie und Wirklichkeit*, pp. 12-17; K.M. O'Conner, *The Confessions of Jeremiah* (SBLDS, 94; Atlanta: Scholars Press, 1988), p. 157.

Against this generally held exilic date, I will discuss evidence that suggests that the Deuteronomic school actively redacted Jer in the post-exilic period. In this context, I assume the validity of the text-critical studies of Cross, Jansen and Tov, all three of whom argued that the *Vorlage* of LXX-Jer preserves an earlier stage of the redaction of Jer in contrast to the expansive character of LXX-Jer.[5] Therefore, I will first discuss the data concerning the date of the Deuteronomic redaction of Jer which are common to both LXX-Jer and MT-Jer and, then, that which is unique to MT-Jer. I will then briefly discuss the implications of this text-critical work concerning the relationship between LXX-Jer and MT-Jer as it applies to the question of dating the Deuteronomic redaction of Jer.

Material Common to MT-Jer and LXX-Jer

In this section, I discuss only that material which is found in both MT-Jer and LXX-Jer.[6] Biblical quotations given in this section follow

---

5.   F. M. Cross, 'The Evolution of a Theory of Local Texts', in *Qumran and the History of the Biblical Text* (ed. F.M. Cross and S. Talmon; Cambridge, MA: Harvard University Press, 1975), pp. 306-20; J.G. Janzen, *Studies in the Text of Jeremiah* (HSM, 6; Cambridge, MA: Harvard University Press, 1973); and Tov, 'Aspects'; Tov, 'L'incidence', and Tov, 'Literary History'. See also B. Gosse, 'Jérémie xlv et la place du recueil d'oracles contre les nations dans le livre de Jérémie', *VT* 40 (1990), pp. 145-51; McKane, *Jeremiah*, I, pp. xv-xli, l-liii; A. Schenker, 'Nebukadnezzars Metamorphose vom Unterjocher zum Gottesknecht. Das Bild Nebukadnezzars und einige mit ihm zusammenhängende Unterschiede in den beiden Jeremia-Rezensionen', *RB* 89 (1982), pp. 498-527; L. Stulman, *The Prose Sermons of the Book of Jeremiah* (SBLDS, 83; Atlanta: Scholars Press, 1986); R.D. Wells, Jr, 'Indications of Late Reinterpretation of the Jeremiah Tradition of the LXX of Jer 21.1–23.8', *ZAW* 96 (1984), pp. 405-20. My argument (like that of some others, most notably Tov) can be described as a deconstruction of Cross's work. That is, I use text-critical arguments concerning DtrH and Jer, on which he has been very influential, to argue against his understanding of the dual redaction of DtrH. In my reading of his work and that of many of his students, I see little integration of these two areas in which he has been widely influential. In fact, his own conclusions in these two areas are contradictory; therefore, the reader must keep in mind when I am appropriating his text-critical arguments and when I am rejecting his arguments concerning redaction history.

6.   MT-Jer and LXX-Jer refer, respectively, to *BHS* and J. Ziegler, *Ieremias, Baruch, Threni, Epistula Ieremias* (Septuaginta Vetus Testamentum Graecum Auctoritate Societatis Göttingensis, 15; Göttingen: Vandenhoeck & Ruprecht, 1957).

LXX-Jer against MT-Jer when they disagree.

The material common to MT-Jer and LXX-Jer does not present us with a unified picture concerning setting. Some of the Jeremianic material predates the destruction of Jerusalem in 587 BCE. Other passages suggest at least an exilic setting, including the following Deuteronomic passage.[7]

> Death shall be preferred to life by all the remnant that remains of this evil family in all the places where I have driven them (Jer 8.3).

There are other Deuteronomic passages, however, which may indicate a post-exilic setting in their use of *vaticinia ex eventu,* for example:

> For thus says the Lord, 'When seventy years are completed for Babylon, I will visit you, and I will fulfill to you my promise and bring you back to this place (Jer 29.10 [LXX 36.10]).

Therefore, there is ambiguity in the determination of the setting of the material common to MT-Jer and LXX-Jer. Given this ambiguity, if we can find enough evidence to argue for a post-exilic setting of some of the material common to MT-Jer and LXX-Jer, we can conclude that the post-exilic redaction(s) did not thoroughly revise all of the exilic material from previous redactions. Below, is an analysis of those elements that suggest a post-exilic date for the Deuteronomic redaction of material common to MT-Jer and LXX-Jer.

The Theme of the Return and the Restoration
The first element considered is that of the possible references to the defeat of the Babylonians by the Persians in 539 BCE and the subsequent return of the exiles to Yehud beginning in 538 BCE. In the material common to MT-Jer and LXX-Jer, a calculation is given for the length of the exile in the Deuteronomic material.[8]

7. See Carroll, *From Chaos to Covenant*, p. 84; Carroll, *Jeremiah*, pp. 224-26; Hyatt, 'Deuteronomic Edition of Jeremiah', pp. 254-55; Hyatt, *Jeremiah*, p. 877; Thiel, *Redaktion von Jeremia 1–25*, pp. 128-34.

8. Tov ('Literary History', p. 236) suggested the possibility of the redaction of the material common to MT and LXX (his 'version 1') to the post-exilic period as possibly indicated in Jer 25.11; 29.10 (LXX 36.10). On Jer 25.11-12 as Deuteronomic, see Carroll, *Jeremiah*, pp. 493-96; Hyatt, 'Deuteronomic Edition of Jeremiah', pp. 258-59; Hyatt, *Jeremiah*, pp. 1000-1001; E.W. Nicholson, *The Book of the Prophet Jeremiah, Chapters 26–52* (CBC; Cambridge: Cambridge University Press, 1975), p. 209. On Jer 29.10 as Deuteronomic, see Carroll, *From Chaos to*

> The whole land shall become a waste, and they shall serve among the
> nations seventy years. Then after seventy years are completed, I will
> punish that nation, for their iniquity, making the land an everlasting waste
> (Jer 25.11-12).

> For thus says the Lord, 'When seventy years are completed for Babylon,
> I will visit you, and I will fulfill to you my promise and bring you back to
> this place (Jer 29.10 [LXX 36.10]).[9]

This calculation of seventy years suggests that the Deuteronomic
redactor may have known of the defeat of Babylon by the Persians.[10]

However, when one does a little adding, how can the seventy years
refer to the defeat of the Babylonians in 539 BCE when only 48 years
have passed since the 587/86 destruction of Jerusalem? Here the reference
to the seventy years in Zech 1.12 (see also 2 Chron 36.21; Dan
9.2) helps us clarify this problem. In Zech 1.12, the seventy-year
period roughly covers the time from the destruction of Jerusalem and
its temple in 587/86 BCE to the time of the rededication of the temple
in 516/15 BCE. This understanding of the seventy-year period is also
suggested in Jer 29.10 in that the return to Yehud is associated with
the seventy-year period. Therefore, it may be that the Deuteronomic
redactor of Jer used the post-exilic reckoning of seventy years to
denote not only the period of Babylonian power, but the period of the
exile from the destruction of Jerusalem in 587/86 BCE to an important
symbol of the restoration of Yehud, the rededication of the temple in
516/15 BCE. In other words, the defeat of the Babylonians by the
Persians (539 BCE) does not demarcate the end of the seventy-year
period, but is included within it (587/86–516/15 BCE).[11]

Covenant, pp. 189-92; Carroll, *Jeremiah*, pp. 555-63; Hyatt, 'Deuteronomic Edition
of Jeremiah', p. 260; Hyatt, *Jeremiah*, pp. 1016-17; Nicholson, *Jeremiah 26–52*,
p. 46.

9. Carroll (*Jeremiah*, pp. 557-59) argued that Jer 29.10-14 is post-exilic, considering its restoration theme as *vaticinia ex eventu* (*Jeremiah*, p. 558). Although his argument was based upon MT, those elements which he used in his argument are found in the material common to LXX and MT.

10. Tov, 'Literary History', 236; Carroll, *Jeremiah*, p. 68.

11. See C.F. Whitley, 'The Term Seventy Years Captivity', *VT* 4 (1954), pp. 60-72. Although he understood this term to be Jeremianic, Whitley also identified the period described by this term to be 586–516 BCE. Against this, see Meyers and Meyers, *Haggai, Zechariah 1–8*, pp. 117-18; D.L. Petersen, *Haggai and Zechariah 1-8* (OTL; Philadelphia: Westminster Press, 1984), pp. 149-51; R.E. Winkle, 'Jeremiah's Seventy Years for Babylon: A Re-Assessment. Part I: The Scriptural

Other Deuteronomic material also suggests the period of the restoration as its setting, including the rebuilding of Jerusalem. For example,[12]

> Return, O faithless children, says the Lord; for I am your master; I will take you one from a city and two from a family, and I will bring you to Zion...It [the ark of the covenant] shall not come to mind, or be remembered, or missed; it shall not be made again (Jer 3.14, 16).

> Behold the days are coming, says the Lord, when I will make a new covenant with the house of Israel and the house of Judah...I will put my law within them, and I will write it upon their hearts; and I will be their God and they will be my people (Jer 31.31, 33).

Within the Deuteronomic redaction of Jer, there is an emphasis upon the Jerusalem temple.[13] Although the narratives refer to the destroyed Solomonic Temple, they make better sense within a Judaean setting, where the people could continue their worship at the temple site, rather than a Babylonian exilic setting. Although worship possibly continued during the Babylonian exile at the temple site, the combination of the restoration language and the thematic emphasis upon the temple in the Deuteronomic material suggests a Second Temple setting of the Deuteronomic redaction evident in the material common to the MT-Jer and the LXX-Jer.[14] In other words, rather than understanding this

Data', *AUSS* 25 (1987), pp. 201-14; R.E. Winkle, 'Jeremiah's Seventy Years for Babylon: A Re-Assessment. Part II: The Historical Data', *AUSS* 25 (1987), pp. 289-99.

12. Carroll, *Jeremiah*, p. 72. Carroll also identified the entire cycles of material in Jer 30–31 and Jer 32–33 as concerning the return and the restoration. Although they assumed these passages are exilic, the following commentators also understood Jer 3.14, 16; 31.31, 33 as Deuteronomic:

On Jer 3.14, 16, see Hyatt, 'Deuteronomic Edition of Jeremiah', p. 254; Hyatt, *Jeremiah*, p. 826; Nicholson, *Jeremiah 1–25*, p. 45.

On Jer 31.31, 33, see Nicholson, *Jeremiah 26–52*, pp. 70-71; Thiel, *Redaktion von Jeremia 26–45*, pp. 23-27.

13. See Jer 7.2-4; 11.2, 6; 16.2-4; 19.3-9; 22.1-5; 26.2-6.

14. Carroll, *Jeremiah*, p. 69. See also D.L. Petersen, 'The Temple in Persian Period Prophetic Texts', in *Second Temple Studies: 1. Persian Period* (ed. P.R. Davies; JSOTSup, 117; Sheffield: JSOT Press, 1991), p. 133; Wells, 'Indications of Late Reinterpretation', pp. 409-10, 420. Petersen argued that Jer 33 is from the Persian period and reflects the cultic practice of the Second Temple. Concerning Jer 21.1–23.8, Wells noted that the theme of hope in LXX concerning the monarchy is downplayed in MT with fuller emphasis on the hope of the exiles. He also discussed briefly the possibility of the postexilic setting of MT.

restoration language as *vaticinia pro eventu*, it is better to understand
the restoration language as *vaticinia ex eventu* and, rather than understanding the emphasis upon the temple as reflecting primarily the
historical Jeremiah and the Solomonic Temple, it is better to understand this emphasis as renewed interest in the temple cult within a
Second Temple setting.[15]

The Plurality of Traditions Represented

The next element that I want to discuss is Carroll's observation that
Jer preserves 'different *interests* represented by the various traditions
in the text'.[16] As examples, he gave the following themes within cycles
of texts, which betray distinctive interests and, therefore, the probability of different social groups:

> the Judean kings (21.11–23.6), the prophets (23.9-40; 27–29), the return
> of the exiles and the reconstructions of the land (30–31; 32–33), ideolo-
> gical criticisms of the cult (6.20; 7.1–8.3; 11.9-13; 19.3-9, 12–13), the
> foreign nations (46–51), the Jewish communities in Egypt (42.7–44.30),
> the Judean community under Gedaliah (40.7–41.18), and relations between
> Jeremiah and important social strata (26; 36; 37–39)…the denigration of
> the Judean communities in favour of the exiles in Babylon (24.4-10;
> 29.10-19), the favouring of the Judean communities over against the
> Jewish exiles in Egypt (42.7–44.30), and the differentiation of various
> strata of people in Jerusalem (e.g. 21.3-10; 35; 38.2; 39.15-18; 45).[17]

This diversity of interests reflects competing traditions. The observation that this diversity is found in one text suggests that the redaction
of Jer occurred over a long period. The collection of various traditions that support such geographically distant groups as the Babylonian
exiles, the exiles in Egypt, and those who remained in Judah suggests

15. This is not to say that there is no historical kernel to the Deuteronomic narrative's emphasis upon the Solomonic Temple. Rather, it is a statement about the purpose and function of these narratives—that is, they are not *merely* descriptive of the
past; they are also normative for the present.

16. Emphasis his. Carroll, *Jeremiah*, p. 69. Although his comments refer to the
stage of the redaction represented in MT-Jer, Carroll's argument in relation to the difference between LXX and MT can, nevertheless, lead to the conclusion that his observations are equally valid for the material common to MT and LXX. In other words, his
observations do not depend entirely upon material unique to MT and thus, with some
refinements, are used here to discuss the material common to MT and LXX.

17. Carroll, *Jeremiah*, p. 70. The versification which he gave is that of MT and
includes some material unique to MT.

the post-exilic period as the most probable setting for bringing these traditions together—that is, the collecting of these various traditions parallels the return of the people of the Diaspora to Yehud and the Second Temple. For this reason, Carroll concluded that these various traditions 'must be seen as the product of different groups within the Judean territory struggling for power and position over a long period after the fall of Jerusalem'[18] and that this observation 'points to a fifth-century dating' of the Deuteronomic redaction of Jer.[19]

In summary, the evidence in the material common to MT-Jer and LXX-Jer suggests a post-exilic setting for its Deuteronomic redaction. This evidence includes the themes of the return and restoration as *vaticinia ex eventu*, including the figure of seventy years from the destruction of Jerusalem in 587 BCE to the rededication of the temple in 516/15 BCE. These themes of the return and the restoration are closely related to the emphasis placed upon the Jerusalem temple, which suggests a Second Temple setting. Also, the plurality of conflicting traditions represented in Jer suggests a long period of time for its redaction. Therefore, the stage of the Deuteronomic redaction of Jer represented in the material common to MT-Jer and LXX-Jer should be located within the postexilic period.[20]

Material Unique to MT-Jeremiah

In this section, I will discuss the material that is unique to MT. All biblical quotations are based upon MT-Jer against LXX-Jer. The material unique to MT-Jer is given in italics.

Material Unique to MT-Jer: Its Post-Exilic Setting

If the redaction represented by LXX-Jer is post-exilic, one would expect the later material unique to MT-Jer to betray its post-exilic setting even more—that is, even though the material common to

18. Carroll, *Jeremiah*, p. 70.

19. Carroll, *Jeremiah*, p. 79. Concerning some of the same material, K.-F. Pohlmann reached a similar conclusion (*Studien zum Jeremiabuch* [FRLANT, 118; Göttingen: Vandenhoeck & Ruprecht, 1978], p. 204). McKane also understood the redaction history of Jer as complex and extending into the post-exilic period (*Jeremiah*, I, pp. lxxxviii-xcii).

20. Although this formulation differs significantly from that of Hyatt concerning the scope of the Deuteronomic redaction, it agrees with Hyatt's conclusion that LXX-Jer is post-exilic.

MT-Jer and LXX-Jer comes from pre-exilic, exilic and post-exilic times, the material which is unique to MT would be exclusively post-exilic in origin.[21] This expectation is confirmed by the following evidence.[22] (Even if one does not agree with the above conclusion of a post-exilic setting for the redaction reflected in the material common to MT and LXX, the following evidence should, standing alone, suffice for the post-exilic setting of the material unique to MT.)

MT-Jer contains additions that describe the fall of the Babylonian empire as *vaticinia ex eventu*. For example,

> Then after seventy years are completed, I will punish *the king of Babylon and* that nation, *the land of the Chaldeans,* for their iniquity, *says the Lord,* making the land an everlasting waste...*For they too shall be enslaved by many nations and great kings; and I will requite them according to their acts and according to their conduct* (Jer 25.12, 14).

In this example, we see an elaboration upon the theme of the defeat of Babylon (Babylon is specifically described), which suggests a post-exilic setting for these additions. Keeping in mind the above argument that the material common to MT-Jer and LXX-Jer in these same verses is post-exilic, this elaboration upon the theme of the defeat of Babylon must be even later in the post-exilic period.

MT-Jer also contains additions that foreshadow the return to Yehud from Babylon as *vaticinia ex eventu*. For example,[23]

---

21. Of course, a later redactor may have added original material, but this does not seem to be the case for the material unique to MT-Jer. The additions in MT-Jer are primarily due to the repetition of sections found in the material common to MT-Jer and LXX-Jer and clarifying additions, such as the addition of titles and names. See Tov, 'Literary History', pp. 215-37.

22. The following is taken from Tov, 'Literary History', pp. 236-37, unless otherwise noted. When available, Tov's translation is followed. In his translation, Tov followed the New Jerusalem Bible 'as much as possible' (p. 218 n. 24). See also Stulman, *Prose Sermons*, p. 146. Stulman agreed with Tov that the additions in MT represent 'repatriates who had returned to Judea' (p. 146).

23. Tov, 'Literary History', pp. 221-22. See also E. Tov, 'Exegetical Remarks on the Hebrew Vorlage of the LXX of Jeremiah 27', *ZAW* 91 (1979), pp. 89-90; Carroll, *Jeremiah*, pp. 529-37. For a lengthier discussion of the difference between LXX and MT concerning the temple vessels, see P.-M. Bogaert, 'Les mécanismes redactionnels en Jér 10,1-16 (LXX et TM) et la signification des supplements', in *Le livre Jérémie* (ed. P.-M. Bogaert; BETL, 54; Leuven: Leuven University Press, 1981), pp. 236-37.

> For thus said the Lord *of Hosts concerning the columns, the tank, the stands and* concerning the rest of the vessels *which remain in this city,* which *Nebuchadnezzar* the king of Babylon did not take when he exiled Jeconiah *son of Jehoiakim, king of Judah* from Jerusalem *to Babylon, with all the nobles of Judah and Jerusalem—thus said the Lord of Hosts, the God of Israel, concerning the vessels remaining in the house of the Lord, in the royal palace of Judah and Jerusalem:* They shall be brought to Babylon *and there they shall remain until I take note of them—*declares the Lord—*and bring them up and restore them to this place* (Jer 27.19-22).

Although the temple vessels may have played some role in the worship among the exiles, the heightened concern of the temple vessels in these verses makes more sense within a setting of the Second Temple, when the worshiping community was struggling with the question of the relationship between the Solomonic Temple and the Second Temple. In other words, within the struggle for the legitimation of the Second Temple these verses where expanded so as to add more specificity to the account of the return of the temple vessels, thereby connecting the Second Temple more closely to the Solomonic Temple.

Some material unique to the MT-Jer not only foreshadows the return to Yehud from Babylon as *vaticinia ex eventu*, but also includes the return from the broader Diaspora. For example,[24]

> I will be found by you, *says the Lord, and I will restore your fortunes and gather you from all the nations and all the places where I have driven you, says the Lord, and I will bring you back to the place from which I sent you into exile* (Jer 29.14).[25]

> *then all the Jews returned from all the places to which they had been driven* and came to the land of Judah, to Gedaliah at Mizpah; and they gathered wine and summer fruits in great abundance (Jer 40.12).

These additions in MT-Jer do not simply refer to the return from the Babylonian exile, but have a much broader focus—that is, the return from all of the Diaspora. In fact, the language used here to refer to the collective of the returnees ('*the Jews*' [היהודים]) occurs primarily in

24. These two examples are given in J. Lust, '"Gathering and Returning" in Jeremiah and Ezekiel', in *Le livre Jérémie* (ed. P.-M. Bogaert), p. 136. The translation used is the RSV.

25. Carroll (*Jeremiah*, pp. 557-59) also argued that Jer 29.10-14 is post-exilic with its restoration theme being *vaticinia ex eventu* (*Jeremiah*, p. 558).

post-exilic literature.[26] Therefore, it would be difficult to understand this addition as coming from the Deuteronomic school's activity in exilic Babylon (or Egypt or Judah). Rather, it is better understood as reflecting the post-exilic period when returnees from throughout the Diaspora came to Yehud.

In the material unique to MT-Jer, we find a heightening of themes which might suggest a post-exilic setting for MT-Jer—that is, the fall of Babylon, the return from Babylon to Yehud, the return from the broader Diaspora to Yehud, and the emphasis upon the Temple. Such heightening betrays a greater interest in these themes in the post-exilic period and is best explained as *vaticinia ex eventu*.

Material Unique to MT-Jer: Its Deuteronomic Redaction
Most of the additions in MT-Jer are quite generic and, therefore, reveal nothing about the identification of the later redactor. Such additions include headings and superscriptions, titles, proper names and place names.[27] However, some of the additions in MT-Jer suggest a Deuteronomic redactor. Tov provides the following examples of MT-Jer additions that contain Deuteronomic language:[28]

> and though I spoke to you *persistently,* you would not listen (7.13; see also 35.15).[29]

> *For I surely warned your fathers on the day that I brought them up from the land of Egypt, persistently until this day, warning 'Listen to me'. And they would not listen and they would not incline their ears but each of them walked in the stubbornness of his evil heart. Therefore I brought to them all the words of this covenant, which I had commanded them to make* (11.7-8).[30]

26. See above, p. 49 n. 30.

27. For examples, see Tov, 'Literary History'.

28. This list is found in Tov, 'Aspects', p. 164; Tov, 'Literary History', p. 233; Tov, 'L'incidence', p. 196. The list provided in 'L'incidence' has some examples not included in the later revisions; these will be noted below. When available, the English translations are from Tov's article, 'Literary History', p. 233. For most of these additions, Tov referred to Bright's list of 'characteristic expressions of the prose sermons of Jeremiah' ('Date of the Prose Sermons', pp. 207-11). These references are also given here as well as references to phrases found in Weinfeld's list of typical Deuteronomic language.

29. Bright, 'Date of the Prose Sermons', p. 207; Weinfeld, *Deuteronomy and the Deuteronomic School*, p. 352.

30. My translation. This example is not given in the lists in Tov, 'Aspects',

This wicked people who refuse to heed my bidding *who follow the will-fulness of their own hearts* (13.10).[31]

because of the desperate straits to which they will be reduced by their enemies *who seek their life* (19.9; see also 34.20; 38.16).[32]

Else my wrath will break forth like fire and burn, with none to quench *because of your wicked acts* (21.12).[33]

I will punish you according to the fruits of your deeds, says Yahweh (21.14).[34]

Do not listen to the words of the prophets *who prophesy to you* (23.16).[35]

From the thirteenth year...I have spoken to you persistently, *but you would not listen* (25.3).[36]

But you would not listen to me *declares the Lord; you vexed me with what your hands made to your own hurt* (25.7).[37]

to repay every man according to his ways, *and with the proper fruit of his deeds* (32.19).[38]

then all the Jews returned from all the places to which they had been driven (40.12).[39]

p. 164; Tov, 'Literary History', p. 233, but is found in Tov, 'L'incidence', p. 196. Cf. Bright, 'Date of the Prose Sermons', pp. 207, 209, 211; Weinfeld, *Deuteronomy and the Deuteronomic School*, p. 352.

31. Bright, 'Date of the Prose Sermons', p. 207.

32. Bright, 'Date of the Prose Sermons', p. 208.

33. Bright, 'Date of the Prose Sermons', p. 208; Weinfeld, *Deuteronomy and the Deuteronomic School*, p. 352.

34. My translation. This example is not given in the lists in Tov, 'Aspects', p. 164; Tov, 'Literary History', p. 233, but is found in Tov, 'L'incidence', p. 196. Bright, 'Date of the Prose Sermons', pp. 208, 211.

35. Bright, 'Date of the Prose Sermons', p. 208.

36. Bright, 'Date of the Prose Sermons', p. 207.

37. Bright, 'Date of the Prose Sermons', p. 207; Weinfeld, *Deuteronomy and the Deuteronomic School*, p. 340.

38. Bright, 'Date of the Prose Sermons', p. 208.

39. My translation. This example is not given in the lists in Tov, 'Aspects', p. 164; Tov, 'Literary History', p. 233, but is found in Tov, 'L'incidence', p. 196. Cf. Bright, 'Date of the Prose Sermons', p. 210; Weinfeld, *Deuteronomy and the Deuteronomic School*, p. 348.

now therefore, hear the word of Yahweh, *O remnant of Judah* (42.15).[40]

the entire remnant of Judah who had returned *from all the countries to which they had been scattered* (43.5).[41]

The following additions in MT-Jer are taken from other Deuteronomic literature:

for there is no rain *in the land* (14.4; see 1 Kgs 17.7).[42]

You shall die this year *for you have urged disloyalty to the Lord* (28.16; see Deut 13.6).[43]

for he has urged disloyalty to the Lord (29.32; see Deut 13.6).[44]

and you must send him free *from your service* (34.14; see Deut 15.12-13).[45]
and every land *in her dominion* (51.28; see 1 Kgs 9.19).[46]

And he [Zedekiah] did evil in the sight of Yahweh, according to all that Jehoiakim had done. For because of the anger of Yahweh it came to pass in Jerusalem and Judah that he cast them out from his presence (52.2-3; see 2 Kgs 24.19-20).[47]

The evidence above is categorized according to two types: (1) MT-Jer additions that betray a Deuteronomic origin because of their phraseology and (2) MT-Jer additions that are taken from other Deuteronomic literature. Because of this evidence, Tov properly concluded that

---

40. My translation. This example is not given in Tov, 'Aspects', p. 164; Tov, 'Literary History', p. 233, but is found in Tov, 'L'incidence', p. 196. Cf. Bright, 'Date of the Prose Sermons', pp. 209-10.

41. Bright, 'Date of the Prose Sermons', p. 210; Weinfeld, *Deuteronomy and the Deuteronomic School*, p. 348.

42. Janzen, *Studies in the Text of Jeremiah*, p. 40. My translation.

43. Tov, 'L'incidence', p. 197; Janzen, *Studies in the Text of Jeremiah*, p. 48. Tov's translation ('Literary History', p. 233). Tov noted that the use of סרה 'disloyalty' with a form of the verb דבר 'to urge' occurs outside MT-Jer only in Deut 13.6.

44. Tov, 'L'incidence', p. 197; Janzen, *Studies in the Text of Jeremiah*, p. 49. The translation is taken from Tov's translation of the previous example with the change to third person. See previous note.

45. Tov, 'L'incidence', p. 197; Janzen, *Studies in the Text of Jeremiah*, p. 51. My translation.

46. Janzen, *Studies in the Text of Jeremiah*, p. 62. My translation.

47. See also Person, 'II Kings 24,18-25,30 and Jeremiah 52'; Weinfeld, *Deuteronomy and the Deuteronomic School*, pp. 335, 339. My translation.

both the LXX-Jer redactor and the MT-Jer redactor belonged to the Deuteronomic school.[48]

Two conclusions emerge concerning the material unique to MT-Jer. First, in comparison to the material common to LXX-Jer and MT-Jer, a heightening of the restoration themes suggests a post-exilic setting. Second, the inclusion of Deuteronomic language and other language that is typical of the Deuteronomic prose sections of Jer suggest that

48. 'L'incidence', p. 199. Nicholson reached a similar conclusion concerning Jer 29.16-20: 'Vv. 16-20 which are missing in the LXX and may represent a later and further expansion of the chapter also show strong indications that they owe their composition to the Deuteronomists' (*Preaching*, p. 99).

The criticisms of the Deuteronomic redaction of Jer generally ignore text critical evidence; however, one recent study takes seriously the text critical evidence and rejects Tov's conclusion concerning the Deuteronomic redaction of MT-Jer (Stulman, *Prose Sermons*). Stulman provided a statistical analysis of the material unique to MT-Jer in 'source C' and concluded that the diction in this material is more conventional, but less Deuteronomic, than the material common to MT-Jer and LXX-Jer. Therefore, he rejected Tov's conclusion that MT-Jer is also a Deuteronomic redaction. However, his statistical data are skewed because of two methodological problems:

a. His analysis was limited to 'source C', the 'prose sermons' (3.6-13; 7.1-8.3; 11.1-14; 16.1-15; 17.19-27; 18.1-12; 19.2b-9, 11b-13; 21.1-10; 22.1-5; 25.1-14; 27.1-22; 29.1-32; 32.1-44; 33.1-26; 34.1-22; 35.1-19; 39.15-18; 44.1-4; 45.1-5). Hence, his analysis did not include some of the passages in which Tov found some of his examples (13.10; 38.16; 21.12, 14; 23.16; 28.16; 40.12; 42.15; 43.5; 52.2-3). Any study that seeks to criticize Tov's conclusion must include, rather than a limited corpus, all of Jer.

b. As Stulman himself noted, 'the vast majority of the [MT] additions...have no significant bearing on the subject-matter in [LXX]. They are essentially elaborations of the text' (*Prose Sermons*, p. 141). He went on to note that these elaborations include adjectives, adverbs, appositions, titles, proper names, divine epithets and prophetic formulae. However, when he devised his word-count system, he ignored the implications of this 'vast majority of additions' on his statistical data. If the 'vast majority of additions' in MT are additions such as proper names, titles and divine epithets, one would expect the diction even of a Deuteronomic redactor to contain a smaller percentage of Deuteronomic phrases. Therefore, his statistical data, especially his word-count system, needs to be corrected to reflect the nature of this 'vast majority of additions'. Any such adjustment will narrow his supposed statistical gap between the diction in the material unique to MT and the material common to LXX and MT, thereby undercutting his conclusions.

The statistical evidence that Stulman provided to reject Tov's conclusion was poorly controlled. The sample was too limited and the word-count system for devising percentages for comparison fails to acknowledge the different types of data in each of his samples. Therefore, Stulman's conclusions must be rejected.

the redactor of MT-Jer also belonged to the Deuteronomic school. Therefore, MT-Jer is the product of a Deuteronomic redactor who reinterpreted an earlier Deuteronomic edition (the material common to LXX-Jer and MT-Jer) within a later, post-exilic setting.

The Relationship of MT-Jer to LXX-Jer and its Implications

The restoration themes in the material common to MT-Jer and LXX-Jer are heightened in the material unique to MT-Jer. This heightening reflects a post-exilic setting for MT-Jer. Other evidence is found in the overall textual relationship between LXX-Jer and MT-Jer. Since it contains material narrating some exilic events, LXX-Jer can be exilic at the earliest; therefore, MT must be even later. In comparing MT-Jer to LXX-Jer, one recognizes the extensive reworking contained in MT-Jer. LXX-Jer is one-eighth shorter than MT-Jer and the locations of the oracles against the foreign nations differ. Such extensive reworking suggests a long lapse of time between LXX-Jer and MT-Jer; therefore, even if LXX-Jer is exilic, the probability for MT-Jer being post-exilic is high.[49]

Summary of Chapter 2:
Conclusions concerning the Book of Jeremiah

A review of the argument for the exilic date for the Deuteronomic redaction of Jer has revealed its weaknesses. The argument that the absence of explicit references to the post-exilic period indicates an exilic redaction seems rooted in Noth's exilic dating of DtrH, which has influenced many Jer scholars directly and indirectly through Hyatt's dating of the Deuteronomic redaction of Jer to the exilic period. Such dating is to be rejected as not adequately established, since it is based solely upon a *terminus a quo*.

Against this generally held view, two types of evidence have been reviewed—namely, text-critical and thematic evidence. The additions in MT-Jer provided by text-critical analysis suggest that MT-Jer is a post-exilic work from the hand of a Deuteronomic redactor. The thematic evidence concerning the restoration and the return appears to

---

49. Tov, 'Aspects', p. 167; Tov, 'Literary History', p. 237. For a fuller discussion of the evidence concerning an extended lapse of time between the two redactions, see Bogaert, 'Mécanismes rédactionnels en Jér 10,1-16'; Lust, 'Gathering and Returning'.

refer to a post-exilic setting. Also, the observation that Jer contains various traditions apparently reflects conflict between different exilic groups and suggests the post-exilic period as the setting in which these traditions came together within one book at the same time as the people came together in Yehud. When both of these types of evidence are combined, the conclusion that MT-Jer is post-exilic is strengthened—that is, the additions in MT-Jer contain a heightened interest in the themes of restoration and return, making these themes even more explicit. Such a tendency to heighten elements that refer to a return to Yehud suggests that the MT-Jer additions are *vaticinia ex eventu* and suggests that MT-Jer is a product of a post-exilic Deuteronomic redactor.

Summary of Part I:
Deuteronomic Redaction in the Post-Exilic Period

The generally held view concerning the final Deuteronomic redaction of both DtrH and Jer is as follows: since the historical narrative stops with the destruction of Jerusalem and the exile, the redaction must be exilic. Against this view, I have provided both text-critical and thematic evidence that suggests a post-exilic setting for the final redaction of both of these works. Significantly, these two independent arguments concerning DtrH and Jer can be easily related to one another and provide two examples of a progression of redactional activity within the Deuteronomic school.

The text-critical evidence for a post-exilic redaction of both DtrH and Jer consists of the divergence between various textual traditions, most notably between LXX and MT. Although this divergence is greater and more easily studied in Jer, some studies suggest a similar phenomenon for DtrH. Deuteronomic redactions of DtrH and Jer in the post-exilic period are suggested by two factors: (1) Textual divergence does not necessarily suggest that the later redactions of DtrH and MT-Jer are Deuteronomic. However, the MT additions contain phrases that betray their Deuteronomic origin. Also, the many scholars who, in their arguments concerning the redaction of DtrH and Jer, base their work primarily upon MT ironically support my thesis by failing to recognize the variants for which we have text-critical evidence suggesting different redactions. (2) The extensive divergence between MT and LXX suggests a long lapse of time between the Deuteronomic redactions represented by MT and LXX in order to account for the redactional activity and its hermeneutical settings. That is, different historical circumstances led to further redaction of DtrH and Jer within the Deuteronomic school. The change of circumstances has generally been argued to be that which occurred between pre-exilic Judah and exilic Babylon (or Egypt or Judah), but this is not necessarily the case. These later Deuteronomic redactions may have occurred in response to the different circumstances that were present in the return to Yehud and the problems associated with the restoration of Jerusalem and the Temple.

The thematic evidence for a post-exilic setting is found in the themes of the defeat of Babylon, the return to Yehud, and the restoration of the temple as *vaticinia ex eventu*. These themes, which are found within both DtrH and Jer and may suggest a post-exilic setting for their redaction, are heightened further in the later, expansive Jer, represented by MT-Jer, wherein the unique material strongly suggests a post-exilic setting.

Although there is sufficient evidence that *some* of the restoration imagery in DtrH and Jer is *vaticinia ex eventu* and is, therefore, post-exilic, this observation does not necessarily lead to the conclusion that *all* of the restoration language in DtrH and Jer is post-exilic. The prevalence of restoration language in some exilic texts (such as II Isa) makes such a generalization just as inappropriate as the generalization that all restoration language is exilic. Hence, although there is evidence for post-exilic restoration language in DtrH and Jer, there may also be exilic restoration language in them.

I have also presented evidence that prolongs the period of Deuteronomic redactional activity. Cross's generally accepted view that Deuteronomic redactional activity began during the time of Josiah and ended in the exilic period has been rejected; this limited period must be broadened to include the post-exilic period too. This new evidence suggests the need for a re-evaluation of the study of DtrH, Jer and other prophetic books redacted by the Deuteronomic school (e.g. Amos) and also suggests that traces of Deuteronomic redaction may be found in post-exilic books, which have until now been understood to fall outside the temporal scope of the redactional activity of the Deuteronomic school. This later point is that which is most important to the present study concerning II Zech—that is, Zech may have been redacted by the Deuteronomic school.

Part II

THE DEUTERONOMIC REDACTION OF ZECHARIAH

INTRODUCTION TO PART II

Mason's conclusion that 'no one source for Zech xiif. can be claimed as exclusive for its inspiration and reinterpretation'[1] is equally valid for all of II Zech, for it depends on various collections, especially II Isa, III Isa, Jer, and Ezek.[2] Although II Zech's dependence upon these prophetic collections has been widely observed, the close connection between II Zech and Deuteronomic literature has not been sufficiently recognized. Even though most of the connections between II Zech and Deuteronomic literature have already been made, the recognition of these connections has led no other commentator to conclude that II Zech was greatly influenced by Deuteronomic literature and, therefore, that it has possibly been edited by a Deuteronomic redactor. The absence of such a conclusion probably stems from the following presuppositions of most commentators: (1) The individual behind II Zech was a 'prophet', not a 'redactor'. (2) Jer is not Deuteronomic literature.[3] (3) The Deuteronomic school ceased in the exilic period. Taken together, these three presuppositions disallowed the possible suggestion that there was a Deuteronomic redaction of II Zech, for not only was the Deuteronomic school presumed to have ended before the time of II Zech, but the relationship of the 'prophet' of II Zech to the Latter Prophets was emphasized rather than any

1. 'Use of Earlier Biblical Material in Zechariah 9–14', p. 205.
2. Delcor, 'Sources'; Mason, 'Some Examples'; Mason, 'Use of Earlier Biblical Material in Zechariah 9–14'. See also Lamarche, *Zacharie IX–XIV*, pp. 124-47; N. Mendecki, 'Deuterojesajanischer und Ezechielischer Einfluss auf Sach 10:8-10', *Kairos* 27 (1985), pp. 340-44.
3. Delcor's work ('Sources'), which is often the basis of later works on inner-biblical exegesis in II Zech, predated Hyatt's thesis of the Deuteronomic redaction of Jer. Mason ('Use of Earlier Biblical Material in Zechariah 9–14') refers to some works that suggested that Jer was redacted by the Deuteronomic school (e.g. Nicholson, *Preaching*, is referred to on p. 95) and briefly discusses the 'Jeremiah/Deuteronomist tradition' (pp. 96-98). However, this connection is not referred to again after p. 98.

possible relationship between the 'redactor' of II Zech and the Deuteronomic redactors of both DtrH and Jer.[4]

These three presuppositions are unfounded and must be replaced with the following: (1) The individual behind II Zech was a redactor with a heightened interest in prophetic themes and forms. (2) The final form of Jer is the product of Deuteronomic redaction. (3) The redactional activity of the Deuteronomic school continued into the post-exilic period. With the combined strength of these three factors, the possibility of Deuteronomic redaction of Zech can be seriously considered, for only then can the full force of the close connections between II Zech and Deuteronomic literature become evident.

Here in Part II, the possibility of the Deuteronomic redaction of II Zech is considered in detail. Chapter 3 presents numerous examples of Deuteronomic language in II Zech. In Chapter 4, various Deuteronomic passages from DtrH and Jer, which significantly influenced the diction and imagery of II Zech, are discussed. Chapter 5 is a verse-by-verse discussion of possible Deuteronomic language and influence in II Zech. Chapter 6 summarizes the results of Chapters 3–5 and applies them to the question of the canonical shape of the book of Zechariah.

The method used in this part compares the language and imagery of II Zech to language and imagery throughout the Hebrew Bible with special reference to Deuteronomic literature. Such a method has been widely used in Jer studies, especially by Hyatt and other proponents of the Deuteronomic redaction of Jer.[5] However, the method employed here differs from that of Hyatt in two significant ways: (1) the results of studies concerning inner-biblical exegesis in II Zech have been incorporated[6] and (2) all of DtrH and Jer are considered part of the

4. Delcor ('Sources') discussed parallels primarily between II Zech and the Latter Prophets. The only literature he discussed that was not in the Latter Prophets is post-exilic (Job, Ezra, Nehemiah, Chronicles). His exclusion of DtrH with these post-exilic books may suggest that he also understood the Deuteronomic school to have ceased during the exile. Mason concluded, 'We seem to have here the work of a prophet or traditio-circle who revered the words of the great prophets' ('Some Examples', p. 353).

5. See especially Hyatt, 'Deuteronomic Edition of Jeremiah'; Nicholson, *Preaching*, pp. 7-10; Thiel, *Redaktion von Jeremia 1–25*, pp. 32-45; Weinfeld, *Deuteronomy and the Deuteronomic School*, pp. 1-3.

6. Although he does not discuss II Zech in any systematic manner, M. Fishbane's discussion of the methodological problems of discerning inner-biblical exegesis is noteworthy (*Biblical Interpretation in Ancient Israel* [Oxford:

Deuteronomic corpus during the time of II Zech. This broader consideration of the Deuteronomic corpus represents a significant change
from the narrower focus of Hyatt's and others' method; nevertheless,
three different means of presentation maintain the narrower comparison of II Zech to the Deuteronomic prose in Jer: (a) All passages
which Hyatt understood as Deuteronomic are indicated by an asterisk
following the reference (e.g. Jer 15.4*).[7] (b) The Deuteronomic
language found in II Zech includes those phrases that appear in
narrower studies concerning Jer, including especially Weinfeld's
comparison of the prose sermons in Jer ('source C') to DtrH. (c) The
discussion of significant Deuteronomic passages is confined to DtrH
and passages in Jer which are generally considered to be heavily
influenced by the Deuteronomic redactor(s). Hence, even though this
study considers all of DtrH and Jer as part of the Deuteronomic
corpus during the time of II Zech, indicators are given in order to
enable the reader to critique the Deuteronomic language given below
against more limited lists of Deuteronomic language (especially that of
Weinfeld).

For the purpose of cross-referencing, each example of Deuteronomic language in Chapter 3 is referred to by a number preceded by
the sign § (e.g. §4); each parallel in Chapter 4 on significant Deuteronomic passages, by a number preceded by the sign † or ‡ (e.g. †4, ‡5).

Digression: Possible Criticism of the Method Used

Hyatt's method and characterization of 'Deuteronomic language' has
been criticized, especially by John Bright and Helga Weippert.[8] These
criticisms have focused upon the significance of lexicographical similarities and dissimilarities between the prose in Jer and DtrH, especially upon the phrases characteristic of the prose in Jer which do not
occur outside of Jer. An excellent discussion of the presuppositions
and logic behind these competing orientations in Jer studies is

Oxford University Press, 1985], pp. 11-12).

7. Hyatt's determination of Deuteronomic prose is utilized because he first
proposed the thesis of the Deuteronomic redaction of Jer and his work is the
narrowest in its scope for what is considered Deuteronomic prose.

8. Bright, 'Date of the Prose Sermons'; Bright, *Jeremiah*; Weippert, *Prosareden
des Jeremiasbuches*.

provided by McKane in his review of Thiel, *Redaktion von Jeremia 1–25* (which follows Hyatt) and Weippert, *Prosareden des Jeremiasbuches* (which follows Bright against Hyatt):

> The absence of parallels to prose vocabulary of the book of Jeremiah in Deuteronomy and the Deuteronomistic literature does not deter [Thiel] from identifying this prose as Deuteronomic or Deuteronomistic. A state of affairs which for [Weippert] is evidence of a distinctive Jeremiah prose—prose disengaged from Deuteronomic or Deuteronomistic connections—is explained by him as the vocabulary of his Deuteronomistic editor of the book of Jeremiah. If the prose of the book of Jeremiah has external connections, he uses these in order to demonstrate that it is Deuteronomic or Deuteronomistic and is the work of a Deuteronomistic editor. If it does not have these external connections, he still maintains that it is derived from this editor, but the mode of argument is one which is internal to the prose of the book of Jeremiah and might be regarded as an argument in a circle. It depends on the discernment of affinities between different passages of prose, their constitution as a group and the conclusion that they all have the marks of the editor D. This is a case which is built up gradually by proceeding from one passage to the next and it has cumulative force only if one is persuaded of the validity of earlier conclusions all the way through. It leans heavily on the identification of the literary habits of the postulated D editor, on a claim to discern his attitude and objectives which sometimes seems exaggerated, and on the assumption that there is a comprehensive, systematic orientation under which all the passages can be subsumed. If one is convinced near the beginning and follows the argument from passage to passage, it takes on the appearance of a superstructure which has been raised on a foundation of sand.[9]

My adaptation of Hyatt's method is open to some of the same criticisms as that of Hyatt and Thiel—that is, it also depends upon the cumulative force of the gradual buildup of the evidence. As such, anyone who basically agrees with Bright and Weippert against Hyatt and Thiel probably disagreed with my previous chapter and will, therefore, disagree with the following arguments concerning II Zech as Deuteronomic.

---

9. 'Relations between Poetry and Prose', p. 273.

Chapter 3

DEUTERONOMIC LANGUAGE IN II ZECH

The method used in this chapter is an adaptation of the method used
by those, beginning with Hyatt, who argue for the Deuteronomc redaction of Jer. An important element in Hyatt's argument is his observation of Deuteronomic language in the prose sermons ('source C').
Building upon Hyatt's method, subsequent studies have provided lists
of Deuteronomic language in DtrH and Jer. This study makes use of
those lists, including ones that reject as well as support Hyatt's thesis.[1]

---

1. Reject: Bright, 'Date of the Prose Sermons', pp. 207-11.

   Support: Stulman, *Prose Sermons*, pp. 33-44; Thiel, *Redaktion von Jeremiah
26–45*, pp. 93-99; Weinfeld, *Deuteronomy and the Deuteronomic School*, pp. 320-
65.

   Other lists used include the following: J.E. Carpenter and G. Harford, *The
Composition of the Hexateuch* (New York: Longmans, Green & Co., 1902), pp. 147-
51; H. Cazelles, 'Jeremiah and Deuteronomy', in *A Prophet to the Nations* (ed.
Perdue and Kovacs), pp. 94-96; J.W. Colenso, *The Pentateuch and the Book of
Joshua Critically Examined* (London: Longman, Roberts, Green, 1862–79), pp. 391-
406; S.R. Driver, *A Critical and Exegetical Commentary on Deuteronomy* (ICC;
Edinburgh: T. &. T. Clark, 1965), pp. lxxviii-lxxxiv, xciii; W.L. Holladay, 'Prototype
and Copies: A New Approach to the Poetry-Prose Problem in the Book of
Jeremiah', *JBL* 79 (1960), pp. 354-66; H.G. May, 'Towards an Objective Approach
to the Book of Jeremiah: The Biographer', *JBL* 61 (1942), pp. 154-55; W.H.
Schmidt, 'Die deuteronomische Redaktion des Amosbuches. Zu den theologischen
Unterschieden zwischen dem Propheten Wort und seinem Sammler', *ZAW* 77
(1965), pp. 168-93.

   Concerning the documentation for these various lists: Weinfeld is always
given when available, and only phrases not given by him are documented for the
other works. Reference made by commentators of II Zech to these phrases will also
be given. The translation used for all phrases given by Weinfeld is his; otherwise the
translation is my own. Since these lists and the concordance used (*The New Concordance of the Bible* [ed. A. Even-Shoshan; Jerusalem: Kiryat Sefer, 1985]) are for
MT, this chapter is based upon MT.

Although the compilers of these various lists reached widely different conclusions, their lists present clearly the issue of the relationship between Jer and DtrH, and therefore require careful consideration in relation to my hypothesis of II Zech as Deuteronomic prose.

Hyatt argued that the predominance of Deuteronomic language within redactional material in Jer strongly suggested the Deuteronomic redaction of the book of Jer. My hypothesis of II Zech as Deuteronomic prose rests upon a similar argument. This chapter will present evidence for a high degree of Deuteronomic language in II Zech. An initial presentation of words and phrases found *only* in Deuteronomic literature (DtrH, Jer) and II Zech will be followed by a discussion of words and phrases found *primarily* in Deuteronomic literature and II Zech. Finally, language which, in its exact wording, is unique to II Zech, but nevertheless has a 'Deuteronomic character',[2] will be considered. Within each of these sections, the strongest evidence is given first.

Only in DtrH and II Zech

The wording in two verses in II Zech suggests the literary dependence of II Zech upon DtrH. These verses contain language not found elsewhere in the Hebrew Bible:

§1. The three terms of madness in Zech 12.4 certainly demonstrate the influence of Deuteronomic literature, specifically Deut 28.28.[3] 'Panic' (תמהון), is found only in Deut 28.28 and Zech 12.4; 'madness' (שגעון), only in Deut 28.28; 2 Kgs 9.20; and Zech 12.4; 'blindness' (עורון), only in Deut 28.28 and Zech 12.4. The combined occurrence of these three terms in Deut 28.28 and Zech 12.4—two of which are found only in these verses—demonstrates that the imagery in Zech 12.4 is dependent upon Deut 28.28.

---

2. Bright criticised Hyatt's hypothesis of the Deuteronomic redaction of Jer because some of the common expressions in 'source C' cannot be found anywhere in DtrH. However, even Bright admitted that some of these expressions had a 'Deuteronomic character' ('Date of the Prose Sermons', p. 193).

3. Fishbane, *Biblical Interpretation*, p. 501; Jones, *Haggai, Zechariah, Malachi*, p. 159; Lacocque, 'Zacharie 9–14', p. 187; Mason, *Haggai, Zechariah and Malachi*, p. 116; Mason, 'Use of Earlier Biblical Material in Zechariah 9–14', p. 214.

§2. The only place in the Hebrew Bible where Deut 6.4-9 is quoted is in Zech 14.9.[4]

יהוה אחד ושמו אחד—'Yahweh will be one and his name one' (Zech 14.9).

יהוה אלהינו יהוה אחד—'Yahweh is our God, Yahweh is one'[5] (Deut 6.4).

Only in Jer and II Zech

Three phrases in II Zech suggest their dependence upon Jer in that they are unique to II Zech and Jer:

§3. The phrase 'the jungle of the Jordan' (גאון הירדן) appears only in Jer (12.15; 49.19; 50.44) and II Zech (11.3).[6]

§4. The phrase 'flock doomed for slaughter' (צאן ההרגה) in Zech 11.4, 7 betrays the influence of Jer in that הרגה appears only in Jer (7.32*; 19.6*) and II Zech (11.4, 7).[7]

§5. The pairing of the noun שקר with a verbal form of דבר is found in Deut 19.18; Isa 59.3; Jer 9.4; 29.23; 40.16; 43.2; Mic 6.12; Zech 13.3; Pss 63.12; 101.7; 109.2. With some exceptions (Deut 19.18; Pss 63.12; 101.7; 109.2), this pairing occurs in prophetic books and most of these occurrences are within redactional material (Isa 59.3; Jer 29.23; 40.16; 43.2; Zech 13.3). However, the *only* instances of this pairing to denote false prophecy are found in Jer (29.23; 43.2) and in II Zech 13.3.[8]

---

4. See Dentan, 'Zechariah 9–14', p. 1112; K. Elliger, *Das Buch der zwölf kleinen Propheten. II. Die Propheten Nahum, Habakuk, Zephania, Haggai, Sacharja, Maleachi* (ATD, 25.II; Göttingen: Vandenhoeck & Ruprecht, 1951), p. 172; Jones, *Haggai, Zechariah, Malachi*, p. 176; Mason, *Haggai, Zechariah and Malachi*, p. 129; Mason, 'Use of Earlier Biblical Material in Zechariah 9–14', p. 279.

5. Although Weinfeld does not include the Shema in his list of Deuteronomic phraseology, he does include similar phrases—e.g. יהוה הוא האלהים—'Yahweh alone is God' in Deut 4.34, 39; 7.9; Josh 2.11; 1 Kgs 8.60 (*Deuteronomy and the Deuteronomic School*, p. 331).

6. M. Bic, *Das Buch Sacharja* (Berlin: Evangelische Verlagsanstalt, 1962), p. 133; Jones, *Haggai, Zechariah, Malachi*, p. 149; Lacocque, 'Zacharie 9–14', p. 171.

7. Delcor, 'Sources', p. 387; Mason, *Haggai, Zechariah and Malachi*, p. 105; Mason, 'Some Examples', p. 348; Mason, 'Use of Earlier Biblical Material in Zechariah 9–14', p. 143.

8. Petersen (*Late Israelite Prophecy*, p. 35) noted that the use of שקר in Zech

כי שקר דברת בשם יהוה—'for you speak lies in the name of Yahweh'
(Zech 13.3).

וידברו דבר בשמי שקר—'and they have spoken in my name lying
words' (Jer 29.23).

שקר אתה מדבר—'You are speaking a lie' (Jer 43.2).

Since the pairing of שקר with a verbal form of דבר within the context of false prophecy occurs only in Jer and Zech 13.3, it is likely
that the diction of false prophecy in Jer influenced that of Zech 13.3.[9]

Only in DtrH, Jer and II Zech

Two phrases in II Zech suggest that the diction of II Zech was influenced by that of DtrH and Jer in that these phrases are contained
solely within DtrH, Jer and II Zech (excluding Chron which used
DtrH as a source):

§6. Other than in Zech 14.10, the toponym 'the Corner Gate'
(שער הפנים) appears only four times in the Hebrew Bible. The first
reference is in DtrH (2 Kgs 14.13), which has influenced its use by the
Chronicler (2 Chron 25.23 [= 2 Kgs 14.13]; 26.9). The other reference is in Jer (31.38). Therefore, all of the references to 'the Corner

---

13.3 came from Jer. Petersen referred to the following passages: Jer 14.14*; 23.25;
29.21.

9.   Other שקר-phrases concerning false prophecy are also found in Jer, some of
which are in the poetry (5.31; 6.13 = 8.10; 13.25; 23.14):

'to prophesy lies'—נבא [ב]שקר 5.31; 23.26; 27.10*, 14*, 16*; see also 23.32 (see
    Holladay, 'Prototypes and Copies', pp. 354-55).
'to prophesy lies in my [Yahweh's] name'—נבא [ב]שקר בשמי: 14.14*; 23.25;
    27.15*; 29.9, 21 (see Holladay, 'Prototypes and Copies', pp. 354-55).
'to trust in lying words/a lie'—בטח על דברי שקר/שקר: 7.4*, 8*; 13.25; 28.15;
    29.31 (see Holladay, 'Prototypes and Copies', p. 356).
'from prophet to priest, all make lies'—ומנביא ועד כהן כלו עשה שקר: 6.13 = 8.10.
'the prophets of Jerusalem walk in lies'—נבאי ירושלם...הלך בשקר: 23.14.

From this survey of the use of שקר in Jer, we note the following: (1) the pairing of
the noun שקר with a verbal form of דבר to denote false prophecy is found only in Jer
(29.23; 49.2) and Zech 13.3; (2) the pairing of שקר and נבא in Jer appears most frequently in Deuteronomic prose; and (3) with one exception (Jer 5.31: נבאו בשקר), the
use of שקר in the context of false prophecy in poetic material in Jer appears in
phrases unique to the poetry (6.13 = 8.10; 23.14). Therefore, the pairing of the noun
שקר with a verbal form of דבר to denote false prophecy suggests the influence of Jer
on Zech 13.3 (*contra* T.W. Overholt, 'Remarks on the Continuity of the Jeremiah
Tradition', *JBL* 91 [1972], pp. 457-62).

Gate' may have the same origin in a particular Deuteronomic way of referring to this gate.[10] This observation is strengthened in that the roughly contemporaneous descriptions of the Jerusalem walls and gates in Neh 2.11–3.32; 12.27-43 omit 'the Corner Gate'.[11] Therefore, we may have here an example of a particularly Deuteronomic way of referring to a specific place.

§7. The use of 'surrounding' (סביב) in phrases denoting non-Israelite people occurs only in Deuteronomic literature and II Zech.[12] The phrase 'all the surrounding nations' (כל הגוים סביב) occurs only in 1 Kgs 5.11; Jer 25.9*; Zech 14.14.

Primarily in DtrH and II Zech

In the preceding sections, evidence for language unique to Deuteronomic literature (DtrH, Jer) and II Zech was given. Because it is confined to Deuteronomic literature and II Zech, the above evidence presents a strong case for the dependence of II Zech on Deuteronomic literature, especially as it concerns distinctively Deuteronomic language. However, this section and the following two sections contain language found *primarily*, but not exclusively, in Deuteronomic literature and II Zech. These sections also present a strong case for literary dependence.

This section includes cases where the language is found primarily in DtrH and II Zech but is lacking in Jer:

§8. The religious feast held during harvest had different names within different traditions. The name used in II Zech (14.16, 18, 19)—

---

10. The following commentators associated Zech 14.10 with Jer 31.38: Delcor, 'Sources', pp. 387, 410; Dentan, 'Zechariah 9–14', p. 1112; Mason, 'Use of Earlier Biblical Material in Zechariah 9–14', pp. 266-67; Mitchell, *Haggai, Zechariah*, pp. 348-49.

11. This omission has led to attempts to identify 'the Corner Gate' with a gate mentioned in Neh, assuming that the description in Neh used another name for the same gate. E.g. G.A. Smith (*Jerusalem: Topography, Economics and History from the Earliest Times to AD 70* [New York: KTAV, 1972], p. 201-202), Avi-Yonah ('Walls of Nehemiah', *IEJ* 4 [1954], p. 240), Mitchell (*Haggai, Zechariah*, p. 350), and H.G.M. Williamson (*Ezra, Nehemiah* [WBC; Waco, TX: Word Books, 1985], pp. 204-205) all identified 'the Corner Gate' with 'the Old Gate'/'the Mishneh Gate' (Neh 3.6; 12.39).

12. See also below §26 concerning the phrase 'all the surrounding peoples' in Zech 12.2, 6.

'the Feast of Booths'—follows that of the Deuteronomic school. The three different ways of referring to this feast are given below, beginning with that of the Deuteronomic school.[13]

חג הסוכות/הסכות—the Feast of Booths: Deut 16.13, 16; 31.10; Zech 14.16, 18, 19. See also Lev 23.24; Ezra 3.4; 2 Chron 8.13.

חג האסיף/האסף—the Feast of Ingathering: Exod 23.16; 34.22.

החג—the Feast: 1 Kgs 8.2, 65; 12.32; Ezek 45.23, 25; Neh 8.14; 2 Chron 5.3; 7.8, 9.

§9. 'The use of 'teraphim' in Zech 10.2 suggests possible Deuteronomic influence, for the word 'teraphim' occurs primarily in Deuteronomic literature.[14] The suggestion that Zech 10.2 was influenced by Deuteronomic literature is strengthened when it is observed that, unlike the use in Deuteronomic literature and Zech 10.2, 'teraphim' are not explicitly condemned in some of the non-Deuteronomic occurrences (Gen 31.19, 34-35). Therefore, the condemnation of 'teraphim' in Zech 10.2 may reflect the influence of what Mason has called 'the Deuteronomistic aversion to teraphim'.[15]

§10. Another temporal phrase that may suggest some Deuteronomic influence is the phrase 'year after year' (שנה בשנה) in Zech 14.16, which is found primarily in DtrH.[16]

§11. In his list of Deuteronomic phraseology, Weinfeld noted that in earlier sources the prevalent term for foreign peoples was 'the inhabitants of the land' (יושב הארץ), but that in Deuteronomic literature the prevalent term is 'these/those nations' (גוים האלה/ההם).[17] The use of 'those nations' (גוים ההם) in Zech 14.3 may, therefore, suggest Deuteronomic influence.

§12. The phrase 'the house of Joseph' (בית יוסף) as a way of referring to the northern kingdom is found primarily in Deuteronomic

13. Mason, *Haggai, Zechariah and Malachi*, p. 132.

14. Gen 31.19, 34, 35; Judg 17.5; 18.14, 17,18, 20; 1 Sam 15.23; 19.13, 16; 2 Kgs 23.24; Hos 3.4; Zech 10.2.

15. 'Some Examples', p. 346. See also Lacocque, 'Zacharie 9–14', p. 164; Mason, 'Use of Earlier Biblical Material in Zechariah 9–14', p. 92; Mitchell, *Haggai, Zechariah*, p. 287.

16. In DtrH (6×): Deut 15.20; 1 Sam 1.7; 7.16; 1 Kgs 5.25; 10.25; 2 Kgs 17.4. Outside of DtrH (5×): Lev 25.53; Zech 14.16; Neh 10.35,36; 2 Chron 9.24 (= 2 Kgs 17.4); 24.5.

17. Deut 7.17, 22; 9.4, 5; 11.23; 12.30; 18.9, 14; 20.15; 31.3; Josh 23.3, 4, 12, 13; Judg 2.23; 3.1; 2 Kgs 7.41. See Weinfeld, *Deuteronomy and the Deuteronomic School*, p. 343.

literature[18] and may suggest Deuteronomic influence.

§13. The use of פדה in the phrase 'for I have redeemed them (פדיתים)...from the land of Egypt' (Zech 10.8, 10) suggests possible Deuteronomic influence. The use of the verb פדה is characteristically Deuteronomic, especially within the context of exodus imagery.[19] In other bodies of literature, the verb generally used is גאל.[20] The following passages contain פדה within the context of exodus language:

> In DtrH: Deut 7.8; 9.26; 13.6; 15.15; 21.8; 24.18; 2 Sam 7.23.
> Outside DtrH: Isa 50.2; 51.11; Mic 6.4; Zech 10.8; Ps 78.42;
> 1 Chron 17.21 (= 2 Sam 7.23).

Primarily in Jer and II Zech

In the cases below, the language is found primarily in Jer and II Zech, but is lacking in DtrH:

§14. In Zech 14.10, 'the Corner Gate' (see above §6) is mentioned in connection with 'the Gate of Benjamin' (שער בנימן). Other than Zech 14.10, 'the Gate of Benjamin' is found only in Ezek 48.32 and in Jer (Jer 20.2; 37.13; 38.7). Therefore, 'the Gate of Benjamin' may be a Deuteronomic name for this gate. This possibility is strengthened by the observation that the roughly contemporaneous descriptions of the Jerusalem walls and gates in Neh 2.11–3.32 and 12.27-43 omit 'the Gate of Benjamin'.[21] Therefore, 'the Corner Gate' (§6) and 'the Gate of Benjamin' are possibly both distinctive Deuteronomic appellations for specific Jerusalem gates, which may have differed from the toponyms used in other traditions.

§15. The 'Tower of Hananel' is mentioned only four times in the

---

18. Josh 17.17; 18.5; Judg 1.22, 35; 25.19, 21; 1 Kgs 11.28; Amos 5.6; Obad 18; Zech 10.6. See Lacocque, 'Zacharie 9–14', p. 166.

19. Weinfeld, *Deuteronomy and the Deuteronomic School*, p. 326. See also Driver, *Deuteronomy*, p. 101; H. Cazelles, 'פדה', in *ThWAT*, VI, pp. 518-19.

20. E.g. Exod 6.6; 15.13; Isa 35.9; 43.1; 44.22, 23; 48.20; 51.10; 52.3, 9; 62.12; 63.9; Pss 74.2; 77.16; 78.35. גאל does not occur in DtrH and is found only once in Jer, where it is in a parallel construction with פדה (31.11).

21. This omission has led to various attempts to identify 'the Gate of Benjamin' with a gate mentioned in Neh, assuming that the description in Neh used another name for the same gate. E.g. Mitchell (*Haggai, Zechariah*, p. 350) identified 'the Gate of Benjamin' with 'the Sheep Gate' (Neh. 12.39). E.W. Cohn ('The History of Jerusalem's Benjamin Gate: A Case of Interrupted Continuity?', *PEQ* 118 [1986], p. 141) identified 'the Gate of Benjamin' with 'the Fish Gate' (Neh 12.39).

Hebrew Bible: Jer 31.38; Zech 14.10; Neh 3.1; 12.39. In each of these works, this name is found in the description of the limits of the city wall of Jerusalem (Jer 31.38; Zech 14.10; Neh 12.39). The previous two conclusions concerning other geographical names (§§6, 14) suggest the possibility that the 'Tower of Hananel' in Zech 14.10 may also be a Deuteronomic name for this tower as reflected in Jer 31.38.[22]

Primarily in DtrH, Jer and II Zech

This section contains language found primarily in DtrH, Jer and II Zech:

§16. Although forms of ישב and בטח are paired together outside Deuteronomic literature as well as within it,[23] only in DtrH, Jer, Zech 14.11 and in the prose in Ezek[24] do they appear in the context of Yahweh providing this security:

וישבה ירושלם לבטח—'and Jerusalem shall dwell in security' (Zech 14.11).

וישבתם בטח—'so that you dwell in security' (Deut 12.10).

יושבת לבטח—'how they dwelt in security' (Judg 18.7).

ותשבו בטח—'and you dwelt in security' (1 Sam 12.11).

וישב יהודה וישראל לבטח—'and Judah and Israel dwelt in security' (1 Kgs 5.5).

והשבתים לבטח—'I will make them dwell in security' (Jer 32.37*).

יושב לבטח—'which dwells in security' (Jer 49.31).

22. The following commentators associated Zech 14.10 with Jer 31.38: Delcor, 'Sources', pp. 387, 410; Dentan, 'Zechariah 9–14', p. 1112; Mason, 'Use of Earlier Biblical Material in Zechariah 9–14', pp. 266-67; Mitchell, *Haggai, Zechariah*, pp. 348-49.

23. In DtrH: Deut 12.10; Judg 18.7; 1 Sam 12.11; 1 Kgs 5.5.

In Jer: 32.37*; 49.31.

Outside of DtrH and Jer: Lev. 25.18, 19; 26.5; Isa 47.8; Ezek. 28.26; 34.25, 28; 38.8, 11, 14; 39.6, 26; Zeph 2.15; Ps. 4.9; Prov. 3.29.

On the pairing of ישב and בטה, see A. Jepsen, ' בטח', *TDOT*, II, pp. 88-94; M. Görg, 'ישב', in *ThWAT*, III, pp. 1021-22.

24. Ezek 28.26; 34.25, 28; 38.8, 11, 14; 39.6, 26. These passages are often considered redactional additions. See W. Zimmerli, *Ezekiel* (Hermeneia; trans. J.D. Martin; Philadelphia: Fortress, 1983), II, *ad loc*. Some works have suggested that the book of Ezekiel contains some Deuteronomic redactional material. See Zimmerli's brief review of this literature (*Ezekiel*, II, pp. xiv-xv).

וישראל ישכן לבטח—'and Israel will live in security' (Jer 23.6).

וירושלם תשכון לבטח—'and Jerusalem will live in security' (Jer 33.16).[25]

§17. The distinctively Deuteronomic use of שם ('name') is its application to Israel and more explicitly to the chosen city and its temple. That is, in contrast to other Pentateuchal sources, שם in Deuteronomic literature refers not simply to Yahweh, but also to Yahweh's chosen city and the temple and is, therefore, closely connected with the Deuteronomic understanding of centralized worship.[26] Although the phrases using שם in II Zech do not closely follow this distinctively Deuteronomic use of שם, their use within contexts which refer to other Deuteronomic themes (e.g. false prophecy) suggests that Deuteronomic literature may have influenced the use of שם in II Zech. Also, the following list of the occurrences in Deuteronomic literature and II Zech shows other possible connections:

ובשמו יתהלכו—'and in his name they shall walk' (Zech 10.12).

כי שקר דברת בשם יהוה—'for you speak lies in the name of Yahweh' (Zech 13.3).

הוא יקרא בשמי ואני אענה אתו—'He will call on my name and I will answer him' (Zech 13.9b).

יהוה אחד ושמו אחד—'Yahweh will be one and his name one' (Zech 14.9).

הבית/העיר אשר נקרא שמי עליו—'the house/city which my name is called upon'[27] (1 Kgs 8.43; Jer 7.10*,11*,14*, 30*; 25.29; 32.34*; 34.15*).

(המקום אשר יבחר) לשכן שמו שם—'(the site that the Lord will choose) to make his name dwell there'[28] (Deut 12.11; 14.23; 16.2, 6, 11; 26.2; Jer 7.12*).

לשום שמו שם—'to put his name there'[29] (Deut 12.5, 21; 14.24; 1 Kgs 9.3; 11.36; 14.21; 2 Kgs 21.4, 7).

להיות שמו שם—'that his name be there'[30] (1 Kgs 8.16, 29; 2 Kgs 23.27).

---

25. Mitchell (*Haggai, Zechariah*, p. 349) relates Zech 14.11 to the 'security' language in Jer 33.16; Ezek 34.27-28.

26. Weinfeld, *Deuteronomy and the Deuteronomic School*, p. 191-209. See also Mettinger, *Dethronement of Sabaoth*, pp. 38-79, 116-34. G. von Rad, 'Deuteronomy's "Name" Theology and the Priestly Document's "Kabod" Theology', in *Studies in Deuteronomy* (trans. D.M.G. Stalker; Chicago: Henry Regnery, 1953), pp. 37-44.

27. Weinfeld, *Deuteronomy and the Deuteronomic School*, p. 325.

28. Weinfeld, *Deuteronomy and the Deuteronomic School*, pp. 193-94, 325.

29. Weinfeld, *Deuteronomy and the Deuteronomic School*, p. 325.

30. Weinfeld, *Deuteronomy and the Deuteronomic School*, p. 325.

בנה/הקדיש בית שם יהוה—'to build/dedicate a house for the name of the Lord'[31] (2 Sam 7.13; 1 Kgs 3.2; 5.17, 18, 19; 8.17, 18, 19, 20, 44, 48; 9.7).

קרא שם על ישראל—'to call his name upon Israel'[32] (Deut 28.10; see also Jer 14.9*; 15.16, referring to the prophet).

יהוה שמו קרא אלי ואענך—'the Lord is his name: Call to me and I will answer you'[33] (Jer 33.2-3*).

The connection between the use of שם in Deuteronomic literature and in II Zech not only includes the contexts of false prophecy and centralized worship but also includes some other similarities. Possible Deuteronomic influence on II Zech is suggested in the use of 'call' (קרא) with 'name' (שם) followed by 'I will answer' in both Jer 33.2-3* and Zech 13.9.

§18. The use of 'devour' (אכל) with '[human] flesh' (בשׂר) in Zech 11.9,16 suggests Deuteronomic influence.[34] This pairing is found primarily in Deuteronomic imagery of curses:

In DtrH and Jer: Deut 28.53; Jer 19.9*. See also 2 Kgs 6.28-29.

Outside of DtrH and Jer: Lev 26.29; Zech 11.9, 16. See also Lam 2.20; 4.10.

§19. The phrase 'on that day' (ביום ההוא)[35] occurs 19 times in II Zech,[36] and can thus be understood as a characteristic of the diction of II Zech. This observation is strengthened further when one notes that this phrase appears 7 times in conjunction with another phrase, 'and it shall come to pass' (והיה).[37] The characteristic use of 'on that

---

31. Weinfeld, *Deuteronomy and the Deuteronomic School*, pp. 193-94, 325.

32. Weinfeld, *Deuteronomy and the Deuteronomic School*, p. 327.

33. This phrase contains the pairing of 'call' (קרא) with 'name' (שם), which is typical of Deuteronomic phraseology (see previous example). Also, Jer 33.2-3* has close affinities with Zech 13.9.

34. Weinfeld, *Deuteronomy and the Deuteronomic School*, p. 349. Lacocque ('Zacharie 9–14', p. 177) noted this connection between the Deuteronomic literature and II Zech.

35. See S.J. de Vries, *Yesterday, Today and Tomorrow* (Grand Rapids, MI: Eerdmans, 1975), pp. 55-136, 279-331.

36. Zech 9.16; 11.11; 12.3, 4, 6, 8 (2×), 9, 11; 13.1, 2, 4; 14.4, 6, 8, 9, 13, 20, 21.

37. Zech 12.3, 9; 13.2, 4; 14.6, 8, 13. Mitchell (*Haggai, Zechariah*, p. 322) noted that the phrase 'and it shall come to pass' occurs 11× in Zech 12–14, 7× with the phrase 'on that day' (ביום ההוא). He concluded, 'The two together may…be regarded as characteristic of these chapters' (*Haggai, Zechariah*, p. 322).

day' (ביום ההוא) suggests some Deuteronomic influence on the basis of the following observations: (1) Although this phrase occurs often throughout the Hebrew Bible (207×), it is prominent in DtrH and Jer (68×).[38] (2) The following similar phrases—none of which is found in II Zech—suggest a heightened interest in temporal language in Deuteronomic literature in that Deuteronomic literature contains a disproportionate number of such temporal phrases.[39]

היום ההוא—'that day' (9×):
    In DtrH (3×): 1 Sam 16.13; 18.9; 30.25.
    In Jer (1×): 46.10.
    Outside of DtrH and Jer (5×): Exod 10.13; Zeph 1.15; Job 3.4; Neh 8.17; 1 Chron 29.21.

ביום הזה—'on this day' (7×):[40]
    In DtrH (3×): Josh 7.25; 1 Sam 11.13; 1 Kgs 2.26.
    Outside of DtrH (4×): Gen 7.11; Exod 19.1; Lev 8.34; 16.30.

(עד) היום הזה—'(until) this day'[41] (144×): the majority of the occurrences of this phrase occur in DtrH and Jer (100 out of 144). This observation is heightened, when one realizes that 8 of the occurrences outside of DtrH are taken from DtrH as a source (Isa 37.3 ; 39.6; 1 Chron 13.11; 17.5; 2 Chron 5.9; 8.8; 10.19; 21.10). Therefore, there are only 36 out of 144 independent occurrences of this phrase outside of Deuteronomic literature.

---

38. May ('Towards an Objective Approach to the Book of Jeremiah', p. 155) included this phrase in his list of phrases characteristic of the prose in Jer (4.9; 25.33; 30.8; 39.16, 17; 48.41; 49.22, 26; 50.30).

39. In his study of the temporal phrases היום הזה and היום הזה, היום הזה, ביום ההוא (*Yesterday, Today and Tomorrow*), de Vries noted that 'in sheer number of occurrences [of *hayyom* and *hayyom hazzeh*], Deuteronomy by itself far outweights the total provided by the rest of the Pentateuch' (pp. 164-65) and that '*hayyom* and *hayyom hazzeh* are even more frequent [in the Former Prophets]' (p. 187). Also, even a quick scan of de Vries' various tables shows that these temporal phrases occur most frequently in Deuteronomic literature.

40. See de Vries, *Yesterday, Today and Tomorrow*, pp. 140-51.

41. See B.S. Childs, 'A Study of the Formula, "Until This Day"', *JBL* 83 (1963), pp. 279-92. Childs showed that (1) there are two distinct ways in the use of this formula, nonetiological and etiological, and (2) that the etiological use is a secondary addition to a received tradition. Most of Child's examples for both usages of this formula are taken from DtrH. See also de Vries, *Yesterday, Today and Tomorrow*, pp. 151-277.

In DtrH (89×): Deut 2.22; 4.14; 5.21; 6.24; 10.8; 11.4; 26.16; 27.9;
29.3; 32.48; 34.6; Josh 3.7; 4.9; 5.9, 11; 6.25; 7.26 (2×);
8.28, 29; 9.27; 10.27; 13.13; 14.14; 15.13; 16.10; 22.3, 17,
22; 23.8,9; Judg 1.21, 26; 6.24; 9.19; 10.4, 15; 12.3; 15.19;
18.1, 12; 19.30; 1 Sam 5.5; 6.18; 8.8; 12.2, 5; 14.45; 17.10,
46 (2×); 24.11, 20; 25.32, 33; 26.21, 24; 27.6; 28.18; 29.3,
6, 8; 30.25; 2 Sam 3.38; 4.3, 8; 6.8; 7.6; 16.12; 18.18, 20
(2×); 1 Kgs 1.30; 8.8; 9.13, 21; 10.12; 12.19; 2 Kgs 2.22;
7.9; 8.22; 14.7; 16.6; 17.23, 34, 41; 19.3; 20.17; 21.15.

In Jer (11×): 3.25; 7.25*; 11.7*; 25.3*; 32.20*, 31*; 35.14*; 36.3;
44.2*, 10*, 22*.

Outside of DtrH and Jer (44×): Gen 7.13; 17.23, 26; 25.33; 29.11;
32.33; 47.26; 48.15; Exod 10.6; 12.14, 17 (2×), 41, 51; 13.3;
Lev. 23.14, 21, 28, 29, 30; Num 11.32; 22.30; Isa 37.3 (= 2
Kgs 19.3); 39.6 (= 2 Kgs 20.17); Ezek 2.3; 20.29; 24.2 (2×);
40.1; Est 1.18; Ezra 9.7 (2×),15; Neh 7.32; 9.10; 1 Chron
4.41,43; 5.26; 13.11 (= 2 Sam 6.8); 17.5 (= 2 Sam 7.6);
2 Chron 5.9 (= 1 Kgs 8.8); 8.8 (= 1 Kgs 9.21); 10.19 (= 1 Kgs
12.19); 21.10 (= 2 Kgs 8.22).

כיום הזה—'as on this day' (23×):[42]

In DtrH (10×): Deut 2.30; 4.20, 38; 6.24; 8.18; 10.15; 29.27; 1 Kgs
3.6; 8.24, 61.

In Jer (6×): 11.5*; 25.18; 32.20*; 44.6*, 22*, 23*.

Outside of DtrH and Jer (7×): Gen 50.20; Dan 9.7, 15; Ezra 9.7, 15;
Neh 9.10; 1 Chron 28.7.

זה היום—'this day' (3×):

In DtrH (2×): Judg 4.14; 1 Kgs 14.14.

Outside of DtrH (1×): Lam 2.16.

בימים ההמה/ההם—'on those days' (40×):[43]

In DtrH (17×): Deut 17.9; 19.17; 26.3; Josh 20.6; Judg 17.6;
18.1(2×); 19.1; 20.27, 28; 21.25; 1 Sam 3.1; 28.1; 2 Sam
16.23; 2 Kgs 10.32; 15.37; 20.1.

---

42. Weinfeld, *Deuteronomy and the Deuteronomic School*, p. 350.

43. May, 'Towards an Objective Approach to the Book of Jeremiah', p. 155. See
Long, *I Kings*, p. 24. Long briefly discussed the use of בימים ההם as a redactional
device in Kgs. This discussion is one part of his discussion concerning the
'hermeneutic of time' in DtrH (pp. 22-26).

In Jer (8×): 3.16*, 18*; 5.18*; 31.29; 33.15, 16; 50.4, 20.
Outside of DtrH and Jer (15×): Gen 6.4; Exod 2.11; Isa 38.1; Ezek
    48.17; Joel 3.2; 4.1; Zech 8.6, 23; Est 1.2; 2.21; Dan 10.2;
    Neh 6.17; 13.15, 23; 2 Chron 32.24 (= 2 Kgs 20.1).

באחרית הימים—'at the end of days' (12×):[44]
In DtrH (2×): Deut 4.30; 31.29; see Josh 3.2.
In Jer (4×): 23.20; 30.24; 48.47; 49.39.
Outside of DtrH and Jer (6×): Gen 49.1; Num 24.14; Ezek 38.16;
    Hos 3.5; Mic 4.7; Dan 10.4.

בעת ההיא/ההוא—'in that time' (68×):[45]
In DtrH (34×): Deut 1.9, 16, 18; 2.34; 3.4, 8, 12, 18, 21, 23; 4.14;
    5.5; 9.20; 10.1, 8; Josh 5.2; 6.26; 11.10, 21; Judg 3.29; 4.4;
    11.26; 12.6; 14.4; 21.14, 24; 1 Kgs 8.65; 11.29; 14.1; 2 Kgs
    8.22; 16.6; 18.16; 20.12; 24.10.
In Jer (7×): 3.17*; 4.11; 8.1; 31.1; 33.15; 50.4, 20.
Outside of DtrH and Jer (27×): Gen 21.22; 38.1; Num 22.4; Isa
    18.7; 20.2; 39.1 (= 2 Kgs 20.12); Joel 4.1; Amos 5.13; Mic
    3.4; Zeph 1.12; 3.19, 20; Est 8.9; Dan 12.1 (2×); Ezra 8.34;
    Neh 4.16; 1 Chron 21.28, 29; 2 Chron 7.8 (= 1 Kgs 8.65);
    13.18; 16.7, 10; 21.10; 28.16; 30.3; 35.17.

The prominence of various temporal phrases in DtrH and Jer (265 out
of 513) suggests that the Deuteronomic school had a heightened interest in time as it related to their theology. Therefore, the frequent use
of 'on that day' in II Zech suggests possible Deuteronomic influence.

§20. The language concerning the breaking of the covenant in Zech
11.10 suggests possible Deuteronomic influence. The use of 'break'
(פרר) with a covenant which was 'cut' (כרת) by Yahweh occurs only in
Deut 31.16; Jer 11.10*; 31.32; Ezek 16.59-60; Zech 11.10.

§21. The phrase כל גויי הארץ ('all the nations of the earth') in Zech
12.3 may suggest Deuteronomic influence, for it occurs in Deut and
Jer.[46]

---

44. May, 'Towards an Objective Approach to the Book of Jeremiah', p. 155.
45. May, 'Towards an Objective Approach to the Book of Jeremiah', p. 155. See
Long, *I Kings*, p. 24. Long briefly discussed the use of בעת ההיא as a redactional
device in Kgs. This discussion is one part of his discussion concerning the
'hermeneutic of time' in DtrH (pp. 22-26).
46. This phrase also reflects the possible influence of the related Deuteronomic
phrase 'all the kingdoms of the earth'—כל (ה)ממלכות (ה)ארץ:

כל גויי הארץ–'all the nations of the earth' (8×):
  In DtrH (1×): Deut 28.1.
  In Jer (3×): 26.6*; 33.9*; 44.8*.
  Outside of DtrH and Jer (4×): Gen 18.18; 22.18; 26.4; Zech 12.3.

Only in II Zech

Above, language unique to Deuteronomic literature, or at least found primarily in DtrH and Jer, was given. Given below is a list of language in II Zech that is Deuteronomic in character, although its exact wording is found nowhere in DtrH and Jer.

Digression: Possible Criticism of 'Deuteronomic Language' in II Zech not found in DtrH

In Jer studies, Bright (and others) has criticized Hyatt and others who argued for the Deuteronomic redaction of Jer in that they did not recognize that some of the characteristic phrases of the prose sermons are not found in DtrH.[47] However, Bright's criticism has been addressed by various proponents of the Deuteronomic redaction of Jer. For example, Weinfeld stated,

> Just as there are expressions in Dtr[H] which do not occur in the book of Deuteronomy, so we find expressions in the prose sermons of Jeremiah which occur neither in Deuteronomy nor Dtr[H]. This fact led Bright to conclude that these Jeremian sermons were composed independently of Dtr[H], and, in fact, much earlier. To our mind, however, this difference in idiom points to the contrary. The fact that the prose sermons in Jeremiah contain idioms—which, as Bright concedes, are of deuteronomic character—yet are not met with elsewhere in deuteronomic literature, indicates rather that the sermons date after Dtr[H] and constitute a new stage in the development of deuteronomic composition. As the Deuteronomist had developed and given more specific sense to the general expression of the book of Deuteronomy, so the deuteronomic editor of Jeremiah developed the terminology of the Deuteronomist.[48]

In DtrH (3×): Deut 28.5; 2 Kgs 19.15, 19.
In Jer (6×): 15.4; 24.9*; 25.26; 29.18*; 34.1, 17* (see May, 'Towards an Objective Approach to the Book of Jer', p. 155).
Outside of DtrH and Jer (5×): Isa 23.17; 37.16 (= 2 Kgs 19.15), 20 (= 2 Kgs 19.19); Ezra 1.2; 2 Chron. 36.23.

  47. 'Date of the Prose Sermons'.
  48. *Deuteronomy and the Deuteronomic School*, p. 6.

In a similar manner, Nicholson noted that the difference simply reflects that the Deuteronomic redactor was reinterpreting the Jeremiah tradition rather than the traditions that made up DtrH.[49]

Although the examples given below do not have exact parallels in DtrH or Jer, they all are Deuteronomic in character. Therefore, a Brightian critique of my thesis—that is, these exact phrases are not found in DtrH (or Jer)–can be addressed in a manner similar to that of Weinfeld and Nicholson. That is, Deuteronomic language was not static, but developed over the lifespan of the Deuteronomic school to reflect new historical situations in relationship to the reinterpretation of different traditions; therefore, even though some of my examples of Deuteronomic language in II Zech do not have exact parallels in DtrH or Jer, they can nevertheless be described as Deuteronomic in character.

§22. The following three phrases found in II Zech are reminiscent of the typical Deuteronomic pairing of 'inhabitants of [name of city]' (יֹשֵׁ[וּ]בִי...) with another noun phrase, which further qualifies the completed pair. Such pairing occurs only in Deuteronomic literature, including Jer, with the exception of similar occurrences in 2 Chron[50] and one occurrence in Dan 9.7.

תִּפְאֶרֶת בֵּית דָּוִיד וְתִפְאֶרֶת יֹשְׁבֵי[51] יְרוּשָׁלַם—'the glory of the house of David and the glory of the inhabitants of Jerusalem' (Zech 12.7).

עַל בֵּית דָּוִיד וְעַל יֹשְׁבֵי[52] יְרוּשָׁלַם—'on the house of David and on the inhabitants of Jerusalem' (Zech 12.10).

---

49. *Preaching*, pp. 25-26.
50. In 2 Chron., these phrases occur:

(כֹּל) יְהוּדָה וְיֹשְׁבֵי יְרוּשָׁלַם—'(all) Judah and the inhabitants of Jerusalem': 20.15, 18, 20; 21.13; 32.33; 33.9; 34.30 (= 2 Kgs 23.2).

הוּא/אֶת יְחִזְקִיָּהוּ וְאֶת יֹשְׁבֵי יְרוּשָׁלַם—'Hezekiah/he and the inhabitants of Jerusalem': 32.22, 26.

51. Reading the plural with some Heb MSS, LXX, Targs. See Zech 13.1. T. Jansma, 'Inquiry into the Hebrew Text and the Ancient Versions of Zechariah ix–xiv', in *Oudtestamentische Studien* (DEEL; ed. P.A.H. de Boer; Leiden: E.J. Brill, 1950), pp. 115-16; Mitchell, *Haggai, Zechariah*, p. 334. *Contra* Otzen, *Studien über Deuterosacharja*, p. 263.

52. Reading the plural with some Heb MSS and the versions. See Zech 13.1. Jansma, 'Hebrew Text and the Ancient Versions', pp. 117-18; Mitchell, *Haggai, Zechariah*, p. 334. *Contra* Otzen, *Studien über Deuterosacharja*, p. 263.

לבית דויד ולישבי ירושלם—'for the house of David and for the inhabitants of Jerusalem' (Zech 13.1).

ואת יושבי [city name] ואת בנותיה—'the inhabitants of [city name] and its villages' (Josh 17.11, 4×; Judg 1.27, 4×).

איש יהודה וישבי ירושלם—'the men of Judah and the inhabitants of Jerusalem'[53] (2 Kgs 23.2; Jer 4.3, 4; 11.2*, 9*; 17.20*, 25*; 18.11*; 32.32*; 35.13*).

ועל ישבי ירושלם ואל איש יהודה—'upon the inhabitants of Jerusalem and upon the men of Judah'[54] (Jer 36.31*).

מלכי יהודה וישבי ירושלם—'the kings of Judah and the inhabitants of Jerusalem' (Jer 19.3*).

עם יהודה וישבי ירושלם—'the people of Judah and the inhabitants of Jerusalem' (Jer 25.2).

ערי יהודה וישבי ירושלם—'the cities of Judah and the inhabitants of Jerusalem' (Jer 11.12*).

את כל ישבי הארץ הזאת ואת המלכים הישבים לדוד על כסאו ואת הכהנים ואת הנביאים ואת כל ישבי ירושלם—'all the inhabitants of this land: the kings who sit on David's throne, the priests, the prophets, and all the inhabitants of Jerusalem' (Jer 13.13).

ערי יהודה ובחיצות ירושלם—'in the cities of Judah and the streets of Jerusalem'[55] (Jer 7.17*, 34*; 11.6*; 33.10*; 44.6*, 9*, 17*, 21*).

This example provides excellent evidence of the variety within Deuteronomic language—that is, various elements within a fairly fixed structure which can vary in length. This variety is found within DtrH and Jer individually as well as taken together. Therefore, this variety within a fixed Deuteronomic structure allowed for the development of different wordings, including the three phrases in II Zech.

§23. The phrase 'from Geba to Rimmon' (מגבע לרמון) appears only in Zech 14.10, but has some indications of Deuteronomic influence. The influence of Deuteronomic style is suggested by the cumulative effect of the following observations. (1) Although the structure of 'from [place name] to [place name]' (מ...ל) appears throughout the Hebrew Bible, the only other occurrence of Geba in this structure is in 2 Kgs 23.8 ('from Geba to Beersheba'). (2) The phrases 'from Geba to Beersheba' (2 Kgs 23.8) and 'from Dan to Beersheba' (Judg

53. Weinfeld, *Deuteronomy and the Deuteronomic School*, p. 353.
54. Weinfeld, *Deuteronomy and the Deuteronomic School*, p. 353.
55. Weinfeld, *Deuteronomy and the Deuteronomic School*, p. 353.

20.1; 1 Sam 3.20; 2 Sam 3.10; 17.11; 24.2, 15; 1 Kgs 4.25)[56] are distinctively Deuteronomic ways to refer to Judah and all of Israel, respectively. (3) Rimmon, situated near Beersheba,[57] was closely related to Beersheba (Josh 15.28-32) and was repopulated in the post-exilic period (Neh 11.29). The change in circumstances from the pre-exilic to the post-exilic period necessitated the change from 'Geba to Beersheba' to 'Geba to Rimmon' as the Deuteronomic manner of referring to Judah/Yehud.[58] (4) The toponym 'Rimmon' occurs primarily in Deuteronomic literature.[59] (5) The place name 'Geba' occurs more frequently in Deuteronomic literature than other literary corpora.[60] Given all of these observations, the phrase 'from Geba to Rimmon' in Zech 14.10 probably represents a development of the distinctively Deuteronomic structure of referring to geographical boundaries of Judah/Yehud (מ...ל) with the necessary changes required by the new circumstances of the post-exilic period.

§24. Although the phrase 'Behold, the day of Yahweh is coming' (הנה יום בא ליהוה) occurs only in Zech 14.1, it is similar to the following Deuteronomic phrase: (נאם יהוה) הנה ימים באים—'Behold, days are coming, (the oracle of Yahweh)' (21×):

In DtrH (2×): 1 Sam 2.31; 2 Kgs 20.17;
In Jer (15×):[61] 7.32*; 9.24; 16.14; 19.6*; 23.5,7; 30.3; 31.27, 31, 38; 33.14; 48.12; 49.2; 51.47, 52.

---

56. The only non-Deuteronomic occurrences of Dan and Beersheba in this structure occur in 1 Chron 21.2 (= 2 Kgs 24.2); 2 Chron 30.5, in which the names are reversed.

57. Mitchell, *Haggai, Zechariah*, p. 348.

58. Although they did not conclude that 'Geba to Rimmon' is Deuteronomic, the following commentators argued that 'Geba to Rimmon' expresses the northern and southern limits of Judah/Yehud as does 'Geba to Beersheba' in 2 Kgs 23.8: Dentan, 'Zechariah 9–14', p. 1112; Elliger, *Buch der zwölf kleinen Propheten*, II, p. 172; Mason, *Haggai, Zechariah and Malachi*, p. 129; Mitchell, *Haggai, Zechariah*, p. 348.

59. In DtrH: Josh 15.32; 19.13; Judg 20.45, 47 (2×); 21.13; 2 Sam 4.2, 5, 9; 2 Kgs 5.18 (3×). Outside of DtrH: Zech 14.10; 1 Chron 4.32 (see Josh 15.32; 19.13).

60. In DtrH: Josh 20.17; 18.24; Judg 20.10, 33; 1 Sam 13.3, 16; 14.5; 2 Sam 5.25; 1 Kgs 15.22; 2 Kgs 23.8. Outside of DtrH: Isa 10.29; Zech 14.10; Ezra 2.26; Neh 7.30; 11.31; 12.29; 1 Chron 6.45 (= Josh 20.17); 8.6; 16.6.

61. May, 'Towards an Objective Approach to the Book of Jeremiah', p. 155.

Outside of DtrH and Jer (4×): Isa 39.6 (= 2 Kgs 20.17); Amos 4.2; 8.11; 9.13.[62]

These two phrases are quite similar in that both proclaim divine intervention in the future within the same linguistic structure. The major difference between these phrases—the change from the plural to the singular—denotes the new context for the Deuteronomic phrase to refer to the eschatological 'day of Yahweh' rather than simply some future days,[63] and may, therefore, simply reflect a latter Deuteronomic view.[64]

§25. The phrase 'to scatter among the peoples' (ואזרעם בעמים) in Zech 10.9 suggests the influence of two phrases that are typically Deuteronomic descriptions of divine punishment:

הפיץ בעמים/בגויים—'to scatter among the peoples/the nations' (Deut 4.27; 28.64; 30.3; Jer 9.15*; 30.11; see Jer 31.10).[65]

These two phrases are closely related to that in Zech 10.9 in that the verb used in Zech 10.9 is זרע instead of the synonymous פוץ.[66] Therefore, although 'to scatter among the peoples' (ואזרעם בעמים) is found only in Zech 10.9, it is Deuteronomic in character, related to the phrases 'to scatter among the peoples/nations (הפיץ בעמים/בגויים).

§26. As noted above (§7), the phrase 'all the surrounding nations' to denote non-Israelite peoples occurs only in Deuteronomic literature (1 Kgs 5.11; Jer 25.9*) and II Zech (14.14). The only other use of 'surrounding' (סביב) in a phrase to denote non-Israelite people occurs in Zech 12.2, 6 (כל העמים סביב—'all the surrounding peoples'). Therefore, the phrase 'all the surrounding peoples' is simply a synonymous

---

62. Some scholars ascribed (all or some of) these passages in Amos to a Deuteronomic redactor. See S. Amsler, 'Amos, prophète de la onzième heure', *TZ* 21 (1965), p. 320; U. Kellerman, 'Der Amosschluss als Stimme deuterono-mistischer Heilshoffnung', *EvT* 29 (1969), pp. 169-83; H.W. Wolff, *Joel and Amos* (trans. W. Janzen, S.D. McBride, Jr, and C.A. Muenchow; Hermeneia; Philadelphia: Fortress Press, 1977), p. 330.

63. Such a change is also evident in the following related phrases:
הנה יום יהוה בא—'Behold, the day of Yahweh comes': Isa 13.9.
הנה היום הנה באה—'Behold the day, behold it comes': Ezek 7.10.
הנה היום בא—'Behold, the day comes': Mal 3.19.

64. See further below, 'Eschatology' in Chapter 8.

65. Weinfeld, *Deuteronomy and the Deuteronomic School*, p. 347.

66. However, זרע is used in the imagery of scattering elsewhere—see Jer 31.10,
†34.

variation of the Deuteronomic phrase 'all the surrounding nations' and
is, itself, Deuteronomic in character.

§27. The covenantal language found in Zech 13.9 is similar to that
of Deuteronomic literature:

אמרתי עמי הוא והוא יאמר יוהו אלהי—'I will say, "They are my people",
and they will say, "Yahweh is our God"' (Zech 13.9);

והייתם לי לעם אנכי אהיה לכם לאלהים—'You will be my people and I will
be your God':

> In Jer: Jer 11.4*; 24.7*; 30.22; 32.38*; see also 7.23*; 13.11*;
> 31.1, 33.[67]

> Outside Jer: Lev 26.12; Ezek 11.20; 14.11; 36.28; 37.23, 27; Zech
> 8.8.

היה לו לעם—'to be a people to him'.[68]
In DtrH: Deut 4.20; 7.6; 14.2; 26.18; 27.9; 2 Kgs 11.17.
Outside of DtrH: see Zech 2.15.

Although the covenantal language in Zech 13.9 could have been
influenced by Deuteronomic literature, another possibility presents
itself in this one example—the covenantal language in Zech 13.9 is
taken from the covenantal language in Zech 2.15 (והיו לי לעם—'to be a
people to me') and 8.8 (והיו לי לעם ואני אהיה להם לאלהים—'and they will be
to me a people and I will be to them their God'). However, since
I Zech itself betrays some Deuteronomic influence,[69] it is possible that
the covenantal language in Zech 2.15, 8.8 and 13.9 was influenced by
Deuteronomic literature.

§28. The phrase 'the Mount of Olives shall be split in two' (Zech
14.4—נבקע הר הזיתים מחציו) suggests the possibility of Deuteronomic
influence. This suggestion stems from two observations: (1) 'The Mount
of Olives' (הר הזיתים) occurs only here in Zech 14.4 (2×); however,
2 Sam 15.30 uniquely refers to 'the Ascent of Olives' (מעלה הזיתים).
(2) The imagery of the earth/mountains splitting in two is found in
prophetic literature (Isa 24.19; Hab 3.9) and in DtrH (1 Kgs 1.40;
19.11). Therefore, together these observations suggest that the phrase
'the Mount of Olives shall be split in two' may have been influenced
by Deuteronomic language.

---

67. May, 'Towards an Objective Approach to the Book of Jeremiah', p. 155.
68. Weinfeld, *Deuteronomy and the Deuteronomic School*, p. 327.
69. See below Chapter 6.

Summary of Chapter 3: Deuteronomic Language in II Zech

How does the evidence gathered above relate to the hypothesis of the Deuteronomic origin for II Zech? It can be broadly divided into three categories: (1) language unique to Deuteronomic literature and II Zech (§§1–7); (2) language found primarily in Deuteronomic literature and II Zech (§§8–21); and (3) language unique to II Zech, but is nevertheless Deuteronomic in character (§§22–28).

Each of these three categories lends a different type of strength to the hypothesis of the Deuteronomic origin of II Zech. First, the language which is unique to Deuteronomic literature and II Zech (§§1–7) provides the strongest and clearest connection of the literary dependence of II Zech upon Deuteronomic literature. Secondly, the examples of language which is primarily Deuteronomic (§§8–21) lends numerical strength to the hypothesis in that the majority of examples of Deuteronomic language in II Zech are of this type. In addition, they also provide some solid instances of language that expresses Deuteronomic theology—for example, the imagery of Jerusalem dwelling in security provided by Yahweh (§16). Thirdly, the observation that II Zech has its own unique phrases, which are Deuteronomic in character (§§22–28), strengthens the possibility of II Zech as an example of Deuteronomic prose from the post-exilic period. Just as some of the Deuteronomic language found in Jer is not found in DtrH,[70] some of the Deuteronomic language in II Zech is not found in DtrH and Jer. Thus these unique phrases do not necessarily refute the hypothesis of II Zech as Deuteronomic prose, but rather they point to the possible dynamism of the Deuteronomic school as it reinterprets a different tradition (I Zech rather than the sources of DtrH and Jer[71]) within a different political environment.

Together, these three categories strongly suggest that II Zech contains a significant number of Deuteronomic words and phrases that it *uniquely* shares with DtrH, Jer and DtrH/Jer combined; that are found *primarily* in DtrH, Jer and DtrH/Jer combined; and that are found *only* in II Zech. Such diversity of evidence suggests that Deuteronomic

---

70. Weinfeld, *Deuteronomy and the Deuteronomic School*, pp. 352-54. Also, some of the Deuteronomic language identified in this study between Jer and II Zech is not found in DtrH (§§3–5, §§14–15).

71. See below Chapter 6.

redactors not only were steeped in a distinctively Deuteronomic style, but that they also applied this style with some flexibility according to differing collections of traditional material as well as differing social settings.

Chapter 4

DEUTERONOMIC PASSAGES THAT SIGNIFICANTLY PARALLEL II ZECH

This chapter concerns those Deuteronomic passages which significantly parallel II Zech. 'Significant' here means that the Deuteronomic passage has a concentration of phrases, themes and/or images that are closely related to II Zech, but does *not* necessarily mean that these passages are the *sole* source of influence for II Zech. However, the concentration of the parallels suggests that these Deuteronomic passages probably influenced the language and imagery of II Zech.

The organization for this chapter follows the canonical sequence of books and chapters and, therefore, does not express any ranking concerning the significance of the Deuteronomic passages. However, the most significant parallels will be emphasized by the use of the double dagger (‡) before their numerical markers.

Deut 13.2-12

‡1.　The theme of false prophecy in Zech 13.2-6 relates closely to Deuteronomic literature, especially the legal material in Deut 13.2-12, which specifies that false prophecy is so serious as to require capital punishment and that the responsibility for executing such punishment includes even family members.[1]

> If a prophet or dreamer of dreams arises among you…, saying,
> 'Let us go after other gods', which you have not known, 'and
> let us serve them'; you shall not obey the words of the prophet
> or the dreamer of dreams for Yahweh your God is testing
> you…But that prophet or dreamer of dreams shall be put to

1.　The following commentators made connections between Zech 13.2-6 and Deut 13.2-12: Elliger, *Buch der zwölf kleinen Propheten*, II, p. 163; Jones, *Haggai, Zechariah, Malachi*, p. 165; Lacocque, 'Zacharie 9–14', p. 195; Mason, 'Use of Earlier Biblical Material in Zechariah 9–14', p. 251; Mitchell, *Haggai, Zechariah*, pp. 337-38; Petersen, *Late Israelite Prophecy*, p. 35.

> death for he spoke rebellion against Yahweh your God...If
> your brother, the son of your mother, or your son, or your
> daughter, or the wife of your bosom, or your friend who is like
> your own soul, secretly incites you saying, 'Let us go after and
> serve other gods', which you or your father have not known...;
> you shall not consent to it and you shall not obey him...But you
> shall kill him...you shall stone him to death with stones (Deut.
> 13.2-4, 6-7, 9-11).

†2.   Deut. 13.2-6 also may have influenced the language concerning false prophecy in Zech 10.1-2, for in both passages
'dream' (חלם) is used within the context of false prophecy
(Deut. 13.2, 4, 6; Zech 10.2).

†3.   The phrase in Deut. 13.6 'and you shall purge the evil from
your midst' (ובערת הרע מקרבך: also in Deut. 17.7; 19.9; 21.21;
22.21, 24; 24.7) may have influenced the threat against the
false prophets in Zech 13.2, wherein Yahweh proclaims,
'And also the prophets and the spirit of uncleanness I will
remove from the land'.[2]

Combined with the other evidence of Deuteronomic influence in the
theme of false prophecy in II Zech,[3] these examples of parallels certainly suggest that Deut 13.2-12 influenced II Zech, especially Zech
13.2-6.

Deut 28

Hyatt noted that the diction of the prose sermons in Jer was influenced
by Deut 28 more than by any other chapter in Deut.[4] An analogous
situation obtains between Deut 28 and II Zech. The following examples
betray the significant influence of Deut 28 upon II Zech:

2.   Petersen, *Late Israelite Prophecy*, p. 35.
3.   See §5 and below on false prophecy in 13.2-6 in Chapter 5, and 'False
Prophecy' in Chapter 8.
4.   'Deuteronomic Edition of Jeremiah', p. 253. Hyatt gave the following
parallels between Deut 28 and Jer: Deut 28.25 // Jer 15.4*; 24.9*; 29.18*; Deut
28.26 // Jer 7.33*; 16.4*; 19.7*; Deut 28.36 // Jer 16.3*; Deut 28.53 // Jer 19.9*;
Deut 28.63 // Jer 32.41*. For Hyatt's understanding of the literary relationship
between Deut 28 and the prose sermons in Jer, see Hyatt, 'Jeremiah and
Deuteronomy', pp. 126-27. Hyatt concluded that Deut 28.1-6, 15-19 is the 'original
nucleus', which was later expanded by a Deuteronomic redactor under influence of
material original to Jeremiah.

†4.   כל גויי הארץ—'all the nations of the earth' (§21) (Deut. 28.1; Zech 12.3).

‡5.   The combination of the imagery concerning curses in Deut. 28 has influenced II Zech in the following ways:

‡5a. The madness imagery in Zech 12.4 certainly demonstrates the influence of Deuteronomic literature, specifically Deut. 28.28, in that the three terms תמהון, שגעון, and עורון are found only in DtrH and II Zech (§1).

‡5b. The use of 'panic' (מהומה/מהומת) is found both in Deut. 28.20 and Zech 14.13.

‡5c. The use of 'devour' (אכל) with '[human] flesh' (בשר) is found in Deut 28.53 and Zech 11.9, 16 (§18).

These parallels suggest an analogous situation between Deut 28 and II Zech to that of Deut 28 and the prose sermons in Jer—that is, Deut 28 significantly influenced the diction and imagery in various sections of II Zech.

Jer 14.1–15.4[5]*

The most significant parallels between Jer 14.1–15.4* and II Zech obtain in Zech 10.1-2.[6]

†6.   Both Jer 14.4, 22 and Zech 10.1 use the image of Yahweh as the giver of rain.

†7.   Jer 14.13–16, 18 and Zech 10.2 condemn the falsity of Israel's leaders, especially the prophets.

---

5.   Although some of the poetic material in Jer 14.1–15.4* is understood as original to the prophet Jeremiah, the following commentators assigned the prose sections (14.11-12; 15.1-4) and the overall final form to a Deuteronomic redactor of Jer: Carroll, *From Chaos to Covenant*, pp. 84, 138, 162; Carroll, *Jeremiah*, pp. 306-21; Nicholson, *Jeremiah 1–25*, pp. 128-35; Nicholson, *Preaching*, pp. 100-101; Thiel, *Redaktion von Jeremia 1–25*, pp. 177-94. Weinfeld included the following phrase in Jer 14.1–15.4* in his list of D phraseology: 'to become a horror to all the kingdoms of earth', Jer 15.4 (*Deuteronomy and the Deuteronomic School*, p. 348).

6.   On the relationship between Jer 14.1–15.4* and Zech 10.1-2, see Elliger, *Buch der zwölf kleinen Propheten*, II, p. 144; Jones, *Haggai, Zechariah, Malachi*, p. 141; H. Junker, *Die zwölf kleinen Propheten* (2 vols.; Bonn: Peter Hanstein Verlagsbuchhandlung, 1938), II, p. 166; Mason, 'Some Examples', p. 345; Mason, 'Use of Earlier Biblical Material in Zechariah 9–14', pp. 93-95; Mitchell, *Haggai, Zechariah*, p. 286.

‡8.   Jer 14.14 and Zech 10.2 utilize a common vocabulary concerning false prophecy (see §5):

Jer 14.14: The prophets are prophesying lies (שׁקר) in my name...They are speaking (דברתי) to you a vision of lies (חזון שׁקר) and worthless divination (קסם)'.

Zech 10.2: 'the teraphim speak (דברו) nonsense and the diviners (הקוסמים) see lies (וחזו שׁקר)'.

Because of these similarities between Jer 14.1–15.4* and Zech 10.1-2, Mason concluded that there is 'a conscious allusion to the Jeremiah passage in Zech x 1f'.[7]

The following connections suggest that Jer 14.1–15.4* may have influenced other sections of II Zech:

†9.   In Jer 14.1–15.4*, the imagery of the sword as a means of Yahweh's judgment occurs (14.12, 13, 15, 16, 18; 15.2). This imagery is also found in II Zech (9.13; 13.7) and may reflect the influence of Jer 14.1–15.4*.

†10.   Paired with the imagery of the sword throughout Jer 14.1–15.4* is the imagery of famine as Yahweh's punishment (14.12, 13, 15, 16, 18; 15.2). Associated with the destruction imagery in Zech 11.4-17 is the imagery of those who remain devouring the flesh of one another (11.9, 16; §18), imagery that occurs within the context of the suffering following destruction. Therefore, it is possible that the famine imagery of Jer 14.1–15.4* is reflected in the imagery of devouring flesh in II Zech.

†11.   As noted above, the close connection between Jer 14.1–15.4* and Zech 10.1-2 concerns the combined themes of Yahweh as the giver of rain and the problem of false prophecy. The problem of false prophecy in Jer 14.1–15.4* may have also influenced Zech 13.2-6. Both Jer 14.14 and Zech 13.3 use שׁקר to denote false prophecy (§5) in connection with Deuteronomic name theology (§17):

Jer 14.14*: 'the prophets are prophesying lies in my name', נבאים בשׁמי שׁקר הנבאים

---

7.   'Some Examples', p. 345. See also p. 347 and Mason, 'Use of Earlier Biblical Material in Zechariah 9–14', p. 95, 97-98.

Zech 13.3: 'for you speak lies in the name of Yahweh', כִּי שֶׁקֶר דִּבַּרְתָּ בְּשֵׁם יהוה.

†12. The form and some of the vocabulary in the curse in both Jer 15.2* and Zech 11.9 are quite similar:[8]

> For the one who belongs to death, death (אֲשֶׁר לַמָּוֶת לַמָּוֶת); and for the one who belongs to the sword, the sword; and for the one who belongs to famine, famine; and for the one who belongs to captivity, captivity (Jer 15.2*).

> What is to die will die (הַמֵּתָה תָמוּת); what is to be destroyed will be destroyed; and those who will remain will devour the flesh of one another (Zech 11.9).

Given these numerous parallels, it is quite probable that Jer 14.1–15.4* significantly influenced the diction and imagery of II Zech.

Jer 23.1-8[9]

The following parallels between Jer 23.1-8 and II Zech concern the shepherd/flock imagery.[10]

---

8. Delcor, 'Sources', p. 408; Lacocque, 'Zacharie 9–14', p. 177; Mitchell, *Haggai, Zechariah*, p. 308.

9. The following commentators assigned Jer 23.1-4 to a Deuteronomic redactor of Jer: Carroll, *From Chaos to Covenant*, pp. 147-49; Carroll, *Jeremiah*, pp. 443-45; Nicholson, *Jeremiah 1–25*, pp. 190-92; Nicholson, *Preaching*, pp. 87-89; Thiel, *Redaktion von Jeremia 1–25*, pp. 246-49.

The following commentators assigned Jer 23.5-6 to a Deuteronomic redactor of Jer: Carroll, *From Chaos to Covenant*, pp. 147-49; Nicholson, *Jeremiah 1–25*, pp. 190-92.

The following commentators assigned Jer 23.7-8 to a Deuteronomic redactor of Jer: Carroll, *From Chaos to Covenant*, pp. 147-49; Nicholson, *Jeremiah 1–25*, pp. 190-92; Thiel, *Redaktion von Jeremia 1–25*, pp. 248-49.

Hyatt assigned Jer 23.1-8 to a post-Deuteronomic editor ('Deuteronomic Edition of Jeremiah', p. 266).

Weinfeld included the following phrase in Jer 23.1-8 in his list of Deuteronomic phraseology: 'be driven there', Jer 23.3, 8 (*Deuteronomy and the Deuteronomic School*, p. 348).

10. Since shepherd/flock imagery is so widespread, it is certainly probable that various prophetic passages influenced the shepherd/flock imagery in II Zech. However, there are some connections between this imagery in Jer and II Zech which suggest that, at the least, II Zech was influenced by this imagery in Jer.

For discussions of the shepherd/flock imagery in II Zech and their relationship

†13.   The only occurrences of shepherd imagery within a woe
       oracle are Jer 10.21; 23.1-4; Ezek 34.1-19; and Zech 11.4-
       17.[11] Therefore, it is possible that this form in Jer 23.1-8
       influenced Zech 11.4-17.

†14.   In Jer 23.3–4, 7-8, the future shepherd is portrayed within
       the context of a new exodus, a theme also found in Zech
       10.6-12 by the shepherd imagery of Zech 10.3 and 11.4-17.

†15.   The judgment imagery of a scattered flock is found in
       Deuteronomic literature (1 Kgs 22.17; Jer 10.21; 23.1-4),
       Ezek 34.5, and II Zech (10.9; 13.7);[12] therefore, this
       imagery may also have come from Jer 23.1-4.

†16.   Only in Jer 23.3 and Zech 10.8 is a form of רבב used in the
       context of shepherd imagery to describe the prosperity of the
       returned and protected flock.

†17.   Also, Jer 23.3 and Zech 10.8 place similar words in
       Yahweh's mouth—respectively, 'I will gather (אקבץ) the
       remnant of my flock' and 'I will gather them (אקבצם)'.

to other prophetic corpora, see A. Caquot, 'Breves remarques sur l'allegorie des
pasteurs en Zach 11', in *Mélanges bibliques et orientalaux en l'honneur de M. Delcor*
(AOAT, 215; ed. A. Caquot, S. Légasse and M. Tardieu; Neukirchen–Vluyn: Neu-
kirchener Verlag, 1985), pp. 45-55; T.J. Finley, 'The Sheep Merchants of Zechariah
11', *GTJ* 3 (1982), pp. 51-65; Mason, 'Use of Earlier Biblical Material in Zechariah
9–14', pp. 101-11, 171-74, 177-79; L.V. Meyer, 'Allegory concerning the Monarchy:
Zech 11: 4-17; 13: 7-9', in *Scripture in History and Theology* (ed. A.L. Merrill and
T.W. Overholt; PTMS, 17; Pittsburgh: The Pickwick Press, 1977), pp. 225-40;
Redditt, 'Israel's Shepherds', p. 636; M. Rehm, 'Die Hirtenallegorie Zach 11,4-14',
BZ 4 (1960), pp. 186-208; G. Wallis, 'Pastor Bonus. Eine Betrachtung zu den Hirtenstücken des Deutero- und Tritosacharja-Buches', *Kairos* 12 (1970), pp. 220-34; A.S.
van der Woude, 'Die Hirtenallegorie von Sacharja 11', *JNSL* 12 (1984), pp. 139-49.

11.   Lacocque ('Zacharie 9–14', p. 180) referred to Jer 23.1; Ezek 34.2; Hab 2.6,
9, 12, 15, 19 as possibly influencing Zech 11.17. However, the 'woe' oracles in Hab
do not use shepherd imagery. Meyer ('Allegory concerning the Monarchy', pp. 228-
29) referred to Jer 23.1-2; 1 Kgs 22.17; Jer 10.21; Ezek 34.1-10; however, 1 Kgs
22.17 is not in the form of a woe oracle. Saebø (*Sacharja 9–14*, pp. 236-38)
compared the form of Zech 11.4-17 to Jer 23.1-8 and Ezek 34.1-31.

12.   On 1 Kgs 22.17 and II Zech, see Mason, 'Use of Earlier Biblical Material in
Zechariah 9–14', pp. 177-78; Meyer, 'Allegory concerning the Monarchy', p. 235.

       On Jer 10.21; 23.1-4 and II Zech, see Mason, 'Use of Earlier Biblical
Material in Zechariah 9–14', pp. 177-78.

       On Ezek 34.5 and II Zech, see Mason, 'Use of Earlier Biblical Material in
Zechariah 9–14', pp. 177-78; Mitchell, *Haggai, Zechariah*, p. 317.

Besides these parallels concerning shepherd imagery, there are two phrases in Jer 23.1-8 that may have influenced the diction of II Zech:

†18. הנה ימים באים נאם יהוה—'Behold, days are coming, the oracle of Yahweh' (Jer 23.5, 7; see §24).

הנה יום בא ליהוה—'Behold, the day of Yahweh is coming' (Zech 14.1).

†19. וישראל ישכן לבטח—'and Israel will live in security' (Jer 23.6; see §16).

וישבה ירושלם לבטח—'and Jerusalem shall dwell in security' (Zech 14.11).

The above parallels suggest the possibility that Jer 23.1-8 significantly influenced the diction and imagery of II Zech, especially concerning shepherd imagery.

Jer 25.15-29, 34-38[13]

The connection between Zech 11.1-3 and Jer 25.34-38 has been widely noted. The two following statements concerning this relationship are representative: Lacocque wrote, 'The model text is Jer 25.34-38'.[14] Jones commented, 'He uses a passage from Jer 25.34-38 and builds on it... This passage the prophet loosely quotes, but gives it a precise reference to Lebanon and adds imagery that suggests the Day of the Lord'.[15] The following observations strongly suggest the relationship of Zech 11.1-3 to Jer 25.34-38:

‡20.　The connection between Zech 11.1-3 and Jer 25.34-38 is based upon their use of identical vocabulary—that is, 'wail'

---

13. Nicholson (*Jeremiah 1–25*, pp. 212-15) assigned Jer 25.15-29 to a Deuteronomic redactor of Jer. Hyatt assigned 25.13b-38 to a post-Deuteronomic editor ('Deuteronomic Edition of Jeremiah', p. 259; see also Thiel, *Redaktion von Jeremia 1–25*, p. 273); Weinfeld (*Deuteronomy and the Deuteronomic School*) included the following phrases in Jer 25.15-29, 34-38 in his list of Deuteronomic phraseology: 'to make them a desolation, a waste, a hiss, a curse', Jer 25.18 (pp. 348-49); 'as at this day', Jer 25.18 (p. 350); 'to send the sword among them', Jer 25.27 (p. 354); 'the city which my name is called upon', Jer 25.29 (p. 325).

14. My translation. 'Zacharie 9–14', p. 170.

15. *Haggai, Zechariah, Malachi*, p. 149.

(היליכו), 'hark' (קול), 'shepherds' (רעים), 'glory' (אדיר/אדרת),
'for' (כי), 'lion' (פיר).[16]

‡21.   The use of 'wail' (יללה) in the phrase 'hark, the wail of the
        shepherds' (קול יללה הרעים) occurs only here in Zech 11.3a.
        'Wail' (יללה) appears elsewhere within the context of shepherd
        imagery only in Jer 25.36: 'Hark (קול), the cry of the shep-
        herds (צעקת הרעים) and the wail of the lords of the flock'
        (ויללת אדירי הצאן). Also, in both Zech 11.3a and Jer 25.36, these
        'hark' phrases are followed by an explanation of the shepherds'
        anguish, which contains a form of the verb 'despoil' (שדד).[17]
        Therefore, the relationship between Zech 11.3a and Jer 25.36
        can be described, in the words of Jones, as one of 'verbal
        dependence'.[18]

The influence of Jer 25.15-29, 34-38 is found elsewhere in II Zech as
well:

†22.   Since Philistia had ceased to be a political rival in the Persian
        period, the reference to the Philistine cities in Zech 9.5-7 must
        have a symbolic meaning; therefore, these cities probably
        represent foreign cities and peoples who were hostile to Israel
        in general. When this list of four Philistine cities is compared
        with other such lists in the Hebrew Bible,[19] it appears that

16. Lacocque, 'Zacharie 9–14', p. 170. See also Delcor, 'Sources', pp. 387, 407-
408; Jones, *Haggai, Zechariah, Malachi*, p. 149; Mason, 'Use of Earlier Biblical
Material in Zechariah 9–14', p. 107; Mitchell, *Haggai, Zechariah*, p. 297.

17. The similarity between Zech 11.3 and Jer 25.36 is so striking that Mitchell
argued that the MT reading 'glory' (אדרתם) in Zech 11.3 is a misreading, which
should be corrected to 'pasture' (מרעיתם) to correspond with Jer 25.36 (*Haggai,
Zechariah*, p. 297). No textual evidence for such an emendation exists, and therefore
his emendation should be rejected. However, it is interesting to note that the similarity
between Zech 11.3 and Jer 25.36 provided the impetus for his argument.

18. *Haggai, Zechariah, Malachi*, p. 149.

19. The following are passages in which one of the four cities given in Zech 9.5-
7 is paired with another Philistine city. The Philistine cities are given in the order in
which they are found in that passage: Josh 11.22 (Gaza, Gath, Ashdod); 13.3 (Gaza,
Ashdod, Ashkelon, Gath, Ekron); 15.45-47 (Ekron, Ashdod, Gaza); Judg 1.18
(Gaza, Ashkelon, Ekron); 1 Sam 6.17 (Ashdod, Gaza, Ashkelon, Gath, Ekron);
7.14 (Ekron to Gath); 17.52 (Gath, Ekron); 2 Sam 1.20 (Gath, Ashkelon); Jer 25.20
(Ashkelon, Gaza, Ekron, Ashdod); 47.5 (Gaza, Ashkelon); Amos 1.6-8 (Gaza,
Ashkelon, Ekron); Zeph 2.4 (Gaza, Ashkelon, Ashdod, Ekron).

Zech 9.5-7 is related to Jer 25.20. In both Jer 25.20 and Zech 9.5-6, the Philistine cities referred to are Ashkelon, Gaza, Ekron and Ashdod, and they are given in the same order.[20]

†23. The use of the judgment imagery of Yahweh's sword with shepherd imagery is found only in Jer 25.34-38 and Zech 13.7.

†24. The Deuteronomic use of name theology is found in both Jer 25.29 and II Zech (§17).

‡25. The judgment imagery of an intoxicating cup is found in various prophetic collections;[21] however, the connections between its use in Jer 25.15-29, 34-38 and Zech 12.2 are much closer. Only in Jer 25.15-29, 34-38 and II Zech are the two judgment images of the intoxicating cup and Yahweh's sword combined and only in them is imagery of bad shepherds combined with these two judgment images. Hence, the image of the intoxicating cup in Jer 25.15-17 was probably a source for that in Zech 12.2.[22]

‡26. Both Jer 25.38 and Zech 11.3 include the imagery of a lion combined with the theme of the land becoming a waste.

†27. Symbolic action can be an important part of a prophetic message. Because of this importance, some redactional narratives resemble accounts of symbolic action. Such a redactional narrative is Jer 25.15-29, wherein it is reported that Jeremiah made the nations drink from a 'cup of the wine of wrath'. Another such account is Zech 11.4-17, wherein the 'prophet' is commanded to 'shepherd' the returnees and then shifts into language suggesting that Yahweh is this shepherd. Since Jer 25.15-29 has other similarities with II Zech, it is possible that the form of a such a fictional symbolic account influenced Zech 11.4-17 by way of Jer 25.15-29.[23]

20. Jones (*Haggai, Zechariah, Malachi*, p. 126) and Mitchell (*Haggai, Zechariah*, pp. 266-67) suggested that Jer 25.20 influenced Zech 9.5-6.

21. Isa 51.17, 22; Jer 25.15-17; 51.7; Hab 2.16. On the influence of Isa 51.17, 22 on Zech 12.2, see Elliger, *Buch der zwölf kleinen Propheten*, II, p. 159; Jones, *Haggai, Zechariah, Malachi*, p. 158; Mason, 'Use of Earlier Biblical Material in Zechariah 9–14', pp. 207-209. On the influence of Jer 51.7 on Zech 12.2, see Delcor, 'Sources', p. 407; Elliger, *Buch der zwölf kleinen Propheten*, II, p. 159; Junker, *Die zwölf kleinen Propheten*, II, p. 177; Mitchell, *Haggai, Zechariah*, p. 321.

22. Junker, *Die zwölf kleinen Propheten*, II, p. 177.

23. Caquot, 'L'allegorie des pasteurs en Zacharie 11', p. 48; Lacocque, 'Zacharie 9–14', p. 174; Meyer, 'Allegory concerning the Monarchy', p. 227; Rehm,

These numerous parallels certainly point to the significant influence that the diction and imagery of Jer 25.15-29, 34-38 played upon II Zech.

Jer 30–31[24]

The following similarities suggest that Jer 30–31 may have influenced II Zech:

†28.   הנה ימים באים נאם יהוה—'Behold, days are coming, the oracle of Yahweh' (Jer 30.3; 31.27, 31, 38; see §24).

הנה יום בא ליהוה—'Behold, the day of Yahweh is coming' (found only in Zech 14.1).

†29.   Both Jer 30.18-21 and Zech 10.4-5 refer to the future leaders of the restored community; therefore, the use of ממנו in Jer 30.21 ('Their prince shall be one of themselves [ממנו]') may have influenced its use in Zech 10.4.[25] Thus, Zech 10.4 can be considered to be, in the words of Mitchell, a 'variation of Jer 30.20f'.[26]

‡30.   The promise in Jer 30.19-20 of multiplying the returnees so that their children will be as numerous as of old may have influenced Zech 10.8, 10.[27] Although the use of the verb 'multiply' (רבב) is found in various places in the Hebrew

'Hirtenallegorie Zach 11,4-14', p. 186; van der Woude, 'Hirtenallegorie von Sacharja 11', p. 144.

24. The following commentators assigned Jer 30–31 to a Deuteronomic redactor of Jer: Nicholson, *Jeremiah 1–25*, pp. 50-73, 83-89; Nicholson, *Preaching*, pp. 85-86, 106-107, 131. Hyatt assigned Jer 30–31 to a post-Deuteronomic editor ('Deuteronomic Edition of Jeremiah', p. 266; see also Thiel, *Redaktion von Jeremia 26–45*, pp. 20-28, 37). Weinfeld (*Deuteronomy and the Deuteronomic School*) included the following phrases in Jer 30–31 in his list of Deuteronomic phraseology: 'to scatter among the nations', Jer 30.11 (p. 347); 'to be a people to him', Jer 30.22, 25; 31.32 (p. 327).

25. This connection is made by the following commentators: Jones, *Haggai, Zechariah, Malachi*, p. 143; Lacocque, 'Zacharie 9–14', p. 166; Mitchell, *Haggai, Zechariah*, p. 289.

26. *Haggai, Zechariah*, p. 289.

27. Delcor ('Sources', pp. 387, 411) suggested that Jer 30.19 was a source for Zech 10.8.

Bible,[28] only in Jer 30.19-20 and Zech 10.8, 10 is 'multiply' applied to the returnees in combination with the Deuteronomic motif of there not being enough land for the prospering people of God (Josh 17.16-17).[29]

†31.   Jer 30.22 and Zech 13.9 have similar covenant language (§27).

†32.   The use of 'break' (פרר) with a covenant 'cut' (כרת) by Yahweh is found in Zech 11.10 and Jer 31.32 (§20).

†33.   The geography in both Jer 31.38-39 and Zech 14.10 describes the rebuilt city walls of Jerusalem. Although there are differences between these two descriptions,[30] there are also significant similarities. Both Jer 31.38 and Zech 14.10 include 'the Tower of Hananel' and 'the Corner Gate',[31] toponyms that may be distinctively Deuteronomic ways of referring to these structures (see §§6, 15).

‡34.   The phrase 'to scatter among the peoples' in Zech 10.9 reflects Deuteronomic phraseology (§25). Of all the Deuteronomic passages which use this phrase, two are found in Jeremiah 30–31 (30.11; 31.10). Also, of all these Deuteronomic passages, Jer 31.10 may be the most significant in relation to Zech 10.9-10 for two reasons. First, like Zech 10.9-10, it also combines the imagery of scattering with that of gathering (קבץ). Secondly, although the Deuteronomic phraseology for 'scattering' generally uses the verb פוץ, Zech 10.9 and Jer 31.10 both use זרע.

†35.   In Jeremiah 31, there is an emphasis upon the inclusion of 'all the families of Israel' (Jer 31.1) and upon the individuality of the giving of the new covenant. Jer 31.34: 'And no longer

28. See Mendecki, 'Deuterojesajanischer und Ezechielischer Einfluss auf Sach 10.8-10', p. 341.

29. Although this motif is also found in 49.19-20, the idiom 'it is not enough' (לא ימצא) is found in both Zech 10.10 and Josh 17.16-17, but is lacking in Isa 49.19-20.

30. Jer 31.38-39 includes 'the hill Gareb', 'Goah', 'the brook Kidron' and 'the Horse Gate', none of which is mentioned in Zech 14.10. Zech 14.10 includes 'Geba', 'Rimmon', 'the Gate of Benjamin' and 'the king's wine presses', none of which is mentioned in Jer 31.38-39.

31. The following commentators associated Zech 14.10 with Jer 31.38: Delcor, 'Sources', pp. 387, 410; Dentan, 'Zechariah 9–14', p. 1112; Mason, 'Use of Earlier Biblical Material in Zechariah 9–14', pp. 266-67; Mitchell, *Haggai, Zechariah*, pp. 348-49.

will each man teach his neighbor, or each man his brother, saying, "Know Yahweh", for all of them will know me, from the least of them to the greatest of them'. This emphasis upon 'all the families' and each individual also occurs in Zech 12.12-14, wherein each family mourns by itself and the men and women mourn by themselves.[32]

These parallels suggest that Jer 30–31 significantly influenced II Zech.

Summary of Chapter 4:
Deuteronomic Passages That Significantly Parallel II Zech

In Chapter 3, Deuteronomic language found in II Zech was listed. In this chapter, I have pointed to various passages from Deuteronomic literature that appear to have significantly influenced II Zech. Deut. 13.2-12 (††1–3) seems to have provided the language of false prophecy in II Zech, especially in Zech 13.2-6. Deut. 28 (††4–5) is a probable source for the curse imagery in II Zech. Jer 14.1–15.4* (††6–12) is a likely source for the judgment imagery in II Zech, especially in the false prophecy imagery in Zech 10.1-2. The imagery in Jer 23.1-8 (††13–19) is close to that of II Zech, especially its shepherd imagery. Jer 25.15-29, 34-38 (††20–27) appears to have influenced II Zech, with the clearest case being the identical vocabulary in Jer 25.34-38 and Zech 11.1-3. The restoration language in Jeremiah 30–31 (††28–35) perhaps contributed to that of II Zech. Although other prophetic literature also clearly influenced II Zech (e.g. Isa, Ezek), the significant influence of these Deuteronomic passages upon II Zech suggests the possibility for the origin of II Zech from the hand of a Deuteronomic redactor.

How does the evidence given in this chapter compare to that given in the previous chapter? First, only 14[33] of the 35 cases given here are repeated from the previous chapter; therefore, the hypothesis of the Deuteronomic origin of II Zech has been quantitatively strengthened. Second, this working hypothesis has been qualitatively strengthened in that the comparisons made in this chapter emphasize the broader context of words, phrases and images more than those in the previous

32. Mason, *Haggai, Zechariah and Malachi*, p. 120; Mason, 'Use of Earlier Biblical Material in Zechariah 9–14', pp. 245-46.

33. ††4, 5a, 5c, 8, 10, 11, 18, 19, 24, 28, 31, 32, 33, 34.

chapter, thereby grouping together possible influences so as to suggest probable direct literary connections. Therefore, when the evidence from this chapter and the previous chapter are combined, the hypothesis for the Deuteronomic origin of II Zech gains both quantitative and qualitative strength.

Chapter 5

DEUTERONOMIC INFLUENCE IN II ZECH

The organization of the previous two chapters did not follow the canonical order of II Zech, but rather dealt categorically with Deuteronomic language and discussed Deuteronomic passages in their canonical order. The organization of this chapter follows the canonical order of II Zech so as to re-present the data given above, with some additional material, to determine more accurately the extent of possible Deuteronomic redaction in II Zech.

Zech 9.1-17

Zech 9.5-6. In these verses there are two possible cases of Deuteronomic influence: (1) The word ממזר, 'bastard', used to describe the people who will dwell in Ashdod, appears only here and in Deut 23.3.[1] (2) The choice of the four Philistine cities and the order in which they are given suggests the influence of Jer 25.20. Of all the possible groupings of Philistine cities, only Jer 25.20 and Zech 9.5-6 have the following sequence of these four Philistine cities: Ashkelon, Gaza, Ekron, Ashdod (†22).

Zech 9.11. The image of captives being set free from a waterless pit recalls the imprisonments of Joseph and of Jeremiah (Gen 37.28; Jer 38.6); only in these three passages is the imagery of a waterless pit used to express captivity.[2] Although this image is also found in Genesis, the close dependence on Jer elsewhere lends support to the probability that Jer 38.6 influenced Zech 9.11.

Summary: Zech 9.1-17. Zech 9.1-17 is generally set off from the rest of II Zech as primarily poetic in contrast to the remaining

---

1. Mason, *Haggai, Zechariah and Malachi*, p. 86; Mitchell, *Haggai, Zechariah*, p. 267.

2. Mason, 'Use of Earlier Biblical Material in Zechariah 9–14', pp. 69-72.

sections of II Zech, which are primarily prosaic.³ Here another observation can be made which likewise sets off Zech 9.1-17 from the rest of II Zech—that is, in contrast to the other sections of II Zech, Zech 9.1-17 has few possible examples of Deuteronomic influence. Because of this relative scarcity, it is unlikely that Zech 9 is primarily the product of a Deuteronomic redactor; rather, Zech 9.1-17 must be viewed as a post-exilic source that originated outside the Deuteronomic school but was perhaps utilized by the Deuteronomic redactor of II Zech. Such a use of a non-Deuteronomic, poetic source in a Deuteronomic redaction of a prophetic book is not without parallel. For example, in Jer the oracles against the nations (Jer 46–51) are not Jeremianic and contain few Deuteronomic phrases; however, they remain part of the Deuteronomic redaction of Jer as a (mostly) poetic source used in the Deuteronomic redaction. Hence, Zech 9.1-17 can be considered a poetic source (most likely also from the post-exilic period)⁴ that was used by the Deuteronomic redactor of II Zech.

Zech 10.1–11.3

Zech 10.1-2. In these two verses, three images are interwoven: Yahweh as the giver of rain, the people as shepherdless sheep, and false prophets. In v. 1, the people are urged to ask for rain from Yahweh, the giver of rain; in v. 2, the necessity for this urging is described as the people wandering like shepherdless sheep because of the leadership of false prophets. Although these images are found throughout the Hebrew Bible,⁵ their juxtaposition is found primarily in Deuteronomic

3.   Hoftijzer, 'Remarks Concerning the Use of the Particle in Classical Hebrew', p. 77; Meyers, 'Messianism in First and Second Zechariah', pp. 8-9, 22 n. 20.

4.   My argument that Zech 9.1-17 is a source used by the Deuteronomic redactor of II Zech does not necessarily imply either that Zech 9.1-17 is pre-exilic/ exilic or that it circulated as an independent unit. My argument requires only the following: (1) Although Zech 9.1-17 must predate Zech 10.1–14.21, they can still be seen as basically contemporary, since no significant lapse of time is required between Zech 9.1-17 and Zech 10.1–14.21. (2) Zech 9.1-17 may have had another original context, such as being circulated independently or as a part of another collection. (3) It may have been produced orally or in a written form.

5.   Yahweh as giver of rain: e.g. Deut 11.10-17; Isa 30.23; Hag 1.5-11; Zech 8.9-13; Mal 3.10-11; Ps 68.8-9. For a fuller discussion of shepherd/flock imagery, see Mason, 'Use of Earlier Biblical Material in Zechariah 9–14', pp. 171-79 and the discussion below on Zech 11.4-17. See also below the discussion of Zech 10.2 in 'False Prophecy' in Chapter 8.

literature. The most significant Deuteronomic passage is Jer 14.1–15.4*, which is similar to Zech 10.1-2 in the following ways: (1) Both use the image of Yahweh as the giver of rain (†6). (2) Both condemn the falsity of Israel's leaders, especially the prophets (†7). (3) They have common vocabulary concerning false prophecy (‡8).

Another Deuteronomic passage, 1 Kgs 22.13-23, combines two of the three images used in Zech 10.1-2. Although the imagery of Yahweh as the giver of rain is not found in 1 Kgs 22.13-23, we find the juxtaposition of the themes of false prophecy and shepherd imagery. Against the message of the false prophets, Micaiah prophesies, 'I saw all Israel scattered upon the mountains, as sheep that have no shepherd' (1 Kgs 22.17). The wording of Micaiah's message— כצאן אשר אין להם רעה, 'as sheep that have no shepherd'—is similar to that of Zech 10.2: 'they wander like sheep; they are afflicted for there is no shepherd' (נסעו כמו צאן יענו כי אין רעה). Micaiah continues by explaining how Yahweh sent a 'lying spirit' (רוח שקר; see §5) among Zedekiah's prophets. Hence, Zech 10.1-2 may also draw from 1 Kgs 22.13-23.[6]

Zech 10.2. The use of 'teraphim' in Zech 10.2 suggests Deuteronomic influence, for the word 'teraphim' occurs primarily in Deuteronomic literature.[7] The observation that 'teraphim' occurs primarily in Deuteronomic literature is even more significant when it is observed that some of the non-Deuteronomic occurrences (Gen 31.19, 34-35) do not explicitly condemn them. Therefore, the use of 'teraphim' in Zech 10.2 may reflect the influence of what Mason has called 'the Deuteronomistic aversion to teraphim'.[8] This observation is strengthened further by the possible allusion to Jer 14.1–15.4*. In addition to the parallels discussed above between Zech 10.1-2 and Jer 14.1–15.4*, Mason noted that there is a possible connection between them concerning 'teraphim'. First, he noted that Jer 14.1–15.4* is 'strongly Deuteronomistic in tone and outlook'.[9] He then understood the 'reference to the sins of Manasseh [in Jer 15.4*]…to include the

6. Jones, *Haggai, Zechariah, Malachi*, p. 142.

7. 'Teraphim' is found in Gen 31.19, 34, 35; Judg 17.5; 18.14, 17, 18, 20; 1 Sam 15.23; 19.13, 16; 2 Kgs 23.24; Hos 3.4; Zech 10.2.

8. 'Some Examples', p. 346. See also Lacocque, 'Zacharie 9–14', p. 164; Mason, 'Use of Earlier Biblical Material in Zechariah 9–14', p. 92; Mitchell, *Haggai, Zechariah*, p. 287.

9. 'Some Examples', p. 346. Here, Mason referred to the work of Nicholson, *Preaching*.

introduction of teraphim into the temple, for it is the Deuteronomistic historian who tells us how they had to be removed by Josiah (II Ki. xxiii 24)'.[10] Therefore, the use of 'teraphim' in Zech 10.2 may be another example of a parallel between Jer 14.1–15.4* and Zech 10.1-2 as well as another example of Deuteronomic influence on these verses.

The characterisation of diviners (הקוסמים) as false prophets may suggest Deuteronomic influence, for divination is forbidden in Deuteronomic legal material (Deut 18.10; see also Jer 14.14*, ‡8).

The use of 'dream' חלם within the context of false prophecy in Zech 10.2 may have been influenced by Deut 13.2,4,6 (†2) and Jer 23.25-28.[11] In Jer 23.25-28, the connection between the interpretation of dreams and false prophecy is made explicit:

> The prophet who has a dream, let him tell his dream; but the one who has my word, let him speak my word truthfully. What does chaff have in common with wheat—oracle of Yahweh? (Jer 23.28)

Therefore, it is possible that dream interpretation as a false means for prophecy in Zech 10.2 reflects the application of a Deuteronomic criterion for true prophecy, which forbids the means of dream interpretation.

Zech 10.4. Mitchell called this verse a 'variation of Jer 30.20-21' which 'borrows a term from Isa 19.13 and another from 22.23',[12] because of their connection of the repetitious use of 'out of them' (ממנו) concerning Israel's future leaders (†29). The terms that Mitchell identified as borrowed from Isa 19.13 and 22.23 are, respectively, two metaphors for Israel's leaders, 'cornerstone' (פנה) and 'tent peg' (יתד). 'Tent peg' occurs only in Isa 22.23 as a metaphor for Israel's leaders and, therefore, Isa 22.23 is probably the source for Zech 10.4.[13] However, it is not necessarily true that the source for 'cornerstone' in Zech 10.4 also came from Isa because, as Mitchell himself noted, 'cornerstone' also appears as a metaphor for Israel's leaders in Judg 20.2 and 1 Sam 14.38.[14] Therefore, it is possible that

10. 'Some Examples', 346.

11. Carroll (*From Chaos to Covenant*, p. 175; *Jeremiah*, p. 473) related Jer 23.28 and Zech 10.2.

12. Haggai, *Zechariah*, p. 289.

13. Mitchell, *Haggai, Zechariah*, p. 289. Also Jones, *Haggai, Zechariah, Malachi*, p. 143; Lacocque, 'Zacharie 9–14', p. 166.

14. Mitchell, *Haggai, Zechariah*, p. 289. Also Junker, *Die zwölf kleinen Propheten*, II, p. 167; Jones, *Haggai, Zechariah, Malachi*, p. 143; Lacocque, 'Zacharie 9–

the use of 'cornerstone' in these Deuteronomic passages was also a source for Zech 10.4. If this is the case, then the combined connection between Zech 10.4 and Jer 30.18-21, on the one hand, and Zech 10.4, Judg 20.2 and 1 Sam 14.38, on the other hand, may suggest that this verse was influenced by Deuteronomic literature.

Zech 10.6. In this verse, the Southern Kingdom is referred to as 'the house of Judah', the Northern Kingdom as 'the house of Joseph'. Although such a term for the southern kingdom is found throughout the Hebrew Bible, the use of 'the house of Joseph' for the Northern Kingdom is limited, being found primarily in Deuteronomic literature (§12).

Zech 10.8a. The use of the verb 'redeem' (פדה) in the context of exodus language is distinctively Deuteronomic; other bodies of litera-ture (e.g. other Pentateuchal sources) generally use the synonym גאל in this context (see §13).

Zech 10.8b. Although the use of the verb 'multiply' (רבב) is found in various places in the Hebrew Bible,[15] two Deuteronomic passages that significantly parallel II Zech contain 'multiply' and have other parallels to Zech 10.8-10 as well. In Jer 23.3, 'multiply' is used within the context of shepherd imagery concerning the return (‡16). In Jer 30.19-20, 'multiply' is applied to the returnees in combination with the Deuteronomic tradition of there not being enough land for the prospering people of God (‡30). Therefore, this use of 'multiply' in relationship to the returnees may suggest Deuteronomic influence.

Zech 10.9. The two phrases describing the Diaspora in Zech 10.9 suggest possible Deuteronomic influence: (1) Although the word 'distant places' (מרחקים) appears elsewhere,[16] it clearly refers to the Diaspora only in Jer 8.19 and Zech 10.9.[17] (2) The phrase 'to scatter among the peoples' reflects Deuteronomic phraseology (§25). Of all the Deuteronomic passages that use this phrase, Jer 31.10 may be the most significant in relation to Zech 10.9-10 for two reasons (‡34): first, like Zech 10.9-10, it combines the imagery of scattering with

14', p. 166; Mason, 'Use of Earlier Biblical Material in Zechariah 9–14', p. 113-14.

15. Mendecki, 'Deuterojesajanischer und Ezechielischer Einfluss auf Sach 10.8-10', p. 341.

16. Isa 10.3; 13.5; 17.13; 30.27; 46.11; Jer 4.16; 5.15; 6.20; 31.10; Ezek 23.40; Prov 25.25.

17. Lacocque (Zacharie 9–14', p. 167) related the use of מרחקים in Zech 10.9 to Jer 8.19.

that of gathering (קבץ); secondly, although the Deuteronomic phrase-ology for 'scattering' generally uses the verb פוץ, Zech 10.9 and Jer 31.10 both use זרע.

Zech 10.10. In the description of the land to which Yahweh's people will return, two locations are included within the borders of the promised land: Gilead and Lebanon. Lebanon is included as part of the promised land only in Deuteronomic literature (Deut 1.7; 3.25; 11.24; Josh 1.4; 9.1; 11.17; 12.7; 13.5,6; Judg 3.3) and in two prophetic passages concerning the return (Isa 29.17; Zech 10.10).[18] Gilead, on the other hand, is included in the promised land in various collections (2 Kgs 15.29; Jer 50.19; Amos 1.3,13; Mic 7.14; Obad 19; Ps 60.9 = 108.9), only two of which express restoration language (Jer 50.19; Mic 7.14).[19] The combination of flock imagery, the theme of the return, and the reference to Gilead in Zech 10.9-10 led Mitchell to conclude that Zech 10.10 was 'a reminiscence of Jer 50.19'.[20] Therefore, it is possible that the references to Lebanon and Gilead suggest Deuteronomic influence. This observation is strengthened further when the motif of there being no room in the land for the numerous returnees is examined—Zech 10.10: 'it will not be enough for them' (לא ימצא להם). Elsewhere, this motif is found only in Josh 17.16-17, Isa 49.19-20 and Jer 30.19-20.[21] Although this motif is found in Isa 49.19-20 and Jer 30.19-20, the idiom 'it is not enough'

---

18. Although they refer to only selected Deuteronomic passages, the following commentators observed this connection to Deuteronomic literature: Jones, *Haggai, Zechariah, Malachi*, p. 146; Lacocque, 'Zacharie 9–14', p. 168.

19. The following commentators referred to various combinations of these passages: Dentan, 'Zechariah 9–14', p. 1101; Jones, *Haggai, Zechariah, Malachi*, p. 146; Lacocque, 'Zacharie 9–14', p. 168; Mendecki, 'Deuterojesajanischer und Ezechielischer Einfluss auf Sach 10.8-10', p. 342; Mitchell, *Haggai, Zechariah*, p. 294.

20. *Haggai, Zechariah*, p. 294. Also, Delcor ('Sources', p. 387) suggested that Jer 50.19 was a source for the occupation of Gilead in Zech 10.10.

21. Lacocque ('Zacharie 9–14', p. 168) and Mitchell (*Haggai, Zechariah*, p. 294) referred to Josh 17.16-17. Mendecki referred to Isa 49.19-20; Jer 31.8; and Mic 2.12 ('Deuterojesajanischer und Ezechielischer Einfluss auf Sach 10.8-10', p. 342). However, Jer 31.8 and Mic 2.12 simply imply that the returnees would be numerous and, therefore, they do not use the 'no room' motif. Jer 30.19-20 also implies that the returnees would be numerous; however, Jer 30.19 may refer to the 'no room' motif with the phrase 'as before'. See †29.

(לא ימצא) within the context of this motif is found only in Zech 10.10 and Josh 17.16-17.[22]

> The sons of Joseph said, 'The hill country is not enough for us (לא ימצא לנו)...' Then Joshua said to the house of Joseph, to Ephraim and Manasseh, 'You are a numerous people...'

(Also, note the reference to 'the house of Joseph' which is similar to that of Zech 10.6. See above.) Therefore, the combined use of the 'no room' motif with the inclusion of Gilead and Lebanon in the promised land in Zech 10.10 suggests Deuteronomic influence.

Zech 10.12. The phrase 'and in his name they will walk' makes use of name theology, which is widely found in Deuteronomic literature (§17).

Zech 11.1-3: As noted above (‡20), a close relationship exists between Zech 11.1-3 and Jer 25.34-38 which is suggested by their use of identical vocabulary—that is, 'wail' (הילילו), 'hark' (קול), 'shepherds' (רעים), 'glory' (אדירי/אדרת), 'for' (כי), 'lion' (פיר). In the following paragraphs, the elements of Zech 11.1-3 will be examined concerning this relationship as well as their relationship to other Deuteronomic literature.

Zech 11.3a. The combination of 'hark' (קול), 'wail' (יללת), and shepherd imagery occurs only in Jer 25.36 and Zech 11.3a (‡21).

Zech 11.3b. Although the combined imagery of a lion and waste land in Jer 25.38 may have suggested its use in Zech 11.3b (‡26), the use of 'lion' in Zech 11.3b has been further developed under the influence of Jer 49.19 = 50.44: 'Behold, like a lion coming up from the jungle of the Jordan'.[23] This development is evident first in that the phrase 'jungle of the Jordan' (גאון הירדן) occurs only in Jer 12.5, 49.19 = 50.44 and Zech 11.3b[24] and, secondly, in that this phrase is combined with the image of a lion only in Jer 49.19 = 50.44 and Zech 11.3b. Therefore, here is another example of lexical dependence of Zech 11.3 on Jer.[25]

Although there is a connection between Zech 11.3 and Jer 25.38;

22. Otzen (*Studien über Deuterosacharja*, p. 250) referred to Num 11.22, Josh 17.16 and Judg 21.14 as the examples of this idiom. However, its use in Num 11.22 does not concern land, but meat.

23. Jones, *Haggai, Zechariah, Malachi*, p. 149.

24. Bic, *Sacharja*, p. 133; Lacocque, 'Zacharie 9–14', p. 171.

25. Jones, *Haggai, Zechariah, Malachi*, p. 149; Mitchell, *Haggai, Zechariah*, p. 297.

49.19 = 50.44, the use of 'lion' in Jer 25.38; 49.19 = 50.44 does not include the image of the lion roaring as does Zech 11.3b. The description of the lion roaring may simply be an effort to parallel the 'roar of the lions' with the 'wail of the shepherds'; however, other passages in Jer suggest a possible connection with Zech 11.3b. Although the image of a roaring lion is widespread,[26] only two other passages using this image also contain the image of the land as a waste, both of which are in Jer: Jer 2.15: 'Against him the lions have roared...they have made his land a waste'; Jer 4.7: 'A lion has gone up from his thicket...to make your land a waste'.

Summary, Zech 10.1–11.3. In this section of II Zech, we have observed some of II Zech's striking similarities to Deuteronomic literature, especially with Jer (14.1–15.4*; 25.34-38; 30.20-21; 49.19 = 50.44). These similarities have led Mason to conclude:

> Some striking similarity of thought, in particular to that of the circles amongst whom the words and traditions of Jeremiah received expansion, can be detected.[27]

Given the connection of Zech 10.1–11.3 to what Mason calls the 'Jeremiah/Deuteronomist tradition',[28] the parallels between Zech 10.1–11.3 and DtrH should receive greater weight than they have previously. These parallels have been discussed above. The similarities between Zech 10.1–11.3 and DtrH include language (§§12, 13, 17), motifs (such as the 'no room' motif), and themes (such as false prophecy). When combined, the similarities between Zech 10.1–11.3 and Jer, on the one hand, and Zech 10.1–11.3 and DtrH, on the other hand, suggest not only Deuteronomic influence, but the possibility that Zech 10.1–11.3 are from the hand of a Deuteronomic redactor.

Zech 11.4-17

Zech 11.4, 7. The phrase 'the flock doomed for slaughter' (צאן ההרגה) betrays the influence of Jer, for the only other occurrences of ההרגה are in Jer 7.32*; 19.6* (§4). This phrase may also have been influenced

---

26. Judg 14.5; Isa 5.29; Jer 2.15; 51.38; Ezek 22.25; Hos 11.10; Amos 3.4, 8; Zeph 3.3; Zech 11.3; Job 4.10; Pss 22.13; 104.21.
27. 'Use of Earlier Biblical Material in Zechariah 9–14', p. 131 (see also p. 108).
28. 'Use of Earlier Biblical Material in Zechariah 9–14', pp. 96-98.

by the synonymous phrase צאן לטבחה which is also found in Jer (12.3).[29]

Zech 11.9. The form and vocabulary of the curse in Zech 11.9 are quite similar to that of Jer 15.2* (†12). The phrase in Zech 11.9, which differs from this common form—'and those who remain will devour one another's flesh'—also betrays Deuteronomic influence, for the use of 'devour' (אכל) with '[human] flesh' (בשׂר) is found primarily in Deuteronomic literature (§18; see also ‡5c). This phrase betrays its Deuteronomic influence even more when its close connection with Jer 19.9* is observed—that is, only in Jer 19.9* and Zech 11.9 does one find the combination of אכל בשׂר with איש רעהו.[30]

Zech 11.9
'and those who remain will devour flesh of one another'
והנשׁארות תאכלנה אשׁה את בשׂר רעותה

Jer 19.9*
'they will devour flesh of one another'
ואישׁ בשׂר רעהו יאכלו

Therefore, this curse contains two elements that suggest Deuteronomic influence: its form (†12) and the combination of אכל בשׂר (§18) with איש רעהו.

Zech 11.10. Although the imagery of Yahweh's breaking the covenant with Israel is found throughout prophetic literature, the language in Zech 11.10 suggests a distinctively Deuteronomic formulation—that is, the use of 'break' (פרר) in connection with a covenant that was 'cut' (כרת) by Yahweh is found primarily in Deuteronomic literature (§20; see also †32).

Zech 11.16. The use of 'devour' (אכל) with '[human] flesh' (בשׂר) betrays Deuteronomic influence (§18; see also †5c).

Zech 11.17. Various elements in Zech 11.17 suggest Deuteronomic influence. (1) Only Jer 23.1-4, Ezek 34.1-19 and Zech 11.4-17 combine the form of a woe (הוי) oracle with the theme of shepherding (†13). (2) The form of 'a sword against...' (חרב על) is modelled after

---

29. Jones, *Haggai, Zechariah, Malachi*, p. 151; Lacocque, 'Zacharie 9–14', p. 175; Mitchell, *Haggai, Zechariah*, p. 303. Lacocque ('Zacharie 9–14', p. 175) also referred to צאן מאכל in Pss 44.12.

30. Lacocque ('Zacharie 9–14', p. 177) noted the similarity of אישׁ רעהו in Exod 11.2; Isa 34.15-16; Jer 19.9*. However, אכל בשׂר does not occur in Exod 11.2 or Isa 34.15-16.

Jer 50.35-38.[31] (3) The imagery of putting out an eye may come from Deut 34.7 or 1 Sam 3.2, 13.[32] (4) The imagery of a hand or arm withering (יבש with יד or זרע) as indication of divine judgment appears only here and in 1 Kgs 13.4.[33]

Zech 11.4-17. Given the influence of Jer 25.15-29 on II Zech, the formal similarity between Zech 11.4-17 and Jer 25.15-29—that is, both are accounts of symbolic action—suggests that the form of Zech 11.4-17 may have been influenced by that of Jer 25.15-29 (†27).

Shepherd Imagery in Zech 11.4-17. Zech 11.4-17 contains within itself three different images using the shepherd motif. (1) The 'prophet'[34] is commanded by Yahweh to become the shepherd in order to lead the people as Yahweh ordained (11.4); however, this 'prophet' finds such a task futile and proclaims to the people 'I will not be your shepherd' (11.9). (2) Before the 'prophet' ceased to be the shepherd, he reported that 'in one month' he destroyed 'the three shepherds' (11.8; see also 11.5-6). (3) Once again, Yahweh commands the 'prophet' to become a shepherd; however, this time the 'prophet' is to represent a 'worthless shepherd' (11.15) because Yahweh proclaims that he is 'raising up in the land a shepherd who does not care for the perishing...' (11.16) and who will later be judged by Yahweh (11.17).

Since II Zech draws so heavily from earlier biblical material (including Isa and Ezek as well as Deuteronomic literature), before one begins to interpret these various shepherd images, one must ask the question 'What are the sources for the shepherd imagery in Zech 11.4-17?' Since shepherd/flock imagery is so widespread, various prophetic passages probably influenced the shepherd imagery in Zech 11.4-17.[35] However, two connections between this imagery in Jer and

31. Jones, *Haggai, Zechariah, Malachi*, p. 156; Lacocque, 'Zacharie 9–14', p. 180; Mitchell, *Haggai, Zechariah*, p. 316.

32. Lacocque, 'Zacharie 9–14', p. 180.

33. Lacocque, 'Zacharie 9–14', p. 180.

34. I use the quotation marks around 'prophet' to remind the reader that this is a literary device created by the redactor, not a preserved oracle from a prophet.

35. For discussions of the shepherd/flock imagery in II Zech and their relationship to other prophetic corpora, see Caquot, 'L'allegorie des pasteurs en Zach 11'; Finley, 'Sheep Merchants of Zechariah 11'; Mason, 'Use of Earlier Biblical Material in Zechariah 9–14', pp. 101-11, 171-74, 177-79; Meyer, 'Allegory concerning the Monarchy'; Redditt, 'Israel's Shepherds'; Rehm, 'Hirtenallegorie Zach 11,4-14'; Wallis, 'Pastor Bonus'; van der Woude, 'Hirtenallegorie von Sacharja 11'.

II Zech suggest that Zech 11.4-17 was influenced, to some degree, by the shepherd imagery in Jer:[36] the use of הרנה in the phrase 'shepherd of the flock doomed for slaughter' (§4) and the unique combination of shepherd imagery and woe oracle (†12).[37]

Summary, Zech 11.4-17. We have noted various parallels between Zech 11.4-17 and DtrH, on the one hand, and Zech 11.4-17 and Jer, on the other. The parallels between Zech 11.4-17 and DtrH concern Deuteronomic phraseology of divine punishment (§§18, 20). The parallels between Zech 11.4-17 and Jer include phraseology concerning divine punishment (§§4, 18, 20), formal similarities (e.g. ††12, 13, 27), and thematic connections (e.g., shepherd imagery). Together, these parallels suggest that the Deuteronomic influence on Zech 11.4-17 is strong enough to imply a possible Deuteronomic redaction.

Excursus: A Possible Interpretation of the Shepherd Allegory

Assuming the validity of the observed relationship between the shepherd imagery in Zech 11.4-17 and Jer as well as my general thesis of a Deuteronomic redaction of Zech, the following allegorical interpretation of the three various uses of the shepherd imagery in Zech 11.4-17 is possible.[38] (1) The 'prophet' who is commanded to become a shepherd (Zech 11.4) represents the prophet Jeremiah, whose prophetic ministry included his own impatience (Zech 11.8; see Jer 17.14-18) and the people's response of detestation (Zech 11.8; see Jer 15.10-21; 17.14-18; 18.18-23). (2) The 'three shepherds' who were destroyed 'in one month' (Zech 11.8) are Jehoahaz, Jehoiakim and Jehoiachin, whose reigns lasted but a relatively brief period of time (2 Kgs 23.31–24.17) and against whom the prophet Jeremiah prophesied (see Jer 22.1-30*).[39] (3) The 'worthless shepherd' (Zech 11.15, 17) represents Zedekiah,

36. This observation does not discount the influence of shepherd imagery in other prophetic books, especially Isaiah and Ezekiel, upon II Zech. Rather, it is simply a statement that Jer influenced II Zech's use of shepherd imagery.

37. The shepherd/flock imagery elsewhere in II Zech also betrays an influence of Jer; therefore, these parallels lend support to the observation that Jer influenced the shepherd imagery in Zech 11.4-17. For example, see †15, ‡16, ‡20.

38. Zech 11.4-17 is widely regarded as allegorical; however, this allegory is understood in various ways. See Caquot, 'L'allegorie des pasteurs en Zach 11'; Mason, 'Use of Earlier Biblical Material in Zechariah 9–14', pp. 101-11, 171-74, 177-79; Mitchell, *Haggai, Zechariah*, pp. 303, 306-07, 315; Meyer, 'Allegory concerning the Monarchy'; Redditt, 'Israel's Shepherds'; Rehm, 'Hirtenallegorie Zach 11,4-14'; Wallis, 'Pastor Bonus'; van der Woude, 'Hirtenallegorie von Sacharja 11'.

39. Delcor ('Sources', pp. 387, 407, 409) and Junker (*Die zwölf kleinen Propheten*, II, p. 172) identified the 'three shepherds' as Jehoahaz, Jehoiakim and Jehoachin and related Zech 11.8 to Jer 22.1-30. In a similar manner, Caquot

who was also the recipient of Yahweh's judgment through the prophetic career of Jeremiah (see Jer 21.1-10*; 34.1-7). Thus, the shepherd imagery of Zech 11.4-17, which draws upon various prophetic sources, nevertheless allegorizes the prophetic career of the prophet Jeremiah in relationship to the last four kings of Judah.

Excursus: Mt 27.9 // Zech 11.12-13

The shepherd imagery in Zech 11.4-17 is relevant to a NT quote of Zech 11.12-13. Mt 27.9-10 reads, 'Then what had been spoken by the prophet Jeremiah was fulfilled, "And they took the thirty pieces of silver, the price the man whose price was set by the sons of Israel, and they gave them to the potter's field, as the Lord has ordered"'. The attribution of the quote from II Zech to Jer has been variously explained. In his work on Matthew's use of the Hebrew Bible, R.H. Gundry summarizes such previous explanations:

> (1) It is a mistake by Mt. (2) The textual evidence for omission is to be accepted. (3) 'Jer' is a general reference to the prophetic section of the OT canon, in which in ancient time Jer stood first. (4) In a vulgar Hebrew text the passage from Zech has been inserted into Jer. (5) Zech 9–11 was written by Jer and inserted into Zech, a theory originated by Joseph Mede to account for the misascription, but eventuating in the Deutero-Zech hypothesis. (6) Ζριου was confounded with Ιριου. (7) Διὰ τοῦ προφήτου reflects ביד נבייא, which was misread as ביר and taken for an abbreviation of the name 'Jeremiah'. (8) The quotation was taken from a Testimony Book, in which it stood close to or in connection with a quotation (or quotations) from Jer. (9) The quotation comes from an apocryphal text of Jer. (10) The Jews deleted the passage from Jer.[40]

To this list, Gundry added his own explanation: Matthew understands that two prophecies (Zech 11.12-13; Jer 19.1-13) are fulfilled in one event, but simply chose to name only one of the prophets. Since the verbal resemblance is stronger between the quote and Zech 11.12-13, Matthew chose to name Jer so that 'the Jer-side of the prophecies [would not] be lost'.[41] Assuming that the above interpretation of the shepherd allegory in Zech 11.4-17 is correct, another explanation presents itself: even though Matthew may have been drawing his quote from II Zech, he understood the shepherd allegory in Zech 11.4-17 to refer to the prophet Jeremiah and his prophetic ministry and, therefore, attributed the quote to him.

('L'allegorie des pasteurs en Zach 11', p. 54) identified the 'three shepherds' as the last three Judaean kings, Jehoiakim, Jehoiachin and Zedekiah.

40. R.H. Gundry, *The Use of the Old Testament in St Matthew's Gospel* (NovTSup, 18; Leiden: E.J. Brill, 1967), pp. 125-26 n. 3. I have removed all bibliographic information from this quote.

41. *Use of the Old Testament in St Matthew's Gospel*, p. 125.

Zech 12.1–13.6

Zech 12.2. The judgment imagery of an intoxicating cup in Zech 12.2 probably originated from the influence of Jer 25.15-17 (‡25).

Zech 12.2, 6. The phrase 'all the surrounding peoples' (כל העמים סביב) suggests Deuteronomic influence in that the word 'surrounding' (סביב) is used to denote non-Israelite peoples only in Deuteronomic literature and II Zech (§26).

Zech 12.3. Likewise, the phrase 'all the nations of the earth' (כל גויי הארץ) perhaps suggests Deuteronomic influence in that it is found primarily in Deuteronomic literature (§21).

Zech 12.3, 9; 13.2, 4; 14.6, 8, 13. The temporal phrase 'And it will come to pass on that day' (והיה ביום ההוא) occurs seven times in II Zech (12.3, 9; 13.2, 4; 14.6, 8, 13) and the phrase 'on that day' (ביום ההוא) occurs an additional twelve times by itself (9.16; 11.11; 12.4, 6, 8 (2×), 11; 13.1; 14.4, 9, 20, 21; see §19). When one surveys the use of temporal phrases in Deuteronomic literature, one observes the interest in time reflected in the disproportionly large amount of temporal phrases in Deuteronomic literature (see §19). This observation suggests a possible Deuteronomic origin for the frequently occurring phrase 'on that day' in II Zech.

Zech 12.4. The three terms of madness imagery in Zech 12.4 certainly demonstrate Deuteronomic influence. 'Panic' (תמהון) is found only in Deut 28.28 and Zech 12.4; 'madness' (שגעון), only in Deut 28.28, 2 Kgs 9.20 and Zech 12.4; 'blindness' (עורון), only in Deut 28.28 and Zech 12.4. The combined occurrence of these three terms in Deut 28.28—two of which appear elsewhere only here—demonstrates that the imagery in Zech 12.4 is drawn from Deut 28.28 (‡5a):

> Yahweh will smite you with madness and blindness and confusion of
> mind—יככה יהוה בשגעון בעורון ובתמהון לבב

Although Deut 28.28 probably influenced Zech 12.4, are there any possible passages that could help explain the change concerning the recipient of the judgment from Yahweh's people (Deut 28.28) to the war horses and their foreign riders (Zech 12.4)? One such passage contains enough connections with Deut 28.28 and Zech 12.4 to explain this change—that is, the account of the Syrian attack against Israel and

Elisha's intervention (2 Kgs 6.15-23).[42] In Zech 12.4, Yahweh says, 'I will open my eyes' (אפקח את עיני); in 2 Kgs 6.17, 20, Elisha prays that Yahweh will open (פקח) the eyes of the king's servants and his prayer is answered. Also in both accounts, Yahweh strikes the invading armies, which include horses and cha..ots, with blindness (Zech 12.4: עורון; 2 Kgs 6.18: בסנורים). Therefore, Zech 12.4 apparently combines themes from two Deuteronomic passages: Deut 28.28 and 2 Kgs 6.15-23.

Zech 12.6. The phrase used to describe Judah's power among the nations—that is, 'a torch of fire among sheaves'—is an image that 'recalls Samson's exploits'[43] in Judg 15.4-5 and perhaps suggests Deuteronomic influence.

Zech 12.7, 10; 13.1. Although the three phrases containing the combination of 'the house of David' and 'inhabitants of Jerusalem' appear only here, their structure suggests Deuteronomic influence. The structure of the phrase 'inhabitants of [name of city]' ([...]שב[ו]י) paired with another noun phrase is found primarily in Deuteronomic literature (§22).

Zech 12.10-11. The reference to the plain of Megiddo in 12.11 possibly recalls Josiah's death as recorded in 2 Kgs 23.29-30 and 2 Chron 35.20-24; therefore, the 'pierced' one in 12.10 may be identified as Josiah. The identification of Josiah with the 'pierced' one is reflected in Targ and Syr and was also made by Jerome.[44] Such an identification of mourning for the 'pierced' one (= Josiah) would be in line with Deuteronomic thought, since Josiah is given such a favorable portrayal in DtrH.

Zech 12.12-14. The representation of each family mourning by itself with the men and women in each family mourning by themselves may be influenced by the emphasis upon 'all the families of Israel' (Jer 31.1) and the individual nature of the 'new covenant' in Jer 31.31-34 (†35).

Zech 13.2-6: The theme of false prophecy in Zech 13.2-6 has close

42. Bic, *Sacharja*, p. 145; Elliger, *Buch der zwölf kleinen Propheten*, II, p. 159; Mason, *Haggai, Zechariah and Malachi*, p. 116.

43. Mason, 'Use of Earlier Biblical Material in Zechariah 9-14', p. 216. See also Mason, *Haggai, Zechariah and Malachi*, p. 116; Meyers, 'Messianism in First and Second Zechariah', p. 12.

44. Mitchell, *Haggai, Zechariah*, pp. 331-32. See also Bic, Sacharja, p. 152; Junker, *Die zwölf kleinen Propheten*, II, p. 180.

affinities with Deuteronomic literature, as the following observations suggest.[45]

1. The phrase 'for you speak lies in the name of Yahweh' (13.3) suggests Deuteronomic influence for two reasons. First, the pairing of the noun 'lie' (שֶׁקֶר) with a verbal form of 'speak' (דבר) suggests Deuteronomic influence (§5). Secondly, this accusation of false prophecy is connected to the improper use of name theology, which is distinctively Deuteronomic (§17; see also 'the names of idols' in 13.2).

2. The punishment given in Zech 13.3 for false prophecy—that is, capital punishment—comes from legal material in Deut:

> If a prophet...arises among you..., saying, 'Let us go after other gods', ...you shall not obey the words of the prophet...But that prophet...shall be put to death for he spoke rebellion against Yahweh your God (Deut 13.2-4, 6; ‡1).

> The prophet who presumes to speak a word in my name which I have not commanded him to speak, or who speaks in the name of other gods, that prophet shall die (Deut 18.20).[46]

3. The emphasis upon the responsibility of the parents of false prophets to carry out the capital punishment also comes from Deuteronomic legal material, for in Deut it is explicitly stated that family members are also responsible for such duty. The passage from Deut 13, quoted above, continues:

> If your brother, the son of your mother, or your son, or your daughter, or the wife of your bosom, or your friend who is like your own soul, secretly incites you saying, 'Let us go after and serve other gods', which you or your father have not known...; you shall not consent to it and you shall not obey him...But you shall kill him...you shall stone him to death with stones (Deut 13.7, 9-11; ‡1).

This emphasis is also found in Deut 21.18-21, which specifies that parents of 'stubborn and rebellious' children must bring such children to the elders who will condemn them to death by stoning.[47]

---

45. See below 'False Prophecy' in Chapter 8 for a more developed discussion of this theme in Deuteronomic thought.

46. The following commentators made connections between Zech 13.2-6 and Deut 18.20: Elliger, *Buch der zwölf kleinen Propheten*, II, p. 163; Lacocque, 'Zacharie 9–14', p. 195.

47. Bic (*Sacharja*, p. 155) and Petersen (*Late Israelite Prophecy*, p. 35) suggested that Zech 13.3 is related to Deut 21.18-21.

4. The threat in Zech 13.2 suggests Deuteronomic influence for three reasons.[48] First, the threat echoes the Deuteronomic formula 'and you shall purge the evil from your midst' (ובערת הרע מקרבך: Deut 13.6; 17.7; 19.9; 21.21; 22.21, 24; 24.7; †3). Second, such a violent depiction of the removal of improper religious practices also appears in Deut 12.3. Third, the language of removal from the land recalls the result of the people of Israel following the false prophets as expressed in Jer 27.10:

> for they are prophesying a lie to you with the result that you will be far removed from your land.

5. The prophetic symbol of the 'hairy mantle' (אדרת שער) recalls Jacob's trick (Gen 25.25) and the prophets Elijah and Elisha.[49] The prophet Elijah is said to have worn a mantle (אדרת: 1 Kgs 19.13, 19) and a 'garment of haircloth' (בעל שער: 2 Kgs 1.8). As a symbol of his prophetic authority, Elisha wore Elijah's mantle (אדרת: 2 Kgs 2.13, 14). Therefore, the 'hairy mantle' in Zech 13.4 reflects this symbol of prophetic authority found elsewhere in Deuteronomic literature.

6. Various suggestions concerning the nature of the 'wounds' on the false prophet's back (Zech 13.6) draw upon Deuteronomic literature. First, Mitchell understood the wounds to come from the punishment of flogging as described in Deut 25.2.[50] Second, Jones suggested the possible reference to the wound which Joram received from Jehu's arrow (2 Kgs 9.24).[51] Third, Petersen related the wounds to the prophet's disobedience of Deut 14.1, 'You shall not cut yourselves'.[52] Fourth, both Jones and Lacocque suggested that Zech 13.6 alludes to the masochistic practices of the prophets of Ba'al represented in 1 Kgs 18.28.[53] The suggestion that Zech 13.6 refers to the practice of false prophets wounding themselves is to be preferred because it is the only suggestion that is directly linked to the theme of false prophecy;

48. Petersen, *Late Israelite Prophecy*, p. 35.

49. Petersen, *Late Israelite Prophecy*, p. 36; H.L. Ginsburg, 'Oldest Record of Hysteria with Physical Stigmata, Zech 13.2-6', in *Studies in Bible and Ancient Near East* (ed. Y. Avishur and J. Blau; Jerusalem: E. Rubinstein's Publishing House, 1978), p. 23; Lacocque, 'Zacharie 9–14', p. 195.

50. *Haggai, Zechariah*, p. 339.

51. *Haggai, Zechariah, Malachi*, p. 168.

52. *Late Israelite Prophecy*, p. 35.

53. Jones, *Haggai, Zechariah, Malachi*, p. 168; Lacocque, 'Zacharie 9–14', p. 195.

however, it is interesting that all of these interpretations draw upon Deuteronomic literature.

Summary, Zech 12.1–13.6. In this section, various parallels between Zech 12.1–13.6 and Deuteronomic literature have been noted. The parallels between Zech 12.1–13.6 and DtrH include language (§§17, 19, 21, 22, 26) and two clear cases of direct borrowing from Deut (Zech 12.4 // Deut 28.28 [‡5a]; Zech 13.2-6 // Deut 13.2-12 [‡1]). The parallels between Zech 12.1-13.6 and Jer concern phraseology (§§17, 19, 21, 22, 26), imagery (‡25) and theme (†35). Such strong Deuteronomic influence certainly commends itself to the interpretation of the Deuteronomic redaction of Zech 12.1–13.6.

Zech 13.7-9

Zech 13.7. The imagery of a scattered flock in Zech 13.7 suggests Deuteronomic influence in two different ways: (1) The judgment imagery against 'the little ones' (הצערים) betrays the influence of Jer 49.20 and 50.45—'the little ones of the flock (צעירי הצאן) shall be dragged away'—for a form of צער is used within the imagery of a scattered flock only in these three passages.[54] (2) The judgment imagery of a scattered flock is found in Deuteronomic literature (1 Kgs 22.17; Jer 10.21; 23.1-4, †15) and Ezek. 34.5. Also, the scattered flock imagery here is probably related to the Deuteronomic phrases 'to scatter among the nations/peoples' (§25).

Zech 13.7. Only in Jer 25.34-38 and Zech 13.7 is the judgment imagery of Yahweh's sword applied to the imagery of a bad shepherd (†23).

Zech 13.9. This verse contains two instances of possible Deuteronomic influence: (1) The phrase 'he will call on my name and I will answer him' utilizes Deuteronomic name theology (§17) and has its closest connection with Jer 33.2-3: 'the Lord is his name: Call to me and I will answer you'. (2) Another phrase—'I will say, "They are my people", and they will say, "The Lord is my God"'—suggests possible Deuteronomic influence, especially in light of the phrase 'You will be my people and I will be your God' which occurs frequently in Jer (§27; †31).

Summary, Zech 13.7-9. In this brief section, the parallels with DtrH

---

54. Mitchell, *Haggai, Zechariah*, p. 317.

consist of language (§§17, 25, 27) and imagery (scattered flock); the parallels with Jer also consist of language (§§17, 25, 27) and imagery (shepherd/flock imagery, ††15, 23). This concentration of possible Deuteronomic influence in such a brief section suggests Deuteronomic redaction.

Zech 14.1-21

Zech 14.1. The phrase 'behold, the day of Yahweh is coming' betrays Deuteronomic influence (§24; ††18, 28).

Zech 14.3. In contrast to the term 'the inhabitants of the land' (יושבי הארץ) in earlier sources, the prevalent term for foreign peoples in Deuteronomic literature is 'these/those nations' (גוים האלה/ההם)(§11). Therefore, the use of 'those nations' here may suggest Deuteronomic influence.

Zech 14.4. The phrase 'the Mount of Olives shall be split in two' (Zech 14.4) suggests the possibility of Deuteronomic influence (§28).

Zech 14.6, 8, 13; 12.3, 9; 13.2, 4. The temporal phrase 'And it will come to pass on that day' (והיה ביום ההוא) occurs seven times in II Zech (12.3, 9; 13.2, 4; 14.6, 8, 13) and the phrase 'on that day' (ביום ההוא) occurs an additional twelve times by itself (9.16; 11.11; 12.4, 6, 8 (2×), 11; 13.1; 14.4, 9, 20, 21; see §19). The repetitive use of this phrase in Zechariah 14 suggests the influence of the heightened interest of the Deuteronomic school in time (see §19).

Zech 14.9. The phrase 'Yahweh will be one and his name one' certainly demonstrates Deuteronomic influence, for no where else in the Hebrew Bible is Deut 6.4 quoted (§2) and the quote here is expanded by the use of Deuteronomic name theology (§17).

Zech 14.10. The geographical names used here possibly betray Deuteronomic influence. The following observations concerning these toponyms are the basis for this suggestion:

1. Although the phrase 'from Geba to Rimmon' occurs only here, it nevertheless suggests Deuteronomic influence for the following reasons (§23): (a) The only other occurrence of Geba in the structure of 'from [place name] to [place name]' occurs in 2 Kgs 23.8. (b) Its use here is similar to the Deuteronomic use of 'from Geba to Beersheba' (2 Kgs 23.8) and 'from Dan to Beersheba' (Judg 20.1; 1 Sam 3.20; 2 Sam 3.10; 17.11; 24.2, 15; 1 Kgs 4.25) to denote the extent of a

territory. (c) Rimmon, situated near Beersheba, was closely
related to Beersheba (Josh 15.28-32), and was repopulated in
the post-exilic period (Neh 11.29). Therefore, the change in
circumstances from the pre-exilic to the post-exilic period
necessitated the change from 'Geba to Beersheba' to 'Geba to
Rimmon' as the Deuteronomic manner of referring to
Judah/Yehud. (d) The place names 'Geba' and 'Rimmon'
occur more frequently in Deuteronomic literature.

2. The toponym 'Corner Gate' occurs only here, in Deuteronomic literature (2 Kgs 14.13; Jer 31.38, †33), and in
   2 Chron (25.23 [= 2 Kgs 14.13]; 26.9) (§6).

3. Likewise, 'the Gate of Benjamin' is found primarily in
   Deuteronomic literature (Jer 20.2; 37.13; 38.7; Ezek. 48.32;
   Zech 14.10) (§14).

4. The 'Tower of Hananel' is mentioned only in Jer 31.38; Zech
   14.10; Neh 3.1; 12.39. Given the close connection between
   Jer 31.38 and Zech 14.10 elsewhere (§14, †33), it is reason-
   able to assume that Zech 14.10 was influenced by Jer 31.38
   here as well (§15).

Zech 14.11. The phrase 'and Jerusalem will dwell in security'
betrays Deuteronomic influence in that the combinations of forms of
ישׁב and בטח within the context of Yahweh as the source of this security
are found primarily in Deuteronomic literature (§16).

Zech 14.13. The madness imagery of Zech 12.4 apparently draws
upon Deuteronomic language, especially that of Deut 28.28 (‡5a).
Likewise, the panic imagery of Zech 14.13 suggests Deuteronomic
influence, for the word used here for 'panic' (מהומת) is also found in
Deut 28.20 (‡5b). Also, of all the occurrences of מהומה, those in DtrH
are thematically closer to Zech 14.13 than the others:

Deut 7.23: 'But Yahweh your God will give them [these nations]
over to you and he will throw them into a great panic (מהומה גדלה)
until they are destroyed'.[55]
Deut 28.20: 'Yahweh will send upon you curses, panic (המהומה), and
frustration in all you do with your hand until you are destroyed...'
1 Sam 5.9: 'the hand of Yahweh was against the city [Ashdod],
causing an exceedingly great panic' (מהומה גדלה מאד).

55. Jones (*Haggai, Zechariah, Malachi*, p. 177) related Zech 14.13 to Deut 7.20-
23.

1 Sam 5.11: 'for there was a panic (מהומת) of death in all of the city'
[Ashdod].

1 Sam 14.20: 'and behold, each man's (איש) sword was against his
neighbor (רעהו), causing an exceedingly great panic' (מהומה גדלה מאד).

2 Chron 15.5: 'In those times, there was no peace... for many panics
(מהומות) were against the inhabitants of the lands'.[56]

Isa 22.5; Ezek. 7.7: 'a day of panic' (מהומה) [concerning Jerusalem].

Ezek 22.5: 'and they will mock you [Jerusalem] who are infamous
and full of panic' (רבת המהומה).

Amos 3.9: 'see the great panic (מהומות) within her' [mountains of
Samaria].

Zech 14.13: 'a great panic (מהומת רבה) of Yahweh will be upon them,
so that each (איש) will seize the hand of his neighbor (רעהו) and his
hand will be raised against the hand of his neighbor' (רעהו).

Taken together, the following observations suggest that the use of
'panic' (מהומת) in Zech 14.13 is thematically closer to those in Deuteronomic literature: (1) Only in Deut 7.23; 1 Sam 5.9, 11; 14.20; Amos
3.9; Zech 14.13 is 'panic' (מהומה/מהומות) used within the context of the
consequences concerning foreign nations. (2) Only 1 Sam 14.20 and
Zech 14.13 use the idiomatic pairing of 'each' (איש) and 'his neighbor'
(רעהו). (3) The imagery of panic in Zech 12.4 definitely draws from
Deut 28 (‡5a); therefore, Deut 28.20 probably influenced the use of
panic imagery here.

Zech 14.14. The phrase 'all the surrounding nations' (כל הגוים סביב)
suggests Deuteronomic influence in that the word 'surrounding' (סביב)
is used to denote non-Israelite peoples only in Deuteronomic literature
and II Zech (§7).

Zech 14.16. Since the phrase 'year after year' occurs frequently in
Deuteronomic literature, this phrase may be another indication of the
heightened interest in time in Deuteronomic thought (§10).

Zech 14.16, 18, 19. The annual harvest festival is referred to in
different bodies of literature in different ways. Since 'Feast of Booths'
(חג הסוכות/הסכות) occurs primarily in Deuteronomic literature, its presence in Zech 14 suggests possible Deuteronomic influence (§8).

Summary, Zech 14.1-21. In this section, the evidence of Deuteronomic influence in the form of Deuteronomic language is significantly

---

56. Rather than מהומות רבות, LXX reads ἔκστασις κυρίου = מהומת יהוה, which
agrees with Zech 14.13.

abundant. Examples of Deuteronomic language common to Zech 14 and DtrH are §§2, 7, 10, 11, 16, 17, 19, 23, 28; see also ‡5b. Examples of Deuteronomic language common to Zech 14 and Jer are §§6, 7, 14, 15, 17, 19. This abundance of Deuteronomic language suggests possible Deuteronomic redaction.

Summary of Chapter 5: Deuteronomic Influence in II Zech

In this chapter the results of the previous two chapters have been brought together with some new data to show the extent of Deuteronomic influence in the different larger units of II Zech. In every section of II Zech a significant amount of possible Deuteronomic influence suggests that II Zech was perhaps redacted by a Deuteronomic scribe, with one notable exception (Zech 9.1-17). The relative sparcity of Deuteronomic influence in Zech 9.1-17 in comparison to the rest of II Zech suggests that Zech 9.1-17 was probably a post-exilic source used by the Deuteronomic redactor of II Zech. This contrast concerning Deuteronomic influence combines with the contrast concerning the issue of poetry versus prose to suggest that Zech 9.1-17 is a poetic source used within the Deuteronomic prose of II Zech (10.1–14.21). Such a use of a poetic source within a Deuteronomic redaction is not without parallel, for in Jer the oracles against the foreign nations appear to be a poetic source which did not come from the prophet Jeremiah nor from the hand of a Deuteronomic redactor, but was a source used in the Deuteronomic redaction. Therefore, I conclude that a Deuteronomic redactor may have authored much of II Zech (the prose of 10.1–14.21), but also used a poetic source (9.1-17).

Chapter 6

THE CANONICAL SHAPE OF THE BOOK OF ZECHARIAH

In the previous three chapters, I have adapted the method used to argue for the Deuteronomic redaction of Jer and applied it to II Zech. In doing so, I have claimed that the prose in II Zech, like that in Jer, comes from a Deuteronomic redactor. Chapter 3 presented the language common to Deuteronomic literature (DtrH and Jer) and II Zech. Chapter 4 dealt with Deuteronomic passages that probably influenced II Zech; one of which (Deut 28) appears to have significantly influenced both II Zech and the prose sermons in Jer. Chapter 5 provided verse-by-verse examples of possible Deuteronomic influence upon the language and imagery of II Zech and concluded with the observation that II Zech is the product of a Deuteronomic redactor who used a poetic source (9.1-17) within his own prose (10.1–14.21). In this chapter, this conclusion concerning the Deuteronomic origin of II Zech will be explored in relationship to the larger question of the present book of Zech.

It is widely agreed that the present book should be divided into I Zech and II Zech and that II Zech was appended to I Zech, which was already in its present form. However, questions remain concerning the relationship of II Zech to I Zech. Was II Zech intended to be an appendix to I Zech? Or was II Zech written independently of I Zech and only subsequently associated with I Zech? Below, I will present evidence which suggests that II Zech was written as a reinterpretation of I Zech and was, therefore, probably intended to be an appendix to I Zech. If this is the case, then the possible Deuteronomic redactor of II Zech produced a Deuteronomic edition of Zech when he appended his work (II Zech) to the existing Zecharianic corpus (I Zech).

Relationship of II Zech to I Zech

As noted in the introduction, the work of Delcor and Mason on inner-biblical exegesis in II Zech suggests the unity of II Zech. Their argument for this unity is strengthened by my thesis that perhaps II Zech was produced by a Deuteronomic redactor, who used a poetic source (Zech 9). But, the question remains, what unity, if any, is there between I Zech and II Zech?[1] There are a number of ways to answer this question, two of which are discussed below: (1) There is a theological unity between I Zech and II Zech in that I Zech has theological affinities with Deuteronomic literature and II Zech is itself Deuteronomic literature. (2) There is a literary unity in that II Zech depends upon I Zech.

Concerning the theological affinities between I Zech and Deuteronomic thought, a number of commentators have noticed the Deuteronomic message and language of the introductory section of I Zech (1.1-6). For example, Joseph Blenkinsopp wrote,[2]

> This is the message and the language of the Deuteronomists, and there are indications that both Malachi and the author of Zech 1.1-6 have modeled themselves on this source. Zech 1.1-6 reminds the hearers that 'the former prophets' (1.4; cf. 7.7, 12) or 'my servants the prophets' (1.6; a Deuteronomic expression) preached repentance to the Israel of an earlier day, that their message fell on deaf ears, and that the result was disaster. Their predictions were verified, and it was left to the forefathers to acknowledge the justice of God and lament their mistakes during the exile. It will be obvious that this is nothing else but a summary of Deuteronomic teaching.

---

1. Although the thesis of C. Meyers and E. Meyers that Haggai–Zech 1–8 is a composite work (*Haggai, Zechariah 1–8*, pp. xliv-xlvii) is convincing, I assume that this composite work had divided into the two separate authoritative works before II Zech was added to I Zech. This assumption is based on the observation that the material in II Zech reflects no knowledge of Hag, an observation that is often made to suggest that Zech 9–14 is distinct from Zech 1–8 (e.g. Mitchell, *Haggai, Zechariah*, pp. 236-39). Also, Mason only makes one reference to Hag in his work on inner-biblical exegesis in II Zech ('Use of Earlier Biblical Material in Zechariah 9–14', p. 93). Since II Zech is so heavily dependent on earlier prophetic literature, including I Zech, it would be difficult to imagine why the redactor of II Zech would ignore Hag, especially if Hag was still connected to I Zech as a composite work. Therefore, my discussion will concern the addition of II Zech to I Zech, not to Hag–Zech 1–8.

2. *A History of Prophecy in Israel* (Philadelphia: Wesminster Press, 1983), p. 235.

In a similar manner, Meyers and Meyers noted that Zech 1.1-6 contains language borrowed from Deuteronomic literature ('earlier prophets' in 1.4; 'words and statues' in 1.6; 'overtake' in 1.6) and was familiar with Jer; thus, they concluded that Zech 1.1-6 has a 'Deuteronomic flavor'.[3]

Stephen Swanson looked more closely at the 'Deuteronomistic stream of tradition' in which he understood I Zech.[4] As with Blenkinsopp and the Meyerses, Swanson's comments also focused upon Zech 1.2-6. He compared Zech 1.2-6 with the following key passages in DtrH and Deuteronomic prose in Jer: Deut 30.1-10; Judg 2.10-23; 1 Sam 12.1-25; 1 Kgs 8.46-53; 2 Kgs 17.7-23; Jer 7.22-29*; 25.3-11*; 32.30-44*; 35.12-17*. His comparison revealed that the following elements in Zech 1.2-6 are found frequently in this Deuteronomic literature: (1) 'Yahweh's anger at the sins of the people'; (2) the use of 'return' (שוב); (3) 'reference to the "evil ways" of the people'; (4) 'the "decrees" of Yahweh, which were given to the people'; and (5) the phrase, 'my servants the prophets'.[5] Besides these similarities, he noted that the theological presentation of history is similar:

> The logical progression of the pattern discernible in the dtr passages and Zech 1.2-6 and 7.1-14 is consistent throughout: 1) the sins of the people, 2) the anger of Yahweh, 3) the warning given by the prophets, 4) the rejection of these warnings, and 5) the execution of judgment.[6]

As seen in these observations on Zech 1.1-6, I Zech was influenced by Deuteronomic thought. II Zech was also influenced by Deuteronomic language and themes so much that Deuteronomic redaction is suggested. Hence, it is not difficult to imagine the Deuteronomic school of the post-exilic period accepting I Zech as authoritative and including it in their working canon. At a later time, when the promises that the prophet Zechariah connected with the rededication of the Temple did not occur (e.g. Zech 8.1-7), the Deuteronomic school reinterpreted

3. *Haggai, Zechariah 1–8*, pp. 94-96.
4. 'Zechariah 1–8 and the Deuteronomistic Stream of Tradition', paper presented to the Annual Meeting of SBL, Chicago, 1988.
5. 'Zechariah 1–8 and the Deuteronomistic Stream of Tradition', pp. 8-9.
6. 'Zechariah 1–8 and the Deuteronomistic Stream of Tradition', p. 9. Similar summaries of the Deuteronomic understanding of history have been suggested by others. E.g. Nicholson, *Preaching*, p. 57; von Rad, 'Deuteronomistic Theology of History in the Books of Kings', in *Studies in Deuteronomy* (trans. D.M.G. Stalker; Chicago: Henry Renery Company, 1953), pp. 37-44.

I Zech with a heightened eschatology,[7] thus producing II Zech and the Deuteronomic redaction of Zech. Hence, there is a theological unity to Zech in that I Zech was influenced by Deuteronomic thought and the prose in II Zech is itself Deuteronomic.

There is another type of unity between I Zech and II Zech—that is, a literary unity in that II Zech depends upon I Zech. In his work on inner-biblical exegesis in II Zech, Mason has demonstrated convincingly that II Zech is a reinterpretation of I Zech with the heavy influence of other biblical material.[8] He showed a continuity of themes between I Zech and II Zech concerning 'the prominence of the Zion tradition; the divine cleansing of the community; universalism; the appeal to earlier prophets; and the provision of leadership as a sign of the new age'.[9] This observation gives more credence to the possibility that the Deuteronomic school accepted I Zech as authoritative and later reinterpreted it with the addition of II Zech. Therefore, the unity of Zech is based upon the theological similarities between the Deuteronomic influence upon I Zech and the Deuteronomic redaction of II Zech as well as the Deuteronomic reinterpretation of I Zech in II Zech.

The Analogy between the Deuteronomic Redaction of Jer and the Deuteronomic Redaction of Zech

The similarities between the Deuteronomic redactions of Jer and Zech have been discussed in the previous chapters. One more similarity deserves comment. The way in which I Zech is a reservoir from which II Zech draws is analogous to the relationship between Jeremianic poetry and Deuteronomic prose in Jer, wherein Deuteronomic redactors reinterpreted the earlier poetic material within their prose sections.[10] However, the analogy between Jeremianic poetry and

7. See further below 'Eschatology' in Chapter 8.

8. See especially 'Relation of Zech 9-14 to Proto-Zechariah'. Mason's approach is also followed in Meyers, 'Messianism in First and Second Zechariah', p. 10. *Contra* Childs, *Introduction*, pp. 479-85; Hanson, *Dawn of Apocalyptic*, pp. 292-93, 400. However, Childs and Hanson did not refer to the work of Mason.

9. 'Relation of Zech 9–14 to Proto-Zechariah', p. 227.

10. McKane, *Jeremiah*, I, pp. l-lxxxiii. McKane's argument builds upon the study by Holladay, entitled 'Prototypes and Copies'. Although Holladay rejects the thesis of the Deuteronomic redaction of Jer, McKane has appropriately used Holladay's insights to clarify further the development the Deuteronomic redaction of Jer.

Deuteronomic prose in Jer, on the one hand, and I Zech and II Zech, on the other hand, is limited because of an important difference—that is, Deuteronomic prose is scattered throughout Jer, whereas the Deuteronomic prose of Zech is confined to the appended II Zech.

This difference may provide some insights concerning the literary history of both Jer and Zech, including the following: (1) The Jeremianic poetry and I Zech may have come into the hands of Deuteronomic redactors in different forms in that the Jeremianic poetry was probably a loose collection of oracles and I Zech may have been a finished literary work. Therefore, Jer evinces Deuteronomic redaction throughout whereas Zech has only the appended Deuteronomic prose in II Zech. (2) The Jeremianic poetry and I Zech may have come into the hands of Deuteronomic redactors with different theologies in relationship to Deuteronomic theology. The purpose of the Deuteronomic redaction of Jer was, in Hyatt's words, an 'attempt to show that Jeremiah did approve of the Deuteronomic reforms, or, in other words, to claim for Deuteronomy the sanction of the prophet'.[11] However, I Zech already presented strong Deuteronomic influence, and therefore the theology in I Zech did not initially need to be adjusted to suit Deuteronomic theology in the same way that the Jeremianic poetry did. Hence, Deuteronomic prose is scattered throughout Jer but is confined to II Zech in Zech. (3) Jeremianic material underwent at least two Deuteronomic redactions over an extended period of time,[12] whereas Zech probably had a much shorter period of redaction. Taken together, these three possible explanations for the differences between the Deuteronomic redactions of Jer and Zech are based on the putative shape of the material as it was received by the Deuteronomic school. The Jeremianic tradition consisted of a loose collection of poetry, which possibly included theological positions that differed from the Deuteronomic school; therefore, over an extended span of time the Deuteronomic school 'corrected' and expanded the Jeremianic tradition, creating the Deuteronomic redaction of Jer. The Zecharianic tradition came to the Deuteronomic school as a unified literary work (I Zech) which included perspectives that were Deuteronomic in character; therefore, this tradition was initially accepted into the Deuteronomic canon as is, only to be revised at a

11. Hyatt, 'Jeremiah and Deuteronomy', p. 121. This view is widely followed by those who argue for the Deuteronomic redaction of Jer.

12. See above Chapter 2.

later date when the prophetic expectations of I Zech had not been fulfilled. This reinterpretation was accomplished through the addition of II Zech to the already authoritative I Zech.

Even though the analogy between the Deuteronomic redaction of Jer and the Deuteronomic redaction of Zech is imperfect because of the different circumstances under which the Deuteronomic school received earlier material, this analogy nevertheless presents their commonality—that is, Jer and Zech are both the result of the Deuteronomic redaction of prophetic material as a reinterpretation of earlier authoritative themes for new circumstances.

Part III

THE DEUTERONOMIC SCHOOL IN THE POST-EXILIC PERIOD

Chapter 7

THE DEUTERONOMIC SCHOOL IN THE POST-EXILIC PERIOD

I have argued that the Deuteronomic school's redactional activity continued into the post-exilic period and appears in three literary works, DtrH, Jer and II Zech. It remains to consider the possible social setting of the Deuteronomic school in the post-exilic period.

This task involves several problems that are specific to this literature, such as: (1) Both DtrH and Jer probably preserve material from the pre-exilic, exilic, and post-exilic periods; therefore, one would have to isolate the post-exilic material from the pre-exilic and exilic material in order to understand fully how the earlier material was reinterpreted in the post-exilic period. Even if it were possible, this process is certainly beyond the scope of the present work. (2) The narrated time of both DtrH and Jer concerns the pre-exilic and early exilic periods. DtrH concerns the 'time' from Moses to Jehoiachin; Jer concerns the 'days of Josiah...until the captivity of Jerusalem in the fifth month' (Jer 1.2-3), with a brief mention of Jehoiachin's release in Babylon (Jer 52.31-34 [= 2 Kgs 25.27-30]). Hence, even though they are both post-exilic works in their final form, DtrH and Jer narrate pre-exilic and exilic events. (3) That all of II Zech is a product of the post-exilic period would at first seem to make it well suited for reconstructing the social setting of the Deuteronomic school in the post-exilic period. However, two features of the Deuteronomic prose in II Zech (Zech 10-14) suggest that II Zech provides ambiguous information for this purpose: (a) II Zech is heavily dependent upon earlier biblical material and (b) most of II Zech looks into the eschatological future. In other words, II Zech does not deal explicitly with its own time. Therefore, although some material in II Zech may obliquely refer to some contemporary events, II Zech is not well suited for reconstructing the social setting of the Deuteronomic school in the post-exilic period.

Given these problems with the literary sources, another strategy may prove more helpful for reconstructing the post-exilic social setting of the Deuteronomic school—that is, a historical review of Yehud within the context of the Achaemenid period, with special attention to professional scribes and scribal schools. This strategy assumes that the Deuteronomic school was a guild-like organization of scribes, some of whom reached such a respected status that they were much more than mere copyists, becoming redactors in their own right. The imprint of these Deuteronomic redactors (i.e., the most accomplished and respected scribes) can be seen in the literature that they produced (DtrH, Jer, II Zech) in that distinctively Deuteronomic language and imagery is found within these works. The strict line that is often drawn demarcating scribe from redactor is very difficult to maintain (at least in reference to the earliest stages of the literary history of these texts), for the most skilful scribes throughout the ancient Near East were involved not only in transmission of written texts, but also in their composition.

The strategy just suggested—that is, an historical and comparative approach to the Deuteronomic school as a scribal school—will follow a short historical sketch and a discussion of sectarianism in Yehud. I will then suggest that the Deuteronomic school returned to Yehud as part of the Persian policy to re-establish the Jerusalem temple cult. This possible role of the Deuteronomic school in the re-establishment of the Jerusalem temple cult parallels that of other scribal groups elsewhere in the Persian empire—that is, they were responsible for the preservation and transmission of the religious texts associated with the temple cult. Within this 'official' context, the Deuteronomic school undertook its work, which included the composition of its own literary works (such as II Zech) wherein they reinterpreted earlier traditions.

Historical Background[1]

With the deportations of 597 and 587 BCE, the leadership of Judah was removed from the land and taken into exile in Babylonia. In 539

1.   The following works were consulted for this section: P.R. Ackroyd, 'The Jewish Community in Palestine in the Persian Period', in *Cambridge History of Judaism*. I. *The Persian Period* (ed. W.D. Davies and L. Finkelstein; Cambridge: Cambridge University Press, 1984), pp. 130-61; E.J. Bickerman, 'Babylonian

BCE, the Babylonian empire fell to the Persian king, Cyrus the Great. In the following year, Cyrus gave an edict which proclaimed royal support for the return of the exiles to Jerusalem under Sheshbazzar and the rebuilding of the temple, thus beginning the return of the exiles to Jerusalem and the establishment of the province of Yehud. After Cyrus's death in 530 BCE, his son Cambyses I ascended to the Persian throne. With Cambyses's death in 522 BCE, revolts broke out and a struggle for the accession to the throne occurred. In late 522 BCE, Darius I gained control of the throne and consolidated his empire. Early in his reign, Darius appointed Zerubbabel as governor of Yehud. Zerubbabel, as governor, and Joshua ben Jehozadak, as high priest, led more exiles to Jerusalem in order to renew the effort to rebuild the temple. Zerubbabel and Joshua found prophetic support in the messages of the prophets Haggai and Zechariah. In 516/515 BCE, the Jerusalem temple was rededicated.

During the reign of Darius I (522–486 BCE), the Achaemenid empire, including the province of Yehud, experienced a high degree of stability. However, following Darius's death in 486 BCE, another period of instability in the empire began. In 486 BCE, Egypt rebelled against Persian control and, in 482 BCE, the Babylonians assassinated their satrap. Again in 460 BCE, Egypt revolted against the empire, this time with the support of the Athenian navy. Shortly after this Egyptian revolt had been put down, Megabyzus, the satrap of Beyond the River, rebelled against the Persian throne. Within this context of instability, the missions of two other appointees, Ezra (458 BCE) and Nehemiah

Captivity', in *Cambridge History of Judaism*, I (ed. Davies and Finkelstein), pp. 342-58; F.M. Cross, 'A Reconstruction of the Judean Restoration', *JBL* 94 (1975), pp. 4-18; K.G. Hoglund, *Achaemenid Imperial Administration in Syria-Palestine and the Missions of Ezra and Nehemiah*, (SBLDS, 125; Atlanta: Scholars Press, 1992); E. Meyers, 'The Persian Period and the Judean Restoration: From Zerubbabel to Nehemiah', in *Ancient Israelite Religion* (ed. Miller, Hanson and McBride), pp. 509-21; Meyers and Meyers, *Haggai–Zechariah 1–8*, pp. xxix-xliv; Petersen, *Haggai, Zechariah 1–8*, pp. 19-31; E. Stern, 'The Persian Period and the Political and Social History of Palestine in the Persian Period', in *The Cambridge History of Judaism*, I (ed. Davies and Finkelstein), pp. 70-87; C.C. Torrey, *Ezra Studies* (Chicago: University of Chicago Press, 1910), pp. 285-335.

Where differences exist, this reconstruction follows that found in Cross, 'Reconstruction of the Judean Restoration'; Hoglund, *Achaemenid Imperial Administration*; E. Meyers, 'Persian Period and the Judean Restoration'; and Meyers and Meyers, *Haggai–Zechariah 1–8*, pp. xxix-xliv.

(445 BCE),[2] were carried out. Through the missions of both Ezra and Nehemiah, Artaxerxes I (465–424 BCE) strove to consolidate Persian control of the small, but strategically important, province of Yehud.[3] As with previous appointees and their missions to Jerusalem, both Ezra and Nehemiah were accompanied by more returnees.

A Survey of Secondary Literature on Sectarianism

Although competing factions certainly existed in pre-exilic Judah,[4] this situation was exacerbated by the destruction of Jerusalem in 587 BCE. The destruction of Jerusalem changed the two most unifying conditions of pre-exilic Judah.[5] (1) The somewhat balanced relationship among the pre-exilic leaders—that is, the king, the priests and the prophets—ended with the demise of the state of Judah. (2) The Judeans were no longer confined to a limited geographical area; rather they were scattered from Egypt to Mesopotamia. Because new social structures were required in the lands to which they were exiled (and to which they had fled), the people of Israel followed different adaptive strategies in relationship to the conditions in the places wherein they resided. Some were syncretistic, while others strove to maintain a very distinct ethnic and religious identity. When these differing perspectives were brought together within the post-exilic province of Yehud, conflict naturally arose. Still it is difficult to reconstruct these competing sects and to assess their relationship to late biblical texts. Some of the theories of sectarianism in Yehud will be examined here, with a consideration, when possible, of II Zech's place within these theories.[6]

2.   For a recent discussion of Ezra's and Nehemiah's missions, see Hoglund, *Achaemenid Imperial Administration*, pp. 51-96.

3.   For the most thorough discussion of the context of Ezra and Nehemiah's missions within the Achaemenid empire, see Hoglund, *Achaemenid Imperial Administration*.

4.   See M. Smith, *Palestinian Parties and Politics That Shaped the Old Testament* (London: SCM Press, 1987), pp. 11-42.

5.   See S. Talmon, 'The Emergence of Jewish Sectarianism in the Early Second Temple Period', in *Ancient Israelite Religion* (ed. Miller, Hanson and McBride), pp. 587-616.

6.   For a fuller review of various understandings of the social location of II Zech, see above, 'The Problems of Source and Redaction in II Zech', in the Introduction.

In his review of late biblical literature (Dan; Isa 24–27; II Zech; Joel), Otto Plöger reconstructed the conflicting groups in the Achaemenid and Hellenistic periods along ideological lines. He labelled the ideology of the two conflicting groups as 'theocratic' and 'eschatological'. The former was represented in the Priestly school and the Chronicler and the latter in Dan; Isa 24–27; Joel 3; II Zech. The 'theocratic' group understood the political entity of Yehud/Judea

> not as a specially exalted nation alongside other nations but as a divine creation, incommensurable in terms of this world,...which interprets its existence as the fulfilment of definite promises which Yahweh had once announced by the mouth of the prophets.[7]

In contrast, the 'eschatological' group understood the political entity of Yehud/Judea as temporary and awaited the 'eschatological revolution' wherein Israel will be rehabilitated.[8] Although the tension between theocracy and eschatology probably played some role in post-exilic conflict, Plöger's characterization of the period is exactly what he, himself, called it: a 'terrible simplification'.[9]

Building upon the work of Plöger, Hanson identified two competing groups in post-exilic Yehud: a 'hierocratic' group and a 'visionary' group.[10] The hierocratic group consisted of Zadokite priests and their allies (Haggai, Zechariah, the Chronicler), all of whom espoused the restoration of the temple cult along pre-exilic Zadokite lines in collaboration with the Persian authorities. The visionary group was composed of the 'disciples of Second Isaiah' and Levitical priests, whose views are preserved in III Isa and II Zech. The visionaries understood

---

7.   Plöger, *Theocracy and Eschatology*, p. 109.

8.   Plöger, *Theocracy and Eschatology*, pp. 106-107.

9.   Plöger, *Theocracy and Eschatology*, pp. 108-109. Plöger's reconstruction is assumed in O.H. Steck, 'Theological Streams of Tradition', in *Tradition and Theology in the Old Testament* (ed. D.A. Knight; Philadelphia: Fortress Press, 1977), pp. 183-214. For some criticisms of Plöger's reconstruction, see J. Blenkinsopp, 'Interpretation and the Tendency to Sectarianism: An Aspect of Second Temple History', in *Jewish and Christian Self-Definition* (ed. E.P. Sanders; Philadelphia: Fortress Press, 1981), II, pp. 11-12; Blenkinsopp, *Prophecy and Canon*, pp. 114-16; R.J. Coggins, *Haggai, Zechariah, Malachi* (Sheffield: JSOT Press, 1987), pp. 52, 57-58.

10.   *Dawn of Apocalyptic*. Hanson's dichotomy of 'hierocratic'/'visionary' is dependent on that of Plöger, 'theocratic'/'eschatological'. Also, like Plöger, he defined the main difference between these groups with the dichotomy of this-worldly/other-worldly.

that the restoration would occur with Yahweh's eschatological initiative wherein the present cult would be replaced by the true cult of Yahweh. Like that of Plöger, Hanson's reconstruction of post-exilic conflict is much too simplistic.[11]

In *Palestinian Parties and Politics That Shaped the Old Testament*, Morton Smith began with a review of sectarian tendencies in pre-exilic Judah. He noted that the two opposing tendencies—that is, the tendency toward cultic syncretism within Yahwism versus that of a 'Yahweh-alone' party—stretched from the pre-exilic period into the Hellenistic period. With the destruction of the northern kingdom in 722 BCE, the syncretistic form of Yahwish was spread over a wide geographical area and attracted considerable numbers of Gentiles. The 'Yahweh-alone' party, on the other hand, continued to be centralized in Jerusalem and then was mostly carried off into exile after the destruction of Jerusalem in 587 BCE where they continued to provide religious leadership to the Jewish exiles. After the defeat of the Babylonians, the 'Yahweh-alone' party received Persian support and returned to Jerusalem where they controlled the rebuilt temple. Their control of the temple led to conflict with those who had remained in Judah during the exile who were syncretistic Yahwists.[12] Thus, conflict ensued between the 'Yahweh-alone' returnees and the syncretistic adherents in Judah. In further describing this conflict, Smith identified the 'Yahweh-alone' returnees with 'followers of the Deuteronomic tradition [who] had a reason which most Judeans did not for returning to the city—Deuteronomy had both required sacrificial worship and limited it to Jerusalem'.[13] Although adherents to any 'Yahweh-alone party' would certainly be in conflict with what they would perceive as 'syncretistic' groups, his dichotomy does not present the complexity of conflict, for certainly different factions within both the 'Yahweh-alone

---

11. For some other criticisms of Hanson's reconstruction, see Blenkinsopp, 'Interpretation and the Tendency to Sectarianism', p. 13; Blenkinsopp, *Prophecy and Canon*, p. 113; Coggins, *Haggai, Zechariah, Malachi*, pp. 52, 54-56, 58-59; E. Meyers, 'Persian Period and the Judean Restoration', pp. 509-10, 518 n. 6; E. Meyers, 'The Use of *tora* in Haggai 2:11 and the Role of the Prophet in the Restoration Community', in *The Word of the Lord Shall Go Forth* (ed. C.L. Meyers and M. O'Conner; Winona Lake, IN: Eisenbrauns, 1982), pp. 70, 72-74.

12. *Palestinian Parties and Politics*, p. 62.

13. *Palestinian Parties and Politics*, p. 81.

party' and the 'syncretistic cult' fought among themselves.[14]

Building upon the work of the Soviet social historian Sarkisan, Joël P. Weinberg (= I.P. Vejnberg)[15] has described a community made up of temple personnel and landed citizens, who exerted social control in Yehud through their control of the Jerusalem temple. This *Bürger-Tempel-Gemeinde* ('civic-temple-community') gained limited control of the internal affairs of the province of Yehud by its collaboration with the Persian administration. Because the *Bürger-Tempel-Gemeinde* was made up primarily of returnees who came from Babylon, as the numbers of Babylonian returnees swelled so did the membership of the *Bürger-Tempel-Gemeinde*.[16]

Although Weinberg has been criticized in his details, his basic understanding of a social entity that controls, to some extent, the internal affairs of Yehud has found its supporters.[17] The most recent

14. For a criticism of Smith's reconstruction, see Blenkinsopp, 'Interpretation and the Tendency to Sectarianism', pp. 11-13.

15. J.P. Weinberg has expressed his view of the *Bürger-Tempel-Gemeinde* in various articles. Those consulted for this review are the following: 'Der *'am ha'ares* des 6.–4. Jh. v.u.Z', *Klio* 56 (1974), pp. 325-35; 'Das *beit abot* im 6.–4. Jh. v.u.Z', *VT* 23 (1973), pp. 400-14; 'Demographische Notizen zur Geschichte der nachexilischen Gemeinde in Juda', *Klio* 54 (1972), pp. 45-59; *'netinim* und "Söhne der Sklaven Salomos" im 6.–4. Jh. v.u.Z'. *ZAW* 87 (1975), pp. 355-71; 'Probleme des Sozialökonomischen Struktur Judas vom 6. Jahrhundret v.u.Z. bis 1. Jahrhundert u.Z. Zu einigen wirtschaftshistorischen Untersuchungen von Heinz Kreissig', *Jahrbuch für Wirtschaftsgeschichte* 1973/I, pp. 237-51; 'Zentral- und Partikulargewalt im achämenidischen Reich', *Klio* 59 (1977), pp. 25-43. The following reviews of Weinberg's work were also consulted: J. Blenkinsopp, 'Temple and Society in Achemenid Judah', in *Second Temple Studies. I. Persian Period* (ed. P.R. Davies; JSOTSup, 117; Sheffield: JSOT Press, 1991), pp. 22-53; B. Funck, 'Zur Bürger-Tempel-Gemeinde im nachexilischen Juda', *Klio* 59 (1977), pp. 491-96; H. Kreissig, 'Eine beachtenswerte Theorie zur Organization altvorderorientalischer Tempelgemeinden im Achämenidenreich. Zu J.P. Weinbergs "Bürger-Tempel-Gemeinde" in Juda', *Klio* 66 (1984), pp. 35-39.

16. Weinberg, 'Demographische Notizen zur Geschichte der nachexilischen Gemeinde in Juda'.

17. The following commentators on the one hand criticized Weinberg's methodology and details, but on the other hand accepted the basic validity of the *Bürger-Tempel-Gemeinde* thesis: Blenkinsopp, 'Temple and Society in Achemenid Judah'; H.G. Kippenberg, *Religion und Klassenbildung im antiken Judäa* (Göttingen: Vandenhoeck & Ruprecht, 1978); Kreissig, 'Eine beachtenswerte Theorie zur Organization altvorderorientalischer Tempelgemeinden im Achämenidenreich';

scholar to develop further the *Bürger-Tempel-Gemeinde* hypothesis is Blenkinsopp, who was harshly critical of Weinberg's assumption of the historicity of such biblical material as the numerical list of repatriates in Neh 7. However, after reviewing the biblical material, especially that in Ezra–Neh, he accepts that the 'Babylonian immigrants...succeeded in imposing the social arrangments with which they had become familiar in Mesopotamia' and concludes that 'to this extent, at least, Weinberg's civic-temple community hypothesis appears to be acceptable'.[18]

Since the emphasis in the *Bürger-Tempel-Gemeinde* hypothesis is upon the community as an agent of social control and social cohesion, the work of Weinberg does not suggest possible tensions within the *Bürger-Tempel-Gemeinde* itself.[19] Certainly if the *Bürger-Tempel-Gemeinde* underwent various population explosions, there would have been some internal conflicts. Hence, although the *Bürger-Tempel-Gemeinde* hypothesis illuminates the situation of social control in Yehud, its limitations must also be granted, especially concerning conflicts within the *Bürger-Tempel-Gemeinde* itself.

In concluding this review of reconstructions of sectarianism in Yehud, the work of two commentators on II Zech deserves consideration. Mason has argued that an antiestablishment group with a strong eschatological outlook stood behind II Zech.[20] Redditt claimed that the redactor's views can be discerned in his connecting material in Zech 10.2-3a; 11.1-17; 12.6-7, 10-12; and 13.1-9.[21] Redditt's analysis of

Petersen, *Haggai, Zechariah 1–8*, pp. 29-31; Petersen, 'Temple in Persian Period Prophetic Texts', p. 128.

18. 'Temple and Society in Achemenid Judah', p. 53.

19. Blenkinsopp did not address the possibility of conflict within the *Bürger-Temple-Gemeinde* in 'Temple and Society in Achemenid Judah'; however, his earlier writings on sectarianism (e.g. 'Interpretation and the Tendency to Sectarianism') suggest that his understanding of Achaemenid Yehud may be more nuanced than Weinberg's. See also Alexander Rofé, 'Isaiah 66:1-4: Judean Sects in the Persian Period as Viewed by Trito-Isaiah', in *Biblical and Related Studies Presented to Samuel Iwry* (ed. A. Kort and S. Morschauser; Winona Lake, IN: Eisenbrauns, 1985), pp. 205-17. Rofé did not refer to the *Bürger-Tempel-Gemeinde* hypothesis, but he provided a discussion of conflict within one 'party'—that is, the different views concerning intermarriage between III Isa and Ezra–Neh (pp. 214-15).

20. 'Some Examples', p. 353; 'Use of Earlier Biblical Material in Zech 9–14', p. 308.

21. 'Israel's Shepherds', pp. 632, 639.

this material in II Zech led him to a conclusion somewhat similar from that of Mason—that is, the group responsible for II Zech is a pro-Judean group with strong antiestablishment tendencies. Thus, Mason and Redditt agree that the group responsible for II Zech are in conflict with the Persian-supported leadership of Yehud.

Mason's and Redditt's conclusions fall into the same trap that we saw above in the reconstructions of sectarianism—that is, social conflict is thought of primarily in the context of two well-defined, competing groups: the theocratic and the eschatological, the hierocratic and the visionary, the Yahweh-alone and the syncretistic, the bourgeois and the proletariat, the establishment and the antiestablishment. Such simplistic dichotomization denies, for example, the possibility of a group (or sub-group) within the privileged classes who are (self-) critical of the established order and, therefore, might envision a brighter (eschatological?) future. The likelihood of such a possible situation would, in my opinion, be very significant within a system, such as the Achaemenid empire, wherein groups with ethnic and religious attachments to local temple cults were used by their political rulers to (re-)establish social control over native populations. Such groups would clearly have mixed allegiances which could easily vacillate between their ethnic and religious identity and their loyalty to the Persian empire. Therefore, terminology which suggests such simplifying dichotomization must be avoided.

The Role of Scribes and Scribal Schools in the Ancient Near East[22]

None of the reconstructions described above is sufficient to explain the complexity of Yehud in the Achaemenid period. They all suffer from the oversimplification of dichotomization and also from the failure to consider how scribal schools and their differing literary canons may have functioned. The works of DtrH, Jer, and II Zech are presumably products of Deuteronomic redactors. Still, a discussion of scribes and scribal schools is helpful in understanding of the redactional process since at least some scribes were involved in functions other than copying and transcribing. That is, some scribes were themselves

22. This section is heavily dependent upon J.G. Gammie and L.G. Perdue (eds.), *The Sage in Israel and the Ancient Near East* (Winona Lake, IN: Eisenbrauns, 1990). In this volume, the designation 'sage' is sufficiently broad so as to include discussions of scribes.

composers of literary texts.[23] All redactors were scribes, even though all scribes were by no means redactors. Therefore, a review of the role of scribes and scribal schools in the ancient Near East in the pre-Achaemenid and Achaemenid periods may illumine the role of the Deuteronomic redactors in Yehud.

Scribes and Scribal Schools prior to the Achaemenid Period

During the Old Babylonian period, the institution of the *edubba*s ('tablet-houses') provided for the education of artisans, especially concerning skills associated with reading and writing. According to Å.W. Sjöberg,[24] Sumerian was no longer a living language; therefore, instruction began in Babylonian with the goal of bilingualism (Sumerian and Babylonian). Other than the study of Sumerian, the curriculum in *edubba*s included mathematics, surveying, music, agriculture, construction and literature. The study of literature in the *edubba*s was of primary importance and included dictation, composition, and the ability to identify isolated quotes within their proper literary context. Concerning the leaders within these *edubba*s, Samuel Noah Kramer wrote:

> In the *edubba*s of Nippur and Ur, for example, there flourished the scholar and man of letters, the academic and humanist, who studied, enlarged, and expanded whatever linguistic, literary, and theological lore was current in his day.[25]

In his survey of 'The Sage in Mesopotamian Palaces and Royal Courts',[26] Ronald Sweet included a discussion of the palace scribe, who was 'indispensible for administration of the scale and complexity

---

23. Fishbane has noted the difficulty in distinguishing scribal activity from authorial activity: 'the boundary-line between scribes and authors is often quite difficult to draw in biblical literature, and, in some cases, involves precarious judgements' (*Biblical Interpretation*, p. 85; see also pp. 27, 37, 41, 78-79, 83-88).

24. This paragraph on *edubba*s is based primarily upon Å.W. Sjöberg, 'The Old Babylonian Eduba', in *Sumeriological Studies in Honor of Thorkild Jacobsen on his Seventieth Birthday* (ed. S. Liebermann; AS, 20; Chicago: University of Chicago Press, 1975), pp. 159-79.

25. 'Sage in Sumerian Literature: A Composite Portrait', in *The Sage in Israel and the Ancient Near East* (ed. Gammie and Perdue), pp. 31-32.

26. In *The Sage in Israel and the Ancient Near East* (ed. Gammie and Perdue), pp. 99-107.

practiced in Mesopotamia'.[27] Sweet noted that by the Ur III period the institution of the 'palace scribe' (dub-sar-é-gal) was well established with eighteen different scribal titles used. Although many scribes dealt primarily, or maybe even exclusively, with administrative texts, some scribes were involved in the composition and transmission of various literary genres, including royal inscriptions, collections of legal material, year-lists, king lists, chronicles, hymns of praise, and disputation texts. Therefore, the Mesopotamian palace scribe was not necessarily a mere transcriber or copyist, rather some were composers in their own right.[28]

In his review of Egyptian literature, Ronald Williams has described the practice of scribal training in ancient Egypt, beginning in the Old Kingdom. According to his reconstruction, youths underwent four years of elementary instruction in basic skills (e.g. arithmetic) with a strong emphasis on the art of writing, beginning with hieratic then hieroglyphic script.[29] After this elementary education, there were various types of advanced studies. Some of the youths were granted the title 'scribe' and undertook more advanced classes; others may have continued their studies within an apprenticeship; still others may have attended trade schools.[30] Those who became scribes hoped to attain a position in the 'House of Life', a scribal institution which not only copied texts but also produced them.[31] Usually located near a temple, the 'House of Life' housed archives that included religious texts. Given the functions of the 'House of Life', an accomplished Egyptian scribe would have been much more than a mere copyist, he (or possibly she) would have become a compiler, a librarian, and, possibly, an author.

27. 'Sage in Mesopotamian Palaces', p. 103. His discussion of palace scribes is on pp. 103-105.

28. See R. Harris, 'The Female "Sage" in Mesopotamian Literature (with an Appendix on Egypt)', in *The Sage in Israel and the Ancient Near East* (ed. Gammie and Perdue), pp. 3-17. Harris reached a similar conclusion concerning female scribes in Mesopotamia. Her discussion included the female scribe as bureaucrat, poetess, and scholar.

29. R.J. Williams, 'Scribal Training in Ancient Egypt', *JAOS* 92 (1972), pp. 216, 219.

30. 'Scribal Training in Ancient Egypt', p. 216.

31. R.J. Williams, 'The Sage in Egyptian Literature', in *The Sage in Israel and the Ancient Near East* (ed. Gammie and Perdue), pp. 26-27; Williams, 'Scribal Training in Ancient Egypt', pp. 220-21.

With respect to the Ugaritic evidence, Loren Mack-Fisher criticized Albright's conclusion that there was no didactic material[32] and the continuing influence of his conclusion upon contemporary works. After re-assessing the existing Ugaritic corpus, Mack-Fisher concluded that Ugaritic scribes produced various types of didactic literature, which betray strong Babylonian influence.[33] He then reconstructed a list of Ugaritic scribes in relationship to the Ugaritic kings under whom they served.[34] In his discussion of some of these Ugaritic scribes, he noted various roles that the Ugaritic scribe might play, including counselor to the king, librarian, and composer of literary works. As in Egypt and Mesopotamia, a scribe in Ugarit was not necessarily a mere transcriber or copyist, nor even confined to literary matters such as composition.

Although the extent of the diffusion of educational institutions and literacy in pre-exilic Israel remains widely debated,[35] the existence of schools for professional scribes (especially those in the palace or temple administration) in monarchical Judah is generally affirmed.[36]

Evidence for the existence of scribal schools in pre-exilic Judah is of three kinds: (1) The Hebrew Bible itself contains three kinds of evidence: (a) narratives (e.g. 2 Kgs 22.8-13) that describe the activity of professional scribes,[37] (b) the mention of the existence of source

32. 'A Survey and Reading Guide to the Didactic Literature of Ugarit: Prolegomenon to a Study on the Sage', in *The Sage in Israel and the Ancient Near East* (ed. Gammie and Perdue), p. 67.

33. 'Didactic Literature of Ugarit'.

34. L.R. Mack-Fisher, 'The Scribe (and Sage) in the Royal Court at Ugarit', in *The Sage in Israel and the Ancient Near East* (ed. Gammie and Perdue), pp. 111-12.

35. E.g. J.L. Crenshaw, 'The Sage in Proverbs', in *The Sage in Israel and the Ancient Near East* (ed. Gammie and Perdue), pp. 205-16; M. Haran, 'On the Diffusion of Literacy and Schools in Ancient Israel', in *Congress Volume, Jerusalem 1986* (ed. J.A. Emerton; VTSup, 40; Leiden: Brill, 1988), pp. 81-95; D.W. Jamieson-Drake, *Scribes and Schools in Monarchic Judah* (JSOTSup, 109; Sheffield: Almond Press, 1991); A. Lemaire, 'The Sage in School and Temple', in *The Sage in Israel and the Ancient Near East* (ed. Gammie and Perdue), pp. 165-81; E. Puech, 'Les écoles dans l'Israël preéxilique: données épigraphiques', in *Congress Volume, Jerusalem 1986* (ed. Emerton), pp. 189-203.

36. *Contra* R.N. Whybray, 'The Sage in the Israelite Royal Court', in *The Sage in Israel and the Ancient Near East* (ed. Gammie and Perdue), p. 139.

37. E.g. J. Blenkinsopp, 'The Sage, the Scribe, and Scribalism in the Chronicler's Work', in *The Sage in Israel and the Ancient Near East* (ed. Gammie and Perdue), pp. 308-309; Fishbane, *Biblical Interpretation*, p. 25; Weinfeld, *Deuteronomy and the Deuteronomic School*, pp. 158-78.

materials, which presumably would have come from the royal court,[38] such as 'the Book of the Chronicles of the Kings of Israel'[39] and 'the Book of the Chronicles of the Kings of Judah',[40] and (c) vocabulary reflecting the technical language of scribalism.[41] (2) The administrative complexity of the institution of the monarchy required the service of professional scribes; therefore, in order to fulfil this need, scribal schools were established.[42] (3) Scribal schools existed throughout the ancient Near East; hence, by analogy, ancient Israel may have also had scribal schools.[43] Although such reasoning has been used to make what James Crenshaw has called 'extravagant claims',[44] it nevertheless suggests that schools for the training of professional scribes existed in pre-exilic Judah and that these scribes were not necessarily mere copyists. It is in this context that the emergence of the Deuteronomic school is often located.

Scribes and Scribal Schools in Achaemenid Administration pertaining to Persia and Egypt
In 'Sages and Scribes in the Ancient Court of Iran',[45] James Russell discussed various court activities of Persian scribes, including religious

38. E.g. Halpern, *First Historians*, pp. 207-18; Mayes, *Story of Israel*, pp. 121-24; McCarter, *I Samuel*, pp. 23-27; Noth, *Deuteronomistic History*, pp. 36, 42-43, 63-68; Weippert, '"Deuteronomistischen" Beurteilungen'; J. Van Seters, 'Histories and Historians of the Ancient Near East: The Israelites', *Or* 50 (1981), pp. 137-85.

39. 1 Kgs 14.19; 15.31; 16.5, 14, 20, 27; 22.39; 2 Kgs 1.18; 10.34; 13.8, 12; 14.15, 28; 15.11, 15, 21, 26, 31.

40. 1 Kgs 14.29; 15.7, 23; 22.45; 2 Kgs 8.23; 12.19; 14.18; 15.6, 36; 16.19; 20.20; 21.17, 25; 23.28; 24.5.

41. Fishbane, *Biblical Interpretation*, pp. 29-32.

42. E.g. W. Brueggeman, 'The Social Significance of Solomon as a Patron of Wisdom', in *The Sage in Israel and the Ancient Near East* (ed. Gammie and Perdue), pp. 117-32.

43. E.g. Lemaire, 'Sage in School and Temple', pp. 168-70.

44. 'Education in Ancient Israel', *JBL* 104 (1985), p. 601. Crenshaw used 'extravagant claims' in reference to Lemaire's reconstruction of schools for the general population at all of the major cities of the pre-exilic Judah.

45. In *The Sage in Israel and the Ancient Near East* (ed. Gammie and Perdue), pp. 141-46. Russell's article refers to scribes during three different periods: Achaemenid (550–333 BCE), Parthian (250 BCE–224 CE), and Sasanian (224–651 CE); however, he noted that the 'inherent conservativism in pre-Islamic Iranian thought' allowed some collation of the material.

duties, interactions with non-Persians, and scribal tasks. Among their scribal tasks, Persian scribes kept administrative records and compiled royal annals. He concluded that during the Achaemenid period 'a majority of the *dabirs*—the term refers primarily to transcribers, translators and lower-level bureaucrats—were non-[Persian]'.[46]

His conclusion that most of the *dabirs* were non-Persians brings us closer to the question of the role of scribes in the administration of the Achaemenid empire outside of Persia, for it shows that, because of language barriers, the Achaemenid imperial administration required the service of non-Persian scribes to serve as translators, especially in the outlying satrapies. In addition, since Achaemenid strategy for controlling various ethnic groups involved the re-establishment and preservation of the native religious practices at their original cultic sites and also the codification of religious legal material, local scribes were involved in a wider range of literary activities. This strategy is illustrated well in the mission of Udjahorresnet.[47]

As is known from the inscription on his mortuary statue, Udjahor-resnet was an Egyptian scribe whose duties included the supervision of lesser scribes at Sais.[48] When Cambyses I conquered Egypt, Udjahor-resnet collaborated with the Persians and later influenced Cambyses to restore the dynastic sanctuary at Sais. After this restoration, he went to Susa as a royal counselor on Egyptian affairs. Early in the reign of Darius I, he was commissioned to re-establish the 'House of Life', a scribal institution that had been closely related to the Sais temple.

> The institution known as the House of Life had not one but many locations, usually—but not exclusively—in the proximity of temples. It was more than a mere scriptorium or library, although it was a center for the composition, preservation, study, and copying of texts. These were mainly of a religious nature, intended for cult use. However, the range of

46. 'Sages and Scribes in the Ancient Court of Iran', p. 146.

47. The following discussion of Udjahorresnet's mission is based upon the following works: J. Blenkinsopp, 'The Mission of Udjahorresnet and Those of Ezra and Nehemiah', *JBL* 106 (1987), pp. 409-21; A.B. Lloyd, 'The Inscription of Udjahorresnet: A Collaborator's Testament', *JEA* 68 (1982), pp. 166-80. Blenkinsopp noted that the mission of Udjahorresnet had other parallels within the Achaemenid empire ('Mission of Udjahorresnet', p. 413).

48. Udjahorresnet's role fits with Williams's description of the role of ancient Egyptian scribes ('Sage in Egyptian Literature', p. 25).

works extended to magical and medical texts, dream-books, and hemerologies. Academy may be an inaccurate as well as an anachronistic term for it, but it was the resort of the intellectuals of the day.[49]

Although it is unclear to what extent Williams's above description of this institution can be related to Udjahorresnet's commission to re-establish the 'House of Life' at Sais, Udjahorresnet's 'House of Life' probably served the function of a scriptorium and a library for religious texts associated with the Sais temple. Because the institution of the 'House of Life' was an Egyptian scribal school consisting of priests who redacted and preserved religious texts, Udjahorresnet's mission is in all likelihood associated with Darius I's order (preserved in the *Demotic Chronicle*) that a commission be established in order to codify Egyptian laws which were in force at the end of Amasis's reign (526 BCE).

Scribes and Scribal Schools in Achaemenid Administration pertaining to Yehud

The use of non-Persian scribes in the administration of the Achaemenid empire involved administrative duties, such as record keeping, and also the collection and preservation of native religious texts. It is within this context that the mission of Ezra must be placed.[50]

In Ezra 7.12, Ezra is addressed as 'Ezra the priest, the scribe of the law of the God of Heaven'. Whether or not the phrase 'the scribe of the law of the God of Heaven' is an imperial title or a Jewish title,[51] Ezra is depicted as a learned scribe who was commissioned by the Persian king, Artaxerxes I, to reassert Persian control over the Jerusalem temple cult. This reassertion was to be accomplished by Ezra's reintroducing the 'true' law of Moses and by insuring that this law was strictly obeyed. Ezra's entourage probably included other scribes.[52] Thus, Ezra's mission to Jerusalem paralleled Udjahorresnet's

49. Williams, 'Sage in Egyptian Literature', p. 27.

50. For discussion of the context of Ezra's mission within the Achaemenid empire, see Blenkinsopp, 'Mission of Udjahorresnet'; Blenkinsopp, 'Sage, the Scribe, and Scribalism in the Chronicler's Work'; Hoglund, *Achaemenid Imperial Administration*.

51. See Hoglund, *Achaemenid Imperial Administration*, pp. 226-36 and the literature cited there.

52. Ezra's entourage included 'Levites', some of whom were probably scribes. See 2 Chron 34.13.

mission to Sais in that both were scribes who were sent by Persian kings to their native cultic center to reassert imperial control through the codification of cultic laws.[53]

Summary of Chapter 7:
The Social Setting of the Deuteronomic School in Yehud

As in much of the ancient Near East, scribal schools existed in pre-exilic Judah. Members of these scribal groups probably were among the deportees who were taken from Jerusalem into Babylonian exile. The Deuteronomic school must be placed within this historical context. This scenario of the Deuteronomic school's history is widely accepted, based upon various interpretations of the material contained in DtrH and/or Jer.[54]

Although the Deuteronomic school is also generally assumed to have perished in exile, ample evidence suggests that the Deuteronomic school continued its redactional activity into the post-exilic period. The literary evidence for this post-exilic setting includes DtrH, Jer and possibly II Zech. Can more be said about the post-exilic setting of the Deuteronomic school?

Persian imperial administration included the re-establishment of local sanctuaries and their native cults. This strategy is evident in the various missions to Jerusalem—that is, those of Sheshbazzar, Zerubbabel, Ezra and Nehemiah—as well as missions elsewhere, most notably Udjahorresnet's mission to Sais. An important element of this strategy included the return of scribal groups who were responsible for the codification and preservation of religious literature associated with the restored sanctuary—for example, Udhajorresnet's restoration

53. Blenkinsopp, 'Mission of Udjahorresnet'; Hoglund, *Achaemenid Imperial Administration*, pp. 235-36.

54. For example, Blenkinsopp, *Prophecy and Canon*, pp. 24-35; Nicholson, *Deuteronomy and Tradition*, pp. 1-17; Weinfeld, *Deuteronomy and the Deuteronomic School*, pp. 158-78. See also J.A. Dearman, 'My Servants the Scribes: Composition and Context in Jeremiah 36', *JBL* 109 (1990), pp. 403-21. In this article, he convincingly demonstrated that the scribal roles depicted in Jer 36 are consistent with other Deuteronomic depictions of scribes (2 Kgs 22; Jer 26) and archaeological evidence (e.g., *bullae* and seals which refer to officials mentioned in Jer 36). He therefore concluded that 2 Kgs 22; Jer 26; 36 are 'the best internal evidence for the circles of scriptural editors/authors commonly known as the Deuteronomistic historians' (p. 404).

of the 'House of Life' at Sais, and Ezra's reading of the law. In my opinion, the return of the Deuteronomic school to Yehud occurred within this context—that is, the Deuteronomic school was commissioned to return to Yehud and aid in the restoration of the temple cult by means of its scribal activity.[55]

How would the members of the Deuteronomic school have contributed to the Persian-supported restoration of the Jerusalem temple? The most obvious answer to this question would be that they would have utilized their scribal skills to preserve the texts associated with the Jerusalem temple by their careful copying and transmission. Also, the most accomplished scribes among them (i.e. Deuteronomic redactors) would have reinterpreted and revised earlier traditions in light of new historical and theological circumstances, thereby producing such works as DtrH, Jer and II Zech.[56]

Another possible way in which some of the members of the Deuteronomic school may have functioned within the Jerusalem temple would have been the teaching of the traditions. In *Preaching*

55. In 'The History of the Cities of Refuge in Biblical Law', Rofé discerned three stages concerning these laws: (1) a pre-exilic stage (Deut 19.1-7) wherein the chosen cities were only a place of refuge; (2) a late sixth- or early fifth-century BCE stage (the Priestly writer's texts of Num 35.9-15 and Josh 20, as represented by the shorter LXX), wherein the chosen cities were also only a place of refuge; and (3) a late fifth- or early fourth-century BCE stage (Num 35.25-29 and the Deuteronomic revision of Josh 20 as represented in the MT additions), wherein the notion of banishment rather than simply voluntary refuge was first introduced. After noting that the punishment of banishment gained importance first in the Persian empire, he suggested that the post-exilic Deuteronomic introduction of banishment in relationship to the cities of refuge occurred under the influence of Persian imperial law (p. 238). Assuming the validity of his argument, we have an example of the influence that the Persian administration had upon the Deuteronomic school's scribal activity in relationship to the Jerusalem temple cult.

56. Although adherents to the *Bürger-Tempel-Gemeinde* hypothesis do not make this explicit, it would seem that any such group would, in some way, be significantly influential in relationship to the literature associated with the temple cult. Therefore, my argument here is in some ways an affirmation of the basic logic of the *Bürger-Tempel-Gemeinde* hypothesis, especially as reflected in Blenkinsopp's refinements. That is, the Persian-supported administration of the Jerusalem temple was made up of returned exiles, who gained social control through the economic and religious power associated with the temple cult. A important element of this control was the imposition of an authoritative canon and its preservation, a task which, in my opinion, fell primarily to the Deuteronomic school.

to the Exiles, Nicholson demonstrated the Deuteronomic character of the prose in Jer. This prose, like that of Deuteronomic literature in general, arose within a homiletical tradition of 'preaching to the exiles'.

> [T]he method of the Deuteronomists witnesses to an exegetical principle which had for its basis their acknowledgement of the enduring vitality of the Word of God and for its goal their desire and determination to actualize that Word for the generation to whom they addressed themselves.[57]

This Deuteronomic method included presenting the prophets (in DtrH and Jer) as 'preachers of the Law'.[58] These 'preachers' were said to have produced 'sermons', Deuteronomic compositions which reinterpreted earlier traditions for new circumstances.[59]

Nicholson assumed the validity of Noth's exilic date for DtrH and Hyatt's exilic date for the Deuteronomic redaction of Jer. However, since the Deuteronomic school continued into the post-exilic period, Nicholson's description of Deuteronomic 'preaching' to the Babylonian exiles may reflect the post-exilic as well as the exilic periods.

Somewhat similar to Nicholson's work is the recent work of Mason intitled *Preaching the Tradition.*[60] He re-examined von Rad's thesis of the 'Levitical Sermons' in Chr and placed these addresses within a larger post-exilic literary context (the speeches in Ezra–Neh, Hag, Zech 1–8, Mal). Although he rejected the form critical classification of 'sermon', Mason concluded that this literature reflects a post-exilic homilectical tradition:

57. *Preaching,* p. 7.

58. Nicholson used this phrase in various places, including *Preaching,* pp. 50, 57, 70. Dearman's analysis of the portrayal of scribes in 2 Kgs 22; Jer 26; 36 led him to a similar conclusion for Deuteronomic scribes: 'Indeed they are all scribes, but the role for many of them in the scriptural accounts is the reading, preservation, *and interpretation* of YHWH's word' ('My Servants the Scribes', p. 411, emphasis his). Thus, not only the Deuteronomic school presented prophets as 'preachers', but it also presented scribes who read aloud prophetic texts as 'preachers'.

59. *Preaching,* p. 71.

60. R.A. Mason, *Preaching the Tradition* (Cambridge: Cambridge University Press, 1990). Mason's comments seem to suggest that he understood his work on post-exilic 'preaching' as complementary to Nicholson's work (*Deuteronomy and Tradition*; *Preaching*), which he described as 'the best exposition of the Deuteronomistic work as "preaching" to the exiles' (p. 266 n. 5). Unfortunately, he likewise assumed the exilic date for the Deuteronomic redactions of DtrH and Jer, thereby missing the possible historical connections between the literature he and Nicholson surveyed.

[T]he material does reflect and encapsulate something of the 'preaching' that must have gone on in the second temple. Of course, the term 'preaching' must not necessarily or exclusively conjure up pictures of present-day ₃ermons…By 'preachers' we must think of those who preserved, developed and taught the traditions which must have been becoming increasingly enshrined in Israel's 'Scriptures'. The activity of such tradents must have been both literary and rhetorical and have taken place in the study and the classroom as well as in more formally 'liturgical' settings.[61]

Their terminology of 'preaching' is unfortunate because it does conjure up 'pictures of present-day sermons'.[62] Still, Nicholson's and Mason's basic premise that sections of DtrH, Jer, Chron, Ezra, Neh, Hag, Zech 1–8, and Mal reflect tradents who reinterpreted their 'traditions' for their contemporary audiences is certainly valid, especially given Mason's understanding that this literature may reflect diverse settings (e.g. classroom and liturgy). Their conclusions, as applied to a post-exilic setting of Deuteronomic literature, suggest that the post-exilic Deuteronomic school functioned within such a rhetorical setting and may have been directly involved in educative processes. Also, some of their literature may have been used in more formal liturgical settings. Therefore, perhaps the Deuteronomic school functioned in a variety of ways within the Persian-supported administration in Jerusalem, including a wide range of educational and scribal tasks. Such variety is certainly paralleled in other settings in the ancient Near East, as demonstrated above.

Assuming that the Deuteronomic school was commissioned by the Persian administration to return to Yehud, there are several possible events during which such a return may have occurred: the return under Sheshbazzar, the return under Zerubbabel, Ezra's mission, and Nehemiah's mission. Of these possibilities, the return under Zerubbabel is to be preferred for several reasons. First, there are factors which tend to eliminate the other possibilities. (1) The return under Sheshbazzar occurred early in the Achaemenid period and, since its mission to rebuild the temple was not accomplished, this return may not have

61. *Preaching the Tradition*, p. 2. Mason (*Preaching the Tradition*, p. 264 n. 7) understood his conclusions to agree with the conclusions of Fishbane, who described the tradents as 'rhetors and teachers' (*Biblical Interpretation*, p. 77).

62. Mason, *Preaching the Tradition*, p. 2. As evident in the above quotation, Mason wanted to prevent such conjuring; however, no matter how hard he strove for such prevention, it would have been better to use some other, unloaded term.

had adequate support from the Persian authorities and the Babylonian Jews in exile. Therefore, it is unlikely that the Deuteronomic school accompanied Sheshbazzar to Jerusalem. (2) The missions of Ezra and Nehemiah occurred quite late and were primarily for the maintenance of the temple cult and the re-establishment of Persian control over the existing Jerusalem temple cult. (3) The Deuteronomic school must have been established in Yehud prior to Ezra's mission because, according to statistical linguistics,[63] the date of the Deuteronomic prose in II Zech falls between the return under Zerubbabel and Ezra's mission.

Secondly, several factors point to the return under Zerubbabel: (1) I Zech betrays some Deuteronomic influence; therefore, it is more likely that the Deuteronomic school was associated with the group responsible for the rebuilding of the temple, including Zechariah, Zerubbabel and Joshua ben Jehozadak. (2) Since the contemporary mission of Udjahorresnet included the re-establishment of the 'House of Life' and the codification of religious literature associated with the Sais temple, Zerubbabel's mission probably also included the services of scribes for the codification and preservation of religious texts associated with the Jerusalem temple cult. The Deuteronomic school is a likely candidate for these scribes. These considerations together suggest that the Deuteronomic school's return to Jerusalem may have been linked to the return under Zerubbabel.

What relationship might exist between the Deuteronomic school's cooperation with the Persian authorities and its theology? There is a tension within Deuteronomic theology that may relate to tension arising from the Deuteronomic school's work with Persian authorities. This tension concerns the Deuteronomic view of Yahweh's use of foreign powers in carrying out the divine will concerning Israel. On the one hand, the Assyrians and the Babylonians were viewed as Yahweh's agents of judgment, which was a fulfilment of Yahweh's covenant with Moses (2 Kgs 17.1-18; 25.1-21; Jer 32.26-35; 52.4-27; etc.). On the other hand, the Babylonians were viewed as being divinely judged for their treatment of Israel, a judgment that would ultimately lead to the restoration of Israel (1 Kgs 8.46-50; Jer 25.11-14*; 29.10*; etc.). Like II Isa (44.24–45.13), the Deuteronomic school may have viewed the conquest of Babylon by the Persians and

63. Hill, 'Dating Second Zech'.

their subsequent policy of the restoration of the Jerusalem temple administration as fulfilment of Yahweh's divine plan. That is, Israel had been judged through the Babylonian destruction of Jerusalem and the exile; Babylon had been punished by the Persian conquest; and now Israel will be restored.[64] Such a Deuteronomic view may appear in 1 Kgs 8.46-50:

> If they sin against you..., then you are angry with them, and you give them to an enemy, so that they are carried away captive to the land of the enemy, distant or near. But if they take it to heart in the land to where they have been carried and they repent and they make supplication to you in the land of their captors, saying, 'We have sinned and we have acted perversely and we are evil'; if they return to you with all their mind and with all their heart...and if they pray to you toward their land, which you gave to their fathers, the city which you have chosen, and the house which I have built for your name; then you will hear in heaven your dwelling place their prayer and their supplication, and you will maintain their cause and you will forgive your people who have sinned against you and all their transgressions which they have committed against you; and you will give them compassion in the sight of their captors that they may have compassion on them.

The latter part of this passage can be interpreted as follows: Yahweh will cause their captors (the Persians) to have compassion on the Babylonian exiles, and thus their captors will participate in the divine will to return these exiles to Yehud. Such a view of history would have allowed the Deuteronomists to cooperate with the Persian empire in the restoration of the Jerusalem temple for, from such a theological perspective, their collaboration was not so much with the Persians as it was with Yahweh's divine will.

Although this view of history perhaps allowed Deuteronomic collaboration in the initial stages of the restoration of the Jerusalem temple cult, this same theological position may have led to subsequent conflict. The rebuilding of the Jerusalem temple did not lead to the fulfilment of the expectations of the restoration of Israel as had been

64. The Deuteronomic view of history is generally summarized along the following lines: (1) Israel's disobedience, (2) Yahweh's warning through 'his servants the prophets', (3) Israel's rejection of this prophetic warning, (4) the just, divine punishment for Israel's continued disobedience, and (5) the hope for restoration. E.g. Nicholson, *Preaching*, p. 57; von Rad, 'Deuteronomistic Theology of History'; and Swanson, 'Zechariah 1–8 and the Deuteronomistic Stream of Tradition', p. 9.

proclaimed by various prophets, including II Isaiah, Haggai and Zechariah. In other words, the expectation of the full restoration of Israel was not fulfilled in the Persian-supported restoration of the Jerusalem temple and the province of Yehud; rather, the restoration of the Jerusalem temple simply became part of the Persian strategy of imperial control over Yehud. In fact, not only were these prophetic expectations unmet, but there is some evidence that social conditions in Yehud may have deteriorated between the times of Zerubbabel and Nehemiah, thereby heightening the disparity between prophetic expectations and political realities.[65]

Because of this deterioration, perhaps the Deuteronomists increasingly understood that the full restoration of Israel would not occur within political history, an understanding which may have led to their increasing withdrawal (or even eventual expulsion) from being active participants in the political leadership, including the temple administration. The full restoration of Israel, then, would only occur in the eschatological future, wherein Yahweh would directly initiate the permanent restoration of the true Jerusalem and a new world order (e.g. Zech 14).[66] Thus, the Deuteronomic view of history may have been a two-edged sword. That is, on the one hand, it allowed the Deuteronomic school to collaborate fully in the early stages of the Persian-supported restoration of the Jerusalem temple; on the other hand, it led to their distancing from the Persian-supported temple administration in Jerusalem, in that the restoration of the Jerusalem temple did not bring about what had been anticipated, but rather led to a political administration that remained under Persian control.

This theological tension can be seen to some extent in the three works of Deuteronomic redaction discussed above. DtrH and Jer primarily emphasize Yahweh's use of foreign powers (primarily the Assyrians and the Babylonians) in the just punishment of Israel. Zech emphasizes Yahweh's activity in the (partial) restoration of the Jerusalem temple (I Zech) as a prelude to the final, eschatological restoration (II Zech). Therefore, DtrH and Jer (with I Zech) may represent the time of the early post-exilic collaboration between the Deuteronomists and the Persians, in that they present positively Yahweh's just use of foreign powers. In contrast, II Zech possibly represents the later disillusioned view, which became more

65. See E. Meyers, 'Persian Period and the Judean Restoration'.
66. See further below the section 'Eschatology' in Chapter 8.

eschatological in light of unmet expectations.

This disillusionment with and distancing from the Jerusalem leadership may have affected the fate of the Deuteronomists. The mission of Ezra, who is depicted as bringing with him the 'law of the God of Heaven', might suggest that by 458 BCE the Deuteronomic school had lost favor with the temple administration in Jerusalem and Persian authorities. Although the exact character of Ezra's legal material cannot be ascertained,[67] it most likely was not identical to that of the Deuteronomic school. The description of Ezra, as the one who brings 'the law' with him, itself suggests that this 'law' was to have a new status in Yehud and may thus have been brought into conflict with the establishment of 'law' under previous returns. Hence, Ezra's introduction of 'the law of the God of Heaven' may have been an attempt by the Persian authorities to reassert some control over the Jerusalem political and religious establishment in face of antagonism caused by the increasingly disenfranchised Deuteronomic scribes. This reassertion of Persian control appeared in the form of replacing one legal system (in the Deuteronomic canon) with another (Ezra's law), a strategy not unknown elsewhere in the Persian empire.[68] Ezra's mission, which included social as well as legal reforms, may have thus undermined the political and social support upon which the Deuteronomic school depended, thereby contributing to its demise.

Postscript: The Deuteronomic Canon

I have argued that perhaps the Deuteronomists returned to Jerusalem with a commission from the Persian administration (probably Darius I under Zerubbabel's leadership) to aid in the restoration of the Jerusalem temple by their preservation and transmission of traditional literature. Later, the demise of the Deuteronomists' power may have begun with Ezra's introduction of a different set of authoritative material. Therefore, it is appropriate to consider what the Deuteronomic canon may have included. To this end, it may be helpful to review briefly some of the previous discussions of the early canons

---

67. See Blenkinsopp, 'Interpretation and the Tendency to Sectarianism', pp. 5-6; Hoglund, *Achaemenid Imperial Administration*, pp. 230-31.

68. E.g. Darius's codification of Egyptian laws as reported in the *Demotic Chronicle*.

of prophetic and Deuteronomic literature.[69]

As early as the 1960s,[70] David Noel Freedman proposed that the formation of the 'Primary History' (Gen–Kgs) occurred in the exilic period under the direction of the chief priest Jehozadak. His argument follows the exact logic that Noth used for his exilic dating of the completion of DtrH:

> The terminus ante quem is determined by the next significant historical event, known from other sources, which, so far as we can determine, would have figured in the historical account had the author or editor known of it. For the Primary History, these decisive events would be the fall of Babylon and the consequent return of the exiles. The fact that the Primary History comes to an end before these occurrences indicates that it was compiled and completed before that time.[71]

> I believe that the final sentences of 2 Kings are a statement of the date and place of publication, shortly after the accession of Awil-Marduk, the heir and successor of the great Nebuchadrezzar, as king of Babylonia.[72]

Freedman accepted the Nothian argument, improperly based solely upon a *terminus a quo*, for the exilic completion of DtrH and applied it to his 'Primary History', which included the 'law' (Gen–Deut) and ended with the same verses as DtrH (2 Kgs 25.27-30).

Freedman also posited a supplementary collection of prophetic literature accompanying the 'Primary History'[73] and including 'the bulk of I Isaiah, Jeremiah, Ezekiel, and the major portion of the

69. For a review of scholarship concerning the canonization of prophetic literature, see Blenkinsopp, *Prophecy and Canon*, pp. 9-17; E. Jacob, 'Principe canonique et formation de l'Ancien Testament', in *Congress Volume, Edinburgh 1974* (ed. A. Alonso Schokel *et al.*; VTSup, 28; Leiden: Brill, 1975), pp. 101-22.

70. 'The Law and the Prophets'. See also D.N. Freedman, 'The Formation of the Canon of the Old Testament', in *Religion and Law* (ed. E.B. Firmage, B.G. Weiss and J.W. Welch; Winona Lake, IN: Eisenbrauns, 1990), pp. 315-31; D.N. Freedman, 'The Earliest Bible', *Michigan Quarterly Review* 22 (1983), pp. 167-75. Meyers and Meyers (*Haggai–Zechariah 1–8*, pp. xxix, 16) have followed Freedman's reconstruction of the 'Primary History'.

71. 'The Law and the Prophets', p. 255.

72. 'The Formation of the Canon', pp. 317-18.

73. Once again Freedman's argument concerning the 'Primary History' is similar to other discussions concerning DtrH—that is, since the Latter Prophets are not mentioned in DtrH, they were collected as a supplement to DtrH. On the literature concerning the relationship between DtrH and the Latter Prophets, see Begg, 'A Bible Mystery'.

minor prophets: Amos, Hosea, Micah, Nahum, Zephaniah, Habakkuk and Obadiah'.[74] Once again, he argued for an exilic completion of this prophetic collection:

> The collection of prophetic books...was produced at about the same time (for example, Jeremiah ends with the same chapter with which 2 Kings ends) to provide supporting data and elaborative details concerning the role of the prophets.[75]

Therefore, his 'first bible' consisted of the 'Primary History' (Gen–Kgs) and most of the Latter Prophets (I Isa, Jer, Ezek, Hos–Zeph).

In his recent article, 'The Formation of the Canon of the Old Testament',[76] Freedman elaborated upon his earlier remarks on the expansion of this 'first bible'.[77] He proposed that it was expanded at about 518 BCE in connection with the rededication of the temple. This 'second bible' now included the 'Primary History' (Gen–Kgs), the Prophets (Isa–Mal), the first edition of the Chronicler's work (1–2 Chron, Ezra 1–3) and probably some of the other Writings (Ps, Prov, Ruth, Cant, Eccl)—that is, all of the present books found in the present canon of the Law and the Prophets and some of those found in the present Writings. In line with rabbinic tradition, he argued that this 'second bible' underwent a significant revision under the guidance of Ezra the scribe, thereby producing the 'third bible', which did did not significantly affect the amount of literature within the canon (although Ezra added his memoirs and perhaps at a later time Nehemiah's). Ezra's primary revision was the division of the 'Primary History' into the Law (Gen–Deut) and the Prophets (Isa–Mal).

Freedman's reconstruction of the formation of the canon falls short of the evidence given above. The argument of Noth and many others for the exilic completion of DtrH has been rejected, as well as the argument of Hyatt (assuming Noth on DtrH) and followed by many

---

74. 'The Law and the Prophets', p. 264. In his later article, 'The Formation of the Canon', Freedman expanded his list of prophetic literature included in this collection to include Isa 1–33, Isa 36–39, Jer, Ezek, and the first nine minor prophets (Hos–Zeph) (pp. 318, 324).

75. 'The Formation of the Canon', p. 318.

76. The remaining comments on Freedman's work refer to this article, unless otherwise noted. Freedman's conclusions on the formation of the canon of the Hebrew Bible are outlined on pp. 324-26 of this article.

77. In 'The Law and the Prophets', Freedman concluded with some suggestions concerning the post-exilic expansion of the canon (p. 264).

others for the exilic completion of Jer. The completion of the redaction of DtrH and Jer did not end in the exile, rather the Deuteronomic school was still active well into the post-exilic period. Freedman's reconstruction of the 'first bible' must be rejected because it is built upon his reappropriation of the faulty arguments for the exilic completion of DtrH and Jer to a much later corpus (his 'Primary History' and its prophetic supplement). In fact, the evidence given in Part I would suggest that any 'bible' that contains all of the literature Freedman places in his 'first bible' must have postdated the date he gave for his 'second bible' (518 BCE). Hence, his reconstruction of the formation of the canon of the Hebrew Bible would be much too early.

The most comprehensive discussion of the canonization of prophetic literature is Blenkinsopp's 1977 monograph, *Prophecy and Canon*.[78] As one part of this discussion, he argued that the (almost complete) lack of reference to the Latter Prophets in DtrH is best explained as the avoidance of repetition, since the Deuteronomic school collected a supplementary prophetic collection.[79] Since he accepted Noth's exilic date for the final redaction of DtrH,[80] he also dated this supplementary collection to the exilic period.[81] He later[82] suggested that, on the basis of Deuteronomic superscriptions and/or redactional material, this 'exilic-Deuteronomic collection' included, at least, I Isa, Jer, Hos, Amos, Mic and Zeph.[83] Like Freedman, Blenkinsopp assumed the validity of Noth's argument for the exilic completion of DtrH and Hyatt's argument for the exilic completion of Jer and so his reconstruction must also be rejected as too early.

78. Blenkinsopp (*Prophecy and Canon*, pp. 99-100) briefly reviewed Freedman's hypothesis of the exilic 'Primary History' and its supplementary prophetic canon and also concluded that Freedman's exilic date for the bulk of the Latter Prophets was too early.

79. *Prophecy and Canon*, pp. 98, 102. See also Blenkinsopp, *History of Prophecy in Israel*, p. 191.

80. Blenkinsopp, *Prophecy and Canon*, pp. 40, 46, 162 n. 52.

81. *Prophecy and Canon*, p. 98. See also Blenkinsopp, *History of Prophecy*, p. 191.

82. *History of Prophecy*, p. 191.

83. Gottwald (*The Hebrew Bible: A Socio-Literary Introduction* [Philadelphia: Fortress Press, 1985], p. 465) accepted Blenkinsopp's argument for an exilic prophetic corpus collected by the Deuteronomic school and argued that this prophetc collection may have included I Isa, Jer, Hos, Amos, Mic, Nah, Hab and Zeph.

Nevertheless, Blenkinsopp's suggested 'exilic-Deuteronomic collection' may reflect a first stage in the Deuteronomic canon. In other words, rather than reconstructing the final Deuteronomic canon as he intended, his argument may reflect the *exilic* Deuteronomic canon, which was the precursor to the revised, final, *post-exilic* Deuteronomic canon. Therefore, his reconstructed exilic Deuteronomic canon is assumed below to be included in the post-exilic Deuteronomic canon.

Blenkinsopp's reconstruction can be supported by further discussion of the inclusion of several books (I Isa, Jer, Hos, Amos, Mic, Zeph) in the post-exilic Deuteronomic canon. (Before proceeding further, I must admit to the limitation of the post-exilic Deuteronomic canon which I strive to reconstruct below. Since the primary purpose of this work concerns II Zech, and since II Zech appears to be the latest example of extant Deuteronomic prose, the post-exilic Deuteronomic canon as reconstructed below is really my understanding of the Deuteronomic canon at the time II Zech was produced. Hence, it is possible that some of the works that I have excluded [especially Hag] were part of a later [post-II Zech] Deuteronomic canon.)

First, the inclusion of all the extant literary works which contain Deuteronomic redactional activity must be considered. Arguments have been made above for the Deuteronomic redaction of DtrH, Jer, and Zech; however, there are also indications of possible Deuteronomic redaction in other prophetic books.[84] Most notable in this regard are the arguments for a Deuteronomic redaction of the three minor prophets of the eighth century—that is, Amos, Hos and Mic. The first to propose the Deuteronomic redaction of Amos was Werner Schmidt.[85] He began by discerning intrusions within grammatical structures and grammatical variations (e.g. change in the person of the

---

84. On Isa, see Blenkinsopp, *History of Prophecy in Israel*, p. 210; Blenkinsopp, *Prophecy and Canon*, pp. 104, 178 n. 8. In his brief remarks, Blenkinsopp stated that the placement of Isa 36.1–39.8, which is copied from 2 Kgs 18.13–20.19, as a transitional section from Isa 1–35 to Isa 40–55 suggests Deuteronomic redaction. On Ezek, see Herrmann, *Prophetischen Heilserwartungen*, pp. 241-91. See also Zimmerli, *Ezekiel*, II, pp. xiv-xv.

85. Schmidt, 'Deuteronomische Redaktion des Amosbuches'. See also Amsler, 'Amos, prophète de la onzième heure'; Clements, *Prophecy and Tradition*, pp. 43-44; B. Gosse, 'Le recueil d'oracles contre des nations du livre d'Amos et l'histoire deuteronomique', *VT* 38 (1988), pp. 22-40; Kellermann, 'Der Amosschluss als Stimme deuteronomistischer Heilshoffnung'; Wolff, *Joel and Amos*, pp. 112-13.

speaker) and then studied some of the stylistic variations between the redactional additions and the original prophetic oracles. He noted that these variations often follow a distinction between Amos material and Deuteronomic phraseology (e.g. 3.1: 'his servants the prophets') and themes (e.g. election theology). He then concluded that the super-scriptions (1.1; 3.1) and exegetical additions (1.9-12; 2.4-5, 10-12; 3.7; 5.25-26) are Deuteronomic because they are similar and contain Deuteronomic phrases and/or themes. Hans Walter Wolff has similarly argued for Deuteronomic redactions of Hos and Mic.[86] Hence, the Deuteronomic canon would have included the following works which evince possible Deuteronomic redaction: DtrH, Jer, Zech, Amos, Hos and Mic.

Another way to ascertain the books in the Deuteronomic canon is to look at the reinterpretation of various prophetic books within Deuteronomic redactional material in Jer and II Zech. That is, what prophetic books were considered authoritative so that they influenced Deuteronomic thought in subsequent redactions? In Jer, there is evidence of the influence of II Isa[87] and Mic.[88] II Zech clearly reinter-prets the books which evince Deuteronomic redaction (DtrH, Jer, Amos),[89] but II Zech also shows the strong influence of Isa (I–III Isa) and Ezek.[90] Therefore, the Deuteronomic canon of the Achaemenid period would have included the prophetic books with Deuteronomic redactions and some form of Isa and Ezek.

---

86. H.W. Wolff, *Hosea* (trans. G. Stansell; Hermeneia; Philadelphia: Fortress Press, 1974), pp. xxix-xxxii. See also Clements, *Prophecy and Tradition*, pp. 43-44; Wolff, *Joel and Amos*, pp. 112-13. On the relationship of Hos and Deut, see Weinfeld, *Deuteronomy and the Deuteronomic School*, pp. 366-70.

H.W. Wolff, *Micha* (BKAT, 14.4; Neukirchen–Vlyun: Neukirchener Verlag, 1982), pp. xxxvi-xxxvii.

87. See Hyatt, 'Deuteronomic Edition of Jeremiah', p. 266; Janzen, *Studies in the Text of Jeremiah*, pp. 60-61.

88. In Jer 26.18*, Mic 3.12 is quoted authoritatively in defense of Jeremiah's message of woe. See Carroll, *Jeremiah*, pp. 518-19; W.L. Holladay, *Jeremiah*, (2 vols.; Hermeneia; Philadelphia: Fortress Press, 1986, 1989), II, pp. 107-108; Hyatt, *Jeremiah*, p. 1008.

89. See above Chapter 2 for the evidence of the influence of DtrH and Jer on II Zech. The influence of Amos is suggested in the quote of Am 7.14 in Zech 13.5.

90. Delcor, 'Sources'; Lamarche, *Zacharie IX–XIV*, pp. 124-47; Mason, 'Some Examples'; Mason, 'Use of Earlier Biblical Material in Zechariah 9–14'; Mendecki, 'Deuterojesajanischer und Ezechielischer Einfluss auf Sach 10.8-10'.

The Deuteronomic canon in the post-exilic period would have thus included the following works in some form: DtrH, Isa, Jer, Ezek, Hos, Amos, Mic, Zech. All of these works show some evidence of Deuteronomic redaction and/or they influenced the Deuteronomic prose in Jer and/or II Zech. The other pre-exilic books (Obad, Nah, Hab, Zeph) were probably also included in the Deuteronomic prophetic canon. As for the remaining prophetic books (Joel, Jonah, Hag, Mal), their relative lateness makes it difficult to include them in the Deuteronomic canon, epecially since they do not evince Deuteronomic redaction or any significant influence upon the Deuteronomic prose in Jer and II Zech. However, there is a reason for the exclusion of Jonah—that is, Jonah satirizes the Deuteronomic understanding of prophecy; therefore, it may have incurred Deuteronomic opposition. The remaining three post-exilic prophetic books (Joel, Hag,[91] Mal) may or may not have been included in the Deuteronomic canon.[92]

The Deuteronomists had a distinctive theological perspective to this prophetic canon. The phrase 'my/his servants the prophets' (2 Kgs 9.7; 17.13, 23; 21.10; 24.2; Jer 7.25*; 25.4*; 26.5*; 29.19*; 35.15*; 44.4*; see also Zech 1.6) suggests that 'the prophets were being understood as a well-defined collectivity'.[93] Recent studies in the canonical shape of the prophetic books[94] help reconstruct what this Deuteronomic perspective may have been. The prophetic books of the Hebrew Bible contain the following theological progression: righteous, divine judgment leads to a purification of Yahweh's people and ultimately to the full restoration of the salvific relationship between

91. The thesis of C. Meyers and E. Meyers concerning the composite unity of Hag–Zech 1–8 would at first seem to suggest that Hag should be included in the Deuteronomic canon (*Haggai–Zechariah 1–8*, pp. xliv-xlviii). However, the lack of any influence of Hag in II Zech suggests that the redactor of II Zech did not have access to Hag, and therefore that Hag and I Zech had probably separated by the time of II Zech into separate works on separate manuscripts. If this is the case, then Hag may not have been the Deuteronomic canon at the time of II Zech.

92. This exclusion does not necessarily represent Deuteronomic opposition to these books, but simply reflects that these books may have not yet become authoritative in the Deuteronomic school at the time of II Zech.

93. Blenkinsopp, *Prophecy and Canon*, p. 101.

94. B.S. Childs, 'The Canonical Shape of the Prophetic Literature', *Int* 32 (1978), pp. 46-55; R.E. Clements, 'Patterns in the Prophetic Canon', in *Canon and Authority* (ed. G.W. Coates and B.O. Long; Philadelphia: Fortress Press, 1977), pp. 42-55.

Yahweh and his people. This viewpoint is certainly found in Deuteronomic literature; therefore, the prophetic canon of the Deuteronomists,
as reconstructed above, presents the Deuteronomic understanding of
history.

Chapter 8

THEOLOGICAL THEMES IN II ZECH
AND DEUTERONOMIC LITERATURE

If the Deuteronomic school continued into the post-exilic period, what
then were some of its theological positions within this historical
setting? The previous chapter contains some preliminary remarks
concerning the Deuteronomic theology in relationship to international
politics—that is, DtrH and Jer emphasize the Deuteronomic school's
understanding of Yahweh's use of foreign powers (explicitly, the
Assyrians and Babylonians, and implicitly the Persians) to execute
divine judgment upon a disobedient Israel, which will lead to the
divine restoration of Israel. This understanding of political history
allowed the Deuteronomists to collaborate with the Persian-supported
restoration of the Jerusalem establishment, for they would have felt
that they were supporting Yahweh's plan for restoration. However,
their expectations for the full restoration of Israel (including Davidic
monarchy and autonomous political control) were not fulfilled, and
the Deuteronomists became more eschatological in their outlook, as
represented in II Zech.

These suggestions, especially emphasizing Deuteronomic theology at
the time of the redaction of II Zech, will be expanded in this chapter.
Although the emphasis below is upon the Deuteronomic theology
during the time of II Zech, I will nevertheless present evidence that
suggests that the Deuteronomic theology in II Zech has its roots in
Deuteronomic theology as reflected in some passages in DtrH and Jer.
To do this, three themes will be considered: eschatology, false prophecy, and the end of prophecy. No attempt is made to distinguish
pre-exilic, exilic, and post-exilic strands of the Deuteronomic tradition
within DtrH or Jer. Rather, the comparisons here are based upon
DtrH and Jer in their present canonical form (MT), assuming that these
canonical forms closely reflect the shape of these texts at the time of

II Zech. This chapter thus only concerns Deuteronomic theology on these three specific themes with primary emphasis on the time of II Zech, when the Deuteronomic school perhaps became increasingly distanced from the Jerusalem authorities.

Eschatology

The work of Gerhard von Rad has been influential in the study of Deut,[1] yet his discussion of the theme of eschatology has not received enough attention.[2]

> As a literary work...*Deuteronomy* certainly dates from a time subsequent to the Settlement, and it is therefore only by a singular kind of fiction that it takes Israel back to Horeb once again: Israel has in fact long been dwelling in the promised land, and we must therefore see a clear eschatological thread running through the whole work. All the benefits of which it speaks, and in particular the state of 'rest' which is the sum of them all, are set before the assembly once again as a promise made to those who decide for Yahweh.[3]

Von Rad's understanding of eschatology in Deut is taken seriously in the following discussions of these passages: Deut 4.29-31; 28; 30.1-14; Jer 30–31; and Zech 10–14.

Deut 4.29-31[4]

Following the description of Yahweh's judgment of scattering disobedient Israel among the peoples (Deut 4.25-28), Yahweh's future promise is given—'When you are in tribulation and all of these things

---

1. *Deuteronomy* (OTL; Philadelphia: Westminster Press, 1966); *Studies in Deuteronomy* (SBT, 9; London: SCM Press, 1953).

2. Discussions concerning eschatology in Josh–2 Kgs are even more scarce. In fact, Van Seters (*In Search of History*, p. 8) has gone so far as to conclude that 'there is no eschatology in the Israelite histories'.

3. G. von Rad, 'Promised Land and Yahweh's Land in the Hexateuch', in *The Problem of the Hexateuch and Other Essays* (trans. E.W.T. Dicken; New York: McGraw–Hill, 1966), p. 92.

4. The following works were consulted: P.C. Craigie, *The Book of Deuteronomy* (NICOT; Grand Rapids, MI: Eerdmans, 1976), pp. 138-41; Driver, *Deuteronomy*, pp. 73-75; A.D.H. Mayes, *Deuteronomy* (NCB; Grand Rapids, MI: Eerdemans, 1979), pp. 156-57; A. Phillips, *Deuteronomy* (CBC; Cambridge: Cambridge University Press, 1973), pp. 35-37; von Rad, *Deuteronomy*, pp. 46-52; Wolff, 'Kerygma', pp. 96-97.

come upon you *at the end of days,*[5] you will return to Yahweh and you will obey his voice' (Deut 4.30). This passage follows the standard eschatological progression—that is, tribulation of the people of God followed by their deliverance;[6] therefore, Deut 4.29-31 is considered to be eschatological in its outlook.

Deut 28.1-46[7]

This section has the form of conditional blessings and curses within the covenant between Yahweh and Israel, and therefore does not explicitly contain an eschatology. However, the vision of the blessings may have influenced later visions of the eschaton or may reflect indirectly the Deuteronomic vision of the eschaton: Israel will be set 'high above all the nations of the earth' (28.1). The people, their livestock and their crops will be fruitful (28.2-6, 11-12). The nations will flee in fright from before Israel (28.7-10).

Deut 30.1-14[8]

The influence of the vision behind the blessings in Deut 28.1-14 upon Deuteronomic eschatology is explicit in Deut 30.1-3.[9]

> And after all these things have come upon you, the blessings and the curses,...then Yahweh your God will restore your fortunes and show mercy on you and he will return and gather you from all the peoples where Yahweh your God had scattered you there.

In Deut 30.1-14, Israel's returning to Yahweh comes about through divine intervention. That is, after the tribulation which was called for by the covenant, Yahweh will cause Israel to return to God permanently:

---

5.   See §19 above.

6.   Wolff, 'Kerygma', pp. 98-99. *Contra* Mayes, *Deuteronomy*, p. 157: 'There is no thought here of the establishment of God's universal dominion'.

7.   The following works were consulted: Craigie, *Deuteronomy*, pp. 334-53; Driver, *Deuteronomy*, pp. 302-19; Mayes, *Deuteronomy*, pp. 348-58; Phillips, *Deuteronomy*, pp. 183-93; von Rad, *Deuteronomy*, pp. 170-75. On the relationship between Deut 28 and II Zech, see †4 and ‡5 above.

8.   The following works were consulted: Bruggemann, 'Kerygma', pp. 393-94 Craigie, *Deuteronomy*, pp. 361-73; Driver, *Deuteronomy*, pp. 328-32; Mayes, *Deuteronomy*, pp. 367-70; Mendecki, 'Dtn 30,3-4—nachexilisch?'; Phillips, *Deuteronomy*, pp. 194-202; von Rad, *Deuteronomy*, pp. 182-84; Wolff, 'Kerygma', pp. 93-96.

9.   Wolff, 'Kerygma', p. 94.

And Yahweh your God will circumcise your heart and your children's heart so that you will love Yahweh your God with all your heart and all your soul, so that you might live (30.6).

The external covenant has been fulfilled by the required punishment. In its place, Yahweh 'circumcises' divine will into every Israelite's heart, thereby overcoming the possibility of later human transgression of an outward covenant.

For this [new] commandment which I have commanded you today, it is not too difficult for you and it is not too distant...For the word is exceedingly near to you, in your mouth and in your heart, so that you can do it (30.11, 14).

Because of this inner circumcision which makes obedience to Yahweh much easier, the people of God will prosper greatly—'and [Yahweh your God] will make you prosper and become numerous more than your fathers' (30.5).[10]

Jer 30–31[11]
Jer 30–31 contains the fullest expression of the themes of restoration within Jer. Three eschatological sayings, which begin with the

---

10. Brueggemann, 'Kerygma', p. 393.

11. The following commentators assigned Jer 30–31 to the Deuteronomic redactor of Jer: J.M. Bracke, 'The Coherence and Theology of Jeremiah 30–31' (PhD dissertation, Union Theological Seminary in Virginia, 1983), p. 20; Carroll, *From Chaos to Covenant*, pp. 198-225; Carroll, *Jeremiah*, pp. 568-618; Nicholson, *Jeremiah 26–52*, pp. 49-73; Nicholson, *Preaching*, pp. 82-84; C. Westermann, *Prophetische Heilsworte im Alten Testament* (Göttingen: Vandenhoeck & Ruprecht, 1987), pp. 106-15, 178.

Hyatt assigned Jer 30–31 to a post-Deuteronomic editor ('Deuteronomic Edition of Jeremiah', p. 266. See also Thiel, *Redaktion von Jeremia 26–45*, pp. 20-28, 37).

Weinfeld (*Deuteronomy and the Deuteronomic School*) included the following phrases in Jer 30–31 in his list of Deuteronomic phraseology: 'to scatter among the nations', Jer 30.11 (p. 347); 'to be a people to him', Jer 30.22, 25; 31.32 (p. 327).

On the theme of eschatology in Jer 30–31, the following works were also consulted: Bright, *Jeremiah*, pp. 269-87; Herrmann, *Prophetischen Heilserwartungen*, pp. 179-85, 215-22; Holladay, *Jeremiah*, II, pp. 148-201; Hyatt, *Jeremiah*, pp. 1022-41.

On the relationship between Jer 30–31 and II Zech, see ††28–35 above.

formula 'Behold the days are coming' (31.27-30, 31-34, 38-40), will be discussed here.[12]

In Jer 31.27-30, the restoration of the 'house of Israel and the house of Judah' is proclaimed. In the last days, the means by which the people are judged will change from the present means of judging an entire people/nation on the basis of their collective obedience or disobedience to the future means of judging each person according to each one's sin (31.30).

Jer 31.31-34 expresses the 'new covenant' (31.31):

> I will put my law within them, and on their hearts I will write it. And I will be their God and they will be my people. And no longer will each teach his neighbor and each his brother, saying, 'Know Yahweh', for all of them will know me, from the least to the greatest (31.33-34).

As in Jer 31.27-30, all will be responsible for their own obedience or disobedience. This 'new covenant' reflects the circumcision of the heart in Deut 30.6.[13]

In Jer 31.38-40, the rebuilding of Jerusalem is given in its geographical dimensions (see §§6, 15, †33 above). The eschatological nature of this rebuilding of Jerusalem is suggested by the permanence associated with the rebuilt Jerusalem: 'It shall not be uprooted and it shall not be overthrown again for ever' (31.40).

These three eschatological sections of Jer 30–31 together present the following scenario: after the judgment of Israel and Judah, Yahweh's new covenant with the people will be written on their hearts so that each person will be accountable for his or her own sin and will be more capable of the required obedience. Since obedience will be internalized and no collective judgment will befall the people, the rebuilt Jerusalem will stand forever.

Zech 10–14[14]

The eschatological character of Zech 10–14 (especially 12–14) is widely known; the following remarks, therefore, simply note the close connections to the previous Deuteronomic passages concerning

---

12. Hyatt (*Jeremiah*, p. 1038) also stated that this phrase is eschatological. See †28 above.

13. Nicholson, *Preaching*, pp. 82-84; Nicholson, *Jeremiah 26–52*, p. 71.

14. For a fuller discussion of the Deuteronomic influences in this passage, see above Chapter 5.

eschatology. Following Yahweh's punishment of disobedient Israel, Yahweh will cleanse the people (12.10–13.9) and restore them to their land (10.6-12; 14.1-21). Those peoples who oppose the restored Jerusalem will be severely punished and will flee in great fear (11.1-3; 12.1-9; 14.12-15). A new relationship will exist between Yahweh and the peoples of the earth, a relationship wherein significant changes will occur: Even the nations will receive Yahweh's blessing on the people (14.16-19). There will no longer be any distinction among Yahweh's peoples, thereby abolishing the need for prophets (13.2-6) and priests (14.21). Also, all vessels will become sacred (14.20-21). This new relationship will exist forever (14.6-7).

Summary: Eschatology in Deuteronomic Thought
The trials and tribulations of the exilic and post-exilic periods were considered just punishment according to the Mosaic covenant between Yahweh and Israel. However, the Deuteronomic school understood that a new relationship of the people with their God would be initiated by Yahweh. This new relationship would occur with Yahweh's infusion of divine will into everyone's heart (Deut 30.6; Jer 31.33-34). Such intimate knowledge of Yahweh's will and the change of the human 'heart' will establish human obedience to Yahweh's will (Deut 30.11, 14), thereby allowing for permanence. Because of this new relationship, the institutional forms of the old covenant (priesthood in Zech 14.21; prophecy in Zech 13.2-6) will no longer be necessary because each person will intimately and directly know Yahweh's will. With such divinely-facilitated obedience to Yahweh, the people of God will be greatly blessed (Deut 28.1-14; 30.1-3, 5, 9; Zech 10–14).[15]

15. In *Dawn of Apocalyptic*, Hanson did not consider the possible influence of Deuteronomic thought. However, the above discussion shows that, at least by the post-exilic period, Deuteronomic theology included elements which clearly approximate 'apocalyptic eschatology', even according to Hanson's own definition (pp. 11-12). Concerning his definitions of 'prophetic eschatology' and 'apocalyptic eschatology', Hanson said (p. 12) that these definitions 'attempt to specify the essential difference between prophetic and apocalyptic eschatology: the prophets, affirming the historical realm as a suitable context for divine activity, understood it as their task to translate the vision of divine activity from the cosmic level to the level of the politico-historical realm of everyday life. The visionaries, disillusioned with the historical realm, disclosed their vision in a manner of growing indifference to and independence from the contingencies of the politico-historical realm, thereby leaving the language increasingly in the idiom of the cosmic realm of the divine warrior and his council'.

False Prophecy

In his influential monograph, *Prophetic Conflict*,[16] Crenshaw reviewed the various attempts to identify objective criteria by which the people of ancient Israel could have recognized the authority of those claiming to be prophets. These attempts included 'message-centered criteria', 'criteria focusing upon the man', and 'chronological criteria'.[17] He concluded that none of these criteria was sufficiently valid for any prophet's contemporary audience to distinguish true from false prophecy; therefore, the ancient Israelites, including even the prophets themselves, had no way of objectively distinguishing a true prophet from a false one.[18]

Why is it that no valid criterion existed for distinguishing true from false prophecy? Crenshaw's answer involved attention to both sides of the prophetic process, the human and the divine. He discussed the human limitations of the prophet, how these limitations affect the prophet's message and mission,[19] and how they are heightened by several factors: the prophet's desire for success, the king's control over the cultic institutions including some prophets, the influence of popular theology, the power of the tradition of the election of Israel, and the emergence of individualism in light of the breakdown of tribal ties. Conflict between prophets may have been caused by differences in the influence of these factors upon their messages. Concerning the divine side of prophecy, he discussed the divine responsibility in the conflict between prophets.[20] After noting that Yahweh was sometimes understood as demonic within the strict monotheism of ancient Israelite religion, he stated that 'false' prophecy should be understood within Yahweh's providence—that is, Yahweh is also responsible for the messages of falsehood that led Israel astray. Thus, there would have been no general criterion for true prophecy because of the

Certainly, the Deuteronomic view of Yahweh initiating the eschaton fits Hanson's understanding of 'apocalyptic eschatology' better than 'prophetic eschatology'. Therefore, Hanson's reconstruction of the emergence of apocalyptic eschatology needs to be revised.

16. *Prophetic Conflict* (BZAW, 124; Berlin: de Gruyter, 1971).
17. *Prophetic Conflict*, pp. 49-61.
18. *Prophetic Conflict*, p. 61.
19. *Prophetic Conflict*, pp. 62-76.
20. *Prophetic Conflict*, pp. 77-90.

theological underpinnings of Hebrew prophecy, which included human culpability and the aspect of the demonic in the divine.[21]

Considering the social forces involved in the prophetic process provides another answer to the question of why there was no valid criterion for true prophecy.[22] Based upon comparative studies, Overholt developed a model for the prophetic process that includes three subjective criteria by which a prophet's audience can determine the truth value of the prophetic message:[23] (1) the basic continuity of the message with the broad cultural tradition of the prophet and people, (2) the relationship between the message and the historical situation in which the prophet and people find themselves, and (3) the adequacy, in the eyes of the prophet's audience, in the prophetic response to the problems presented within the people's present historical situation. Later,[24] Overholt was more explicit in how his model related to the problem of prophetic conflict. He suggested that, according to Amos 2.11-12 and 7.12-13, opposition to Amos 'could effectively deter the operation of prophecy by denying a prophet the opportunity to speak and/or refusing to acknowledge his words as authoritative if he did'.[25] He thus claimed that a 'false' prophet is one who receives negative feedback on the basis of the three subjective criteria in his model; a 'true' prophet is one who receives positive feedback. Of course, differing social groups within any society may perceive a prophet differently according to their subjective viewpoints; therefore, social aspects combine with theological concerns to create an environment in which no widely-accepted objective criterion for true prophecy existed.

Despite all these theories, it is also possible that the quest for a systematic set of criteria for validation is a modern concern, which was not operative for the tradents who preserved prophetic literature.[26] Such tradents 'knew' with the clarity of hindsight who were the true

21. *Prophetic Conflict*, pp. 110-11.

22. Although Crenshaw's emphasis was theological, his analysis included social forces, such as the influence of 'popular theology' (*Prophetic Conflict*, pp. 69-71).

23. 'The Ghost Dance of 1890', pp. 39-40, 44-46.

24. T.W. Overholt, 'Commanding the Prophets: Amos and the Problem of Prophetic Authority', *CBQ* 41 (1979), pp. 517-32.

25. 'Commanding the Prophets', p. 518.

26. This position is argued forcefully by Carroll concerning the Jeremianic material. See *From Chaos to Covenant*, pp. 158-59, 180-97; *Jeremiah*, pp. 547-50.

prophets and who were the false prophets. Canonical prophets were thus by definition true, and any prophet (or any other figure, for that matter) who disagreed with or opposed a true (i.e. canonical) prophet was false. Although there are problems concerning fulfilment even for some canonical prophets,[27] the truth of a prophet was based upon the relationship of his prophetic message to how the tradents perceived its fulfilment in history.

Although canonical prophets are assumed to be true, features of true or false prophecy, which appear in narratives concerning prophetic conflict, may reflect the concept of prophecy held by the tradents. These tradents are probably to be seen as belonging to the Deuteronomic school, for several reasons. First, in the words of Sanders, 'Jeremiah 28, with Deuteronomy 13 and 18, is the *locus classicus* of the problem [concerning true and false prophecy]';[28] therefore, the *locus classicus* is within Deuteronomic literature. Secondly, the only legal material in the Hebrew Bible concerning the problem of true and false prophecy occurs in Deut (13; 18). Thirdly, as seen above (§5), the use of שקר in the context of prophecy occurs primarily in Deuteronomic literature. Some of the key Deuteronomic passages concerning this theme—that is, Deut 13.2-6; 18.9-22; 1 Kgs 13; Jer 27–29; and Zech 10.2; 13.2-6—will be considered below in order to understand the Deuteronomic view of prophecy as expressed in the criteria of true and false prophecy.

Deut 13.2-6[29]

This passage gives two criteria by which a prophet is to be judged as a true prophet, who speaks Yahweh's word, or a false prophet, who is sent by Yahweh to test the people. The first criterion concerns fulfilment/non-fulfilment with the implication that miracle-working

---

27. E.g. Isa 44.24–45.13, wherein Cyrus is proclaimed the 'shepherd' who will rebuild Jerusalem; Jer 4.5-31, wherein a 'foe from the north' is prophesied. Such problems of 'dissonance' are the basis of R. Carroll's study, *When Prophecy Failed* (London: SCM Press, 1979). See also Crenshaw, *Prophetic Conflict*, pp. 49-52.

28. J.A. Sanders, 'Hermeneutics in True and False Prophecy', in *Canon and Authority* (ed. Coates and Long), p. 22.

29. The following works were consulted: Craigie, *Deuteronomy*, pp. 220-24; Driver, *Deuteronomy*, pp. 150-52; Mayes, *Deuteronomy*, pp. 232-35; Phillips, *Deuteronomy*, pp. 92-96; von Rad, *Deuteronomy*, pp. 95-98. On the relationship between Deut 13.2-12 and II Zech, see ††1–3 above.

may, in some instances, suggest true prophetic powers: 'If a prophet...
gives you a sign or wonder, and the sign or wonder comes to pass...'
(13.2-3). However, even if a prophet meets this criterion, he or she
must also face a message-centered criterion that requires strict
Yahwistic monotheism (13.3-4). Any prophet judged false by this
criterion must be put to death (13.6).

Deut 18.9-22[30]

In Deut 18.9-14, Yahweh forbids certain 'abominable practices' of the
non-Israelites who live in the land:

> No one who passes his son or his daughter through fire, no diviner, no
> soothsayer, no augur, no sorcerer, no charmer, no medium, and no
> necromancer shall be found among you (18.10-11).

Yahweh proclaims that a 'prophet like Moses' will appear (18.15-19)
and that false prophets (presumably including those intermediaries
listed in 18.10-11) will be punished with death (18.20). But, how is one
to tell a true from a false prophet? The obvious criterion of the falsehood of non-Yahwistic prophets is given first (18.20, 22), but Yahweh
then gives a way to determine the validity of Yahwistic prophets:

> If a prophet speaks in the name of Yahweh and the word does not come
> to pass...that word was that which Yahweh did not speak (18.22).

Here, the criterion of fulfilment/non-fulfilment is given its greatest
endorsement, for it comes in Yahweh's word through Moses.

1 Kgs 13[31]

This passage has two main sections. The first (13.1-10) concerns the
Bethel cult with the man of God as the protagonist and Jeroboam as

---

30. The following works were consulted: Craigie, *Deuteronomy*, pp. 259-64;
Driver, *Deuteronomy*, pp. 221-30; Mayes, *Deuteronomy*, pp. 279-83; Phillips,
Deuteronomy, pp. 123-26; von Rad, *Deuteronomy*, pp. 121-25.

31. The following works were consulted: P.R. Ackroyd, 'A Judgment Narrative
between Kings and Chronicles? An Approach to Amos 7:9-17', in *Canon and
Authority* (ed. Coates and Long), pp. 71-87; A.G. Auld, *I & II Kings* (Philadelphia:
Westminster Press, 1986), pp. 88-96; Crenshaw, *Prophetic Conflict*, pp. 39-49;
de Vries, *1 Kings*, pp. 164-74; S.J. de Vries, *Prophet against Prophet* (Grand
Rapids, MI: Eerdmans, 1978), pp. 59-61; T.B. Dozeman, 'The Way of the Man of
God from Judah: True and False Prophecy in the Pre-Deuteronomic Legend of
1 Kings 13', *CBQ* 44 (1982), pp. 379-93; Gray, *I & II Kings*, pp. 324-32;

the antagonist; the second (13.11-32) deals with prophetic conflict.[32] Hearing of the man of God's actions, an old prophet of the Bethel cult visits the man of God and lies to him in order to deceive him into disobedience against Yahweh. Yahweh then speaks through the old prophet to warn the man of God; nevertheless, the man of God disobeys. Later, the man of God is killed by a lion for his disobedience. The old prophet recovers the corpse of the man of God and buries him in his own grave as a gesture of respect, because he believed that Yahweh's word spoken by the man of God against the Bethel altar would come true (13.32).

This narrative features two criteria for determining the truth of prophecy. The first concerns moral behavior. The man of God was commanded neither to eat nor to drink (13.9), but because of the lie of the old prophet he ate and drank in disobedience and so he was punished with death. The second concerns fulfilment and is evident in two different places in the narrative. The first is in the relationship of Yahweh's words through the old prophet and the fate of the man of God. Although the old prophet lied to get the man of God to eat and drink, Yahweh warned the man of God through the old prophet that he should not eat nor drink lest he die and not be buried in the tomb of his fathers (13.20-22). However, the man of God disobeyed and faced his punishment of death and being buried in Bethel. Hence,

W.E. Lemke, 'Way of Obedience: I Kings 13 and the Structure of the Deuteronomistic History', in *Magnalia Dei* (ed. F.M. Cross; Garden City, NY: Doubleday, 1976), pp. 301-26; Long, *I Kings*, pp. 143-52; J.A. Montgomery, *The Book of Kings* (ICC; Edinburgh: T. &. T. Clark, 1951), pp. 259-65; Nelson, *First and Second Kings*, pp. 82-90; J. Robinson, *The First Book of Kings* (CBC; Cambridge: Cambridge University Press, 1972), pp. 157-64; Rofé, 'Classes in the Prophetical Stories'; U. Simon, '1 Kings 13: A Prophetic Sign—Denial and Persistence', *HUCA* 47 (1976), pp. 81-117; D.W. Van Winkle, '1 Kings XIII: True and False Prophecy', *VT* 39 (1989), pp. 31-43; Würthwein, *1 Könige 1-16*, pp. 166-72; E. Würthwein, 'Die Erzählung vom Gottesmann aus Juda in Bethel. Zur Komposition von 1 Kön 13', in *Wort und Geschichte* (ed. H. Gese and H.P. Rüger; AOAT, 18; Neukirchen–Vluyn: Neukirchener Verlag, 1973), pp. 181-89. On the possible relationship of 'the man of God' to Amos, see Ackroyd, 'A Judgment Narrative between Kings and Chronicles?'; Crenshaw, *Prophetic Conflict*, pp. 41-42; Lemke, 'Way of Obedience', pp. 315-16.

32. See the literary structure of this passage as discussed by Lemke, 'Way of Obedience', pp. 305-306. Also, Lemke discussed the 'integral relationship' between 1 Kgs 13 and the theology of DtrH ('Way of Obedience', pp. 307-12).

Yahweh's word spoken through the old prophet came true. The second case of the fulfilment criterion is suggested in the old prophet's respectful words for the dead man of God: 'For the word which he proclaimed in the word of Yahweh against the altar of Bethel will surely come to pass' (13.32).

Unlike other narratives concerning prophetic conflict, here we have conflict between two prophets who are both judged as false. The man of God is judged false on the basis of his disobedience to Yahweh's command not to eat or drink; the old prophet, on the basis of his deceitful lies and his relationship to the Bethel cult. This narrative thereby shows how Yahweh can use even false prophets to proclaim a message, for the man of God spoke truth concerning the Bethel cult and later Yahweh spoke to the man of God through the old prophet.

Jer 14.11-16[33]

Yahweh commands Jeremiah not to pray for the welfare of Judah, because there is no room for intercession—that is, destruction is coming. Jeremiah tells Yahweh that the prophets are proclaiming that there will be no destruction, only peace:

> Ah, my Lord Yahweh, behold, the prophets are saying to them, 'You shall not see the sword, and famine shall not come to you, for I will give peace and faithfulness to you in this place' (Jer 14.13*).

Yahweh responds,

> The prophets are prophesying lies in my name...They are speaking to you a vision of lies and worthless divination and the deceit of their own minds (Jer 14.14*).

---

33. Although some of the poetic material in Jer 14.1–15.4* is understood as original to the prophet Jeremiah, the following commentators assigned the prose sections (14.11-12; 15.1-4) and the overall final form to the Deuteronomic redactor of Jer: Carroll, *From Chaos to Covenant*, pp. 84, 138, 162; Carroll, *Jeremiah*, pp. 306-21; Nicholson, *Jeremiah 1–25*, pp. 128-35; Nicholson, *Preaching*, pp. 100-101; Thiel, *Redaktion von Jeremia 1–25*, pp. 177-94. On the theme of false prophecy in Jer 14.11-16*, the following works were also consulted: Bright, *Jeremiah*, pp. 97-104; Carroll, *From Chaos to Covenant*, pp. 162-64; Carroll, *Jeremiah*, pp. 311-15; Holladay, *Jeremiah*, I, pp. 418-44; Hyatt, *Jeremiah*, pp. 932-34; McKane, *Jeremiah*, I, pp. 324-28; I. Meyer, *Jeremia und die falschen Propheten* (Göttingen: Vandenhoeck & Ruprecht, 1977), pp. 47-65; T.W. Overholt, *The Threat of Falsehood* (SBT, 2.15; Naperville, IL: Allenson, 1970), pp. 77-79. On the relationship of Jer 14.1–15.4* to II Zech, see ††6–12 above.

This passage features only one criterion—that is, a message-centered criterion. As history later proved, any message of unconditional peace was of human invention and, therefore, always false. In fact, any message of peace for Judah given before 587 BCE was suspect. Therefore, these peace prophets are false, for their message does not reflect Yahweh's will, but their own minds. These false prophets will incur the punishment of death 'by sword and famine' (14.15).

Jer 23.25-28[34]

Jeremiah's opponents, 'the prophets who prophesy lies', are judged false on the basis of two criteria: (1) The form of the prophets receiving their prophetic message (i.e. dreams) is declared unvalid:

> The prophet who has a dream, let him tell his dream; but the one who has my word, let him speak my word truthfully. What does chaff have to do with wheat? (Jer 23.28).

(2) The prophets are also accused of acting immorally by stealing prophetic words from one another (Jer 23.30).

Jer 27–29[*35]

In Jer 27*, Jeremiah wears a yoke to symbolize the divinely-willed subservience of Judah and other nations to Babylon and proclaims:

34. The following commentators assigned Jer 23.25-28 to the Deuteronomic redactor of Jer: Carroll, *From Chaos to Covenant*, pp. 173-79; Carroll, *Jeremiah*, pp. 469-74; Nicholson, *Jeremiah 1–25*, pp. 198-201; Nicholson, *Preaching*, pp. 102-103; Thiel, *Redaktion von Jeremia 1–25*, pp. 252-53. On the theme of false prophecy in Jer 23.25-28, the following works were also consulted: Bright, *Jeremiah*, pp. 147-55; Holladay, *Jeremiah*, I, pp. 641-46; Hyatt, *Jeremiah*, pp. 993-94; McKane, *Jeremiah*, I, pp. 588-97; Meyer, *Jeremia und die falschen Propheten*, pp. 132-40; Overholt, *The Threat of Falsehood*, pp. 63-68.

35. The following commentators assigned Jer 27–29* to the Deuteronomic redactor of Jer: Carroll, *From Chaos to Covenant*, pp. 158-97; Carroll, *Jeremiah*, pp. 523-68; Nicholson, *Jeremiah 26–52*, pp. 29-49; Nicholson, *Preaching*, pp. 93-103. Hyatt assigned Jer 27*; 29.10-20* to the Deuteronomic redactor of Jer ('Deuteronomic Edition of Jeremiah', pp. 259-60; *Jeremiah*, pp. 1009-22; see also Thiel, *Redaktion von Jeremia 26–45*, pp. 5-19). On the theme of false prophecy in Jer 27–29, the following works were also consulted: Bright, *Jeremiah*, pp. 195-212; de Vries, *Prophet against Prophet*, pp. 71-72; Holladay, *Jeremiah*, II, pp. 111-47; B.O. Long, 'The Social Dimensions of Prophetic Conflict', *Semeia* 21 (1981), pp. 31-53; D. Lys, 'Jeremie 28 et le probleme du faux prophete ou la circulation du sens dans le diagnostie prophetique', *RHPR* 59 (1979), pp. 453-82; H. Mottu,

> Do not obey your prophets, or your diviners, or your dreamers, or your
> soothsayers, or your sorcerers, who are saying to you, 'Do not serve the
> king of Babylon', for they are prophesying a lie to you…(27.9-10*. See
> also 27.14-16*).

Following his words against these false prophets, Jeremiah comes into
conflict with Hananiah, who prophesies the message that was exactly
what Jeremiah had denounced:

> Thus says Yahweh of Hosts, the God of Israel, I have broken the yoke of
> the king of Babylon. Within two years, I will bring back to this place all
> the vessels of the house of Yahweh…I will also bring back to this place
> Jeconiah, son of Jehoiakim, king of Judah, and all the exiles, oracle of
> Yahweh, for I will break the yoke of the king of Babylon (28.2-4).

Then Jeremiah gives a criterion by which their competing words
should be judged:

> The prophet who prophesies peace, when the word of the prophet comes
> to pass, it will be known that Yahweh truly sent the prophet (28.9).

Jeremiah then prophesies Hananiah's death within the year. According
to the fulfilment/non-fulfilment criterion, Hananiah is proven false,
for the exile continued. Likewise, Jeremiah is proven true, for
Hananiah died. In his letter to the exiles (Jer 29*), Jeremiah encour-
ages them to settle down in Babylon for the seventy-year period of the
exile and warns them against the message of false prophets:

> Do not let your prophets, who are among you, and your diviners deceive
> you. Do not listen to your dreams, which you dream, for they are pro-
> phesying a lie to you in my name. I did not send them, oracle of Yahweh
> (29.8-9*).

Jeremiah then proclaims the impending judgment upon other false
prophets who, like Hananiah, prophesy the lie of immediate restoration and will be similarly punished with death (29.21-32*). These
prophets are also accused as false for the immoral behavior of
adultery (29.23*).

In Jer 27–29* the following criteria are used to distinquish
true from false prophecy: (1) The central criterion in Jer 27–29* is
that of fulfilment/non-fulfilment: Hananiah's prophecy of impending

'Jeremiah vs Hananiah: Ideology and Truth in Old Testament Prophecy', *Radical
Religion* 2 (1975), pp. 58-67; Overholt, *The Threat of Falsehood*, pp. 24-48;
Wilson, *Prophecy and Society*, pp. 247-51.

restoration proved false; Jeremiah's prophecies of an extended exile and Hananiah's death proved true. This criterion is placed in the words of Jeremiah (28.9) and was most likely taken from Deut 18.21-22.[36] (2) Like the prophets in Jer 14.13*, Hananiah is judged false on the basis of his message of impending restoration (28.2-4). (3) The prophets Zedekiah and Ahab are judged false for the immoral act of committing 'adultery with their neighbors' wives' (29.23*). Any prophet who breaks Yahweh's law brings upon himself the required punishment of that offense and is understood to be a false prophet. Those prophets who are judged false by these criteria deserve the mandated punishment of death (28.16-17; 29.21*,32*; Deut 13.6; 18.20).[37]

Zech 10.2

> For the teraphim speak nonsense, and the diviners see lies; and they tell empty dreams and they give vain consolation. Therefore, they [the people] wander like sheep; they are afflicted, for there is no shepherd.

Here the theme of false prophecy has strong similarities with the Deuteronomic passages discussed above. To begin with, the means of intermediation—that is, the use of teraphim, divination and dream interpretation—is associated with false prophecy. Although the use of teraphim is not directly associated with false prophecy elsewhere, it was clearly considered an 'abomination' in Deuteronomic thought (1 Sam 15.23; 2 Kgs 23.24); therefore, any use of teraphim for the purposes of intermediation would be condemned as false prophecy. Divination is denounced as a false form of prophecy in Deut 18.10-11; Jer 14.14*; 27.9-10*; 29.8-9. Although the practice of dream interpretation appears to be accepted in some Yahwistic thought,[38] dream interpretation is considered false prophecy in Deut 13.2-6; Jer 23.28; 27.9-10*; 29.8-9. Therefore, the individuals depicted in Zech 10.2 are judged to be false prophets on the basis of their use of improper forms of intermediation. Also, the depiction of the people wandering

---

36. Bright, *Jeremiah*, p. 203; Carroll, *From Chaos to Covenant*, p. 187; Hyatt, *Jeremiah*, p. 1015; Nicholson, *Jeremiah 26–52*, p. 38; Nicholson, *Preaching*, p. 97.

37. The following commentators related the death sentence for these false prophets to the legal material in Deut: Bright, *Jeremiah*, p. 203; Carroll, *From Chaos to Covenant*, pp. 185, 187; Nicholson, *Preaching*, p. 97; Thiel, *Redaktion von Jeremia 26–45*, pp. 13-14.

38. For example, Gen 28.10-17; Num 12.6; Joel 3.1; see also 1 Sam 28.6.

aimlessly because they listened to these false prophets is simply the fulfilment of the unheeded warnings of Jeremiah concerning 'the [false] prophets' (Jer 14.13-14*; 23.25-28; 27.9-10*; 29.8-9*). Therefore, the theme of false prophecy in Zech 10.2 certainly reflects the Deuteronomic understanding of false prophecy.

Zech 13.2-6[39]

On the eschatological day of Yahweh ('on that day', 13.2, 4), Yahweh will 'remove the prophets and the spirit of uncleanness from the land' (13.2). Thereafter, any one who claims to be a prophet 'speaks lies in the name of Yahweh' (13.3) and should be put to death (13.3).

Within this passage are various indications of the use of Deuteronomic thought concerning false prophets, the most significant being the following: (1) The characterization of the false prophet as 'speaking lies' (דבר שקר) reflects Deuteronomic terminology (§5). (2) The punishment for false prophecy is capital punishment (Deut 13.6; 18.20; ‡1). (3) The responsibility for carrying out the capital punishment includes all members of the community, including family members (Deut 13.7-11; 21.18-21; ‡1). A new criterion for false prophecy is found here—that is, the chronological criterion stating that prophecy will cease at a certain time. This chronological criterion is consistent with other Deuteronomic literature.[40]

39. Works consulted for Zech 13.2-6 are the following: Bic, *Sacharja*, pp. 153-57; R. Brunner, *Sacharja* (Zürcher Bibelkommentare; Zürich: Zwingli Verlag, 1960), pp. 163-65; Dentan, 'Zechariah 9–14', pp. 1108-109; Elliger, *Buch der zwölf kleinen Propheten*, II, pp. 162-64; F.E. Greenspahn, 'Why Prophecy Ceased', *JBL* 108 (1989), pp. 40-41; Jones, *Haggai, Zechariah, Malachi*, pp. 165-68; Junker, *Die zwölf kleinen Propheten*, II, pp. 182-84; Lacocque, 'Zacharie 9–14', pp. 181-84, 194-95; Lamarche, *Zacharie IX–XIV*, pp. 88-90; Mason, *Haggai, Zechariah and Malachi*, pp. 120-23; Mason, 'Uses of Earlier Biblical Material in Zechariah 9–14', pp. 250-52; Ginsberg, 'Oldest Record of Hysteria'; Mitchell, *Haggai, Zechariah*, pp. 335-40; Otzen, *Studien über Deuterosacharja*, pp. 194-98, 265-66; Petersen, *Late Biblical Prophecy*, pp. 33-37; S.B. Reid, 'End of Prophecy in the Light of Contemporary Social Theory: A Draft', in *SBL 1985 Seminar Papers* (ed. K.H. Richards; Atlanta: Scholars Press, 1985), pp. 515-23.

40. See the following section, 'The "End" of Prophecy'.

Summary: False Prophecy in Deuteronomic Thought
A false prophet is a prophet who speaks lies (see §5) and who was not commanded by Yahweh (Deut 18.20; Jer 14.14*; 23.32; 29.23*);[41] therefore, the false prophet 'speaks rebellion against Yahweh' (Deut 13.6; Jer 28.16). The following criteria are given in Deuteronomic literature to distinguish true from false prophets:

1. The true prophet must be a prophet of Yahweh alone. This criterion is made explicit only in Deut 13.2-6 and 18.20, in which only monotheistic, Yahwistic prophets are considered to be true prophets.

2. The form of intermediation must follow acceptable practices. In Deut 18.10-11, the following types of intermediation are excluded as 'abominable practices' of the non-Israelites: divination, magic and necromancy. These practices are also associated with false prophecy in Jer 27.9-10*.[42] Although the interpretation of dreams is considered genuine elsewhere, three passages suggest that the interpretation of dreams was excluded as a means of true prophecy in Deuteronomic thought. In Deut 13.2-6, the false prophet is paired with 'the dreamer of dreams'. Jer 23.25-28 clearly asserts that dreams are not a means of true prophetic inspiration. Both Jer 14.14* and Zech 10.2 denounce the practices of divination (‡8) and the interpretation of dreams (†2). Also, in Jer 23.30, the practice of 'stealing' a prophetic message from another prophet is condemned. Therefore, any prophet who uses any means other than divinely initiated communication directly from Yahweh is a false prophet.

3. The Deuteronomists already knew who the true prophets were because of their hindsight—in other words, true prophets meet the fulfilment criterion, as explicitly stated in Deut 13.2-3; 18.22; and Jer 28.9. The fulfilment criterion played such an important role in Deuteronomic thought that, as is widely acknowledged, it provided a literary structure in DtrH.[43]

4. Any prophet who disobeys Yahweh's law is a false prophet and

41. Carroll (*Jeremiah*, p. 315) and Thiel (*Redaktion von Jeremia 1–25*, p. 186) noted that the phrase 'nor did I command them' in Deut 18.20; Jer 4.14; 23.32; 29.23 is distinctively Deuteronomic.

42. Nicholson, *Jeremiah 26–52*, p. 33.

43. E.g. von Rad, 'Deuteronomistic Theology of History', especially pp. 78-81. Nicholson (*Jeremiah 26–52*, pp. 40-41; *Preaching*, p. 97) related the fulfilment criterion in Jer 28.17 to the prophecy/fulfilment structure in DtrH.

deserves the punishment associated with the offense. For example, the prophets in Jer 29.21-23* are judged false because of adultery and therefore deserved death for adultery (Deut 22.22-27) and also for false prophecy (Deut 13.6; 18.20).

5. Closely related to the fulfilment criterion is the message-centered criterion focused on 'the promise of weal or woe'.[44] As history later proved, any prophetic message of unconditional peace based on Israel's election was false, especially concerning any prophet who preached such a message before 587 BCE (Jer 4.10; 6.14 = 8.11; 13.10; 14.13*; 23.17; 28.2-4). However, as evident in restoration language in Deuteronomic literature, true prophets were also portrayed as giving messages of hope, but these messages were conditioned upon the people's obedience to Yahweh's laws or announced a future time beyond the necessary period of punishment. Therefore, the false message of hope was either based upon an unconditional understanding of Israel's election and/or lacked the perception of Israel's disobedience to Yahweh's will.

6. Zech 13.2-6 features the chronological criterion, which establishes a time in the eschatological future after which all prophets by definition will be false because true prophecy will have ceased.[45]

Prophets judged false by these criteria are to be put to death (Deut 13.6; 18.20; 1 Kgs 13.22, 24-25; Jer 14.15*; 28.16-17; 29.21*, 32*; Zech 13.3) and no one, including family members, is excluded from the responsibility of carrying out this just punishment (Deut 13.7-11; Zech 13.3).

The 'End' of Prophecy

On the basis of their readings of Jer 23.33-40 and Zech 13.2-6, some scholars have assumed that prophecy ceased in the post-exilic period, declined significantly, or was transformed into something radically different. These same scholars, in attempting to account for this change in prophecy by reconstructing its causes, have reached divergent conclusions about the causes of the end of prophecy as illustrated in the following examples.[46] (1) The destruction of the Judean state in

44. Crenshaw, *Prophetic Conflict*, pp. 52-54.
45. See the following section, 'The "End" of Prophecy'.
46. See also the review of scholarship in T.W. Overholt, 'The End of Prophecy: No Players without a Program', *JSOT* 42 (1988), pp. 104-109.

587 BCE, especially the institution of the monarchy, led to the decline and eventual end of classical prophecy, for the institutions of monarchy and prophecy were closely related. The end of prophecy created a void in Israelite religion which was filled by apocalypticism, the child of a radically transformed prophetic tradition.[47] (2) Crenshaw argued that there were no objective criteria by which the people could discern a true from a false prophet; therefore, prophetic conflict was inevitable. This unresolvable problem of prophetic conflict led to the decline of prophecy and its transformation into apocalyptic and wisdom movements.[48] (3) The success of the pre-exilic prophets who foretold the destruction of Jerusalem and of the exilic prophets who foretold the restoration led to their canonization in written form. With this new emphasis upon prophecy as written text, the nature of prophecy became understood more and more as the process of interpreting these texts rather than listening to the oral messages of the 'prophets'. Therefore, the necessary orality of prophecy became devalued in the society, leading to the end of prophecy and its continuation in other forms, especially apocalypticism.[49]

In his article, 'Why Prophecy Ceased', Greenspahn reviewed literature that has been interpreted to express an end to prophecy, including passages in the Hebrew Bible, the New Testament, rabbinic literature and intertestamental material. He noted that various bodies of late literature assume the existence of prophets (such as 1QH 4.16; Josephus;[50] Lk 1.41, 67; 2.26, 36[51]) and concluded that

47. E.g. F.M. Cross, 'The Early History of the Apocalyptic Community at Qumran', in *Qumran and the History of the Biblical Text* (ed. F.M. Cross and S. Talmon; Cambridge, MA: Harvard University Press, 1975), p. 343. Hanson, *Dawn of Apocalyptic*, pp. 16, 282; Petersen, *Late Israelite Prophecy*, pp. 2-8, 97-98.

48. Crenshaw, *Prophetic Conflict*, p. 109.

49. E.g., Blenkinsopp, *History of Prophecy*, p. 256. Blenkinsopp, *Prophecy and Canon*, pp. 128-31; M.B. Dick, 'Prophetic *Poiesis* and the Verbal Icon', *CBQ* 46 (1984), pp. 226-46; R. Jacobson, 'Absence, Authority, and the Text', in *Glyph: Johns Hopkins Textual Studies* (Baltimore: Johns Hopkins University Press, 1978), III, pp. 140-41; R.A. Mason, 'The Prophets of the Restoration', in *Israel's Prophetic Tradition* (ed. R.J. Coggins, A. Phillips and M.A. Knibbs; Cambridge: Cambridge University Press, 1982), p. 142; E. Meyers, '*tora* in Hag 2.11'; Wilson, *Prophecy and Society*, pp. 106-108.

50. See also D.E. Aune, 'The Use of προπήτης in Josephus', *JBL* 101 (1982), pp. 419-21.

51. On Christian prophecy, see also D.E. Aune, *Prophecy in Early Christianity*

[a]lthough these authors may have held diverse views of prophecy, all of which differed from that of the Hebrew Bible, theirs are still Jewish views, none of which would be conceivable in a community that believed prophecy had come to an end.[52]

He correctly noted that 'one must distinguish what actually happened from what was later believed'.[53] Prophecy may have undergone a transformation, but this transformation was not so radical as to allow prophecy to be subsumed by apocalypticism and/or the wisdom movement.

If prophecy did not cease, then what should be made of the passages in the Hebrew Bible that have been interpreted to proclaim the 'end' of prophecy? In response to this question, the two key passages—Jer 23.33-40 and Zech 13.2-6—are discussed below. Since these two passages belong to Deuteronomic literature, the following discussion places them within the larger context of Deuteronomic thought. Both passages combine the Deuteronomic themes discussed in the two preceding sections, eschatology and false prophecy, within the context of the 'end' of prophecy.

Jer 23.33-40[54]

This passage is widely considered to concern the problem of false prophecy. The criterion given by which to judge false prophets is a

---

and the Ancient Mediterranean World (Grand Rapids, MI: Eerdmans, 1983); M.E. Boring, *Sayings of the Risen Jesus* (Cambridge: Cambridge University Press, 1982). On prophecy in the history of Judaism, see A.J. Heschel, *Prophetic Inspiration after the Prophets* (Hoboken: Ktav, 1990).

52. 'Why Prophecy Ceased', p. 41.

53. 'Why Prophecy Ceased', p. 37. Similarly, Overholt, 'The End of Prophecy', p. 103; Reid, 'End of Prophecy'.

54. The following commentators assigned Jer 23.33-40 to the Deuteronomic redactor of Jer: Carroll, *From Chaos to Covenant*, p. 180; Carroll, *Jeremiah*, pp. 474-80; Nicholson, *Jeremiah 1–25*, pp. 201-202; Nicholson, *Preaching*, pp. 102-103. Petersen (*Late Biblical Prophecy*, p. 29) concluded 'that the author may have been a member of the deuteronomistic school writing decades later than some of his earlier colleagues'. On the theme of the 'end' of prophecy in Jer 23.33-40, the following works were also consulted: Bright, *Jeremiah*, pp. 147-55; Holladay, *Jeremiah*, I, pp. 647-53; Hyatt, *Jeremiah*, pp. 995-96; McKane, *Jeremiah*, I, pp. 597-604; W. McKane, 'משא in Jeremiah 23.33-40', in *Prophecy* (ed. J.A. Emerton; Berlin: de Gruyter, 1980), pp. 35-54; Overholt, *Threat of Falsehood*, pp. 68-71.

chronological criterion—that is, there are no longer any true prophets; therefore, any one who proclaims 'an oracle of Yahweh' is a false prophet.[55] Like other Deuteronomic passages, the false prophet will be severely punished.

Although the problem of false prophecy is properly understood in this passage, its eschatological context has remained unnoticed. Yet, the language of Jer 23.33-40 surely reflects the eschatological time which is also described in Jer 31.31-34 as is evident in a comparison of the following verses:

> I will put my law within them, and on their hearts I will write it. And I will be their God and they will be my people. And no longer will each teach his neighbor and each his brother, saying, 'Know Yahweh', for all of them will know me, from the least to the greatest (Jer 31.33-34).

> Thus you may say, each to his neighbor and each to his brother, 'What has Yahweh answered?' and 'What has Yahweh spoken?' But 'oracle of Yahweh' you shall not mention again, for the oracle has become to each as his own word (Jer 23.35-36).

The similarity between these two passages is striking: in both, a former means of divine communication (respectively, law and prophecy) is made void, because all of the people will have direct, intimate knowledge of Yahweh and his word. The only significant difference between the thought expressed in these two passages concerns the two former modes of divine communication (prophecy and law). I contend that Jer 23.33-40 concerns, rather than the redactor's own time as is generally understood, the eschatological future. Therefore, the application of this chronological criterion to the problem of false prophecy also concerns the eschatological future, allowing for the possibility of true prophecy during the redactor's own time.

---

55. Carroll, *Jeremiah*, pp. 474-80; Overholt, *Threat of Falsehood*, pp. 70-71; Petersen, *Late Biblical Prophecy*, p. 28; Reid, 'End of Prophecy', p. 521. The following commentators did not interpret Jer 23.34-40 as expressing an 'end' to prophecy (however, they still understood Jer 23.33-40 within the context of false prophecy): Bright, *Jeremiah*, pp. 147-55; Carroll, *From Chaos to Covenant*, p. 180; Holladay, *Jeremiah*, I, pp. 647-53; Hyatt, *Jeremiah*, pp. 995-96; McKane, *Jeremiah*, I, pp. 597-604; McKane, 'משא'; Nicholson, *Jeremiah 1–25*, pp. 201-202; Nicholson, *Preaching*, pp. 102-103.

Zech 13.2-6[56]

As in Jer 23.33-40, a chronological criterion is applied to the problem of false prophecy—that is, on the eschatological day of Yahweh, prophecy will cease; thereafter, any one who calls himself a prophet is false and deserves death. The context of this chronological criterion has not been generally understood as eschatological, especially in discussions of the 'end' of prophecy.[57] However, the 17 occurrences of the phrase 'on that day'[58] tie together the various images in Zech 12–14, all of which describe the events that will occur 'on that day'. The nations will be judged (12.1-6; 14.12-15), a remnant of Judah and Jerusalem will be cleansed and protected (12.7–13.2; 13.7-9; 14.1-5, 10-12), 'Yahweh will become king over all the earth' (14.9), a remnant among the nations will worship Yahweh in Jerusalem (14.16-19), and the distinction between sacred and secular will be abolished (14.20-21). In this eschatological context we find an understanding of the end of prophecy (13.2-6).[59] Much like the lack of a need for a priest (14.21), there will be no need for a prophet. Like the abolition of the dichotomy between sacred and secular (14.20-21), the distinctions between prophet (as well as priest) and people will be abolished,

56. For a fuller discussion of the Deuteronomic influences in this passage, see above §§5, 17, ‡1, †3 and Chapter 5. Works consulted for Zech 13.2-6 are the following: Bic, *Sacharja*, pp. 153-57; Brunner, *Sacharja*, pp. 163-65; Dentan, 'Zechariah 9–14', pp. 1108-109; Elliger, *Buch der zwölf kleinen Propheten*, II, pp. 162-64; Ginsberg, 'Oldest Record of Hysteria'; Greenspahn, 'Why Prophecy Ceased', pp. 40-41; Jones, *Haggai, Zechariah, Malachi*, pp. 165-68; Junker, *Die zwölf kleinen Propheten*, II, pp. 182-84; Lacocque, 'Zacharie 9–14', pp. 181-84, 194-95; Lamarche, *Zacharie IX–XIV*, pp. 88-90; Mason, *Haggai, Zechariah and Malachi*, pp. 120-23; Mason, 'Uses of Earlier Biblical Material in Zechariah 9–14', pp. 250-52; Mitchell, *Haggai, Zechariah*, pp. 335-40; Otzen, *Studien über Deuterosacharja*, pp. 194-98, 265-66; Petersen, *Late Biblical Prophecy*, pp. 33-37; Reid, 'End of Prophecy'.

57. E.g. Greenspahn, 'Why Prophecy Ceased', pp. 40-41; Petersen, *Late Biblical Prophecy*, p. 33; Reid, 'End of Prophecy'.

58. Zech 12.3, 4, 6, 8 (2×), 9, 11; 13.1, 2, 4; 14.4, 6, 8, 9, 13, 20, 21. See above §19.

59. Another eschatological reading of Zech 13.2-6 is that of Mason. Mason concluded that Zech 13.2-6 'is really another instance of the fulfillment of Jeremiah's new covenant, that there will be no need for anyone to teach another saying' ('Uses of Earlier Biblical Material in Zechariah 9–14', p. 251). See also Jones, *Haggai, Zechariah, Malachi*, pp. 165-68; Lacocque, 'Zacharie 9–14', pp. 181-84, 194-95; Mason, *Haggai, Zechariah and Malachi*, pp. 120-23.

for each person will experience Yahweh directly.

Since this chronological criterion concerns the eschatological future, this criterion does not necessarily suggest that the author understood true prophecy as impossible within his own time. It is quite possible that the Deuteronomic redactor of II Zech understood some of the prophets of his own time to be true prophets, possibly including a prophet who produced the poetic source which he used in Zech 9. Therefore, the previous interpretations of Zech 13.2-6, which suggested that II Zech understood true prophecy to have already ceased, must be rejected.

However, it is also quite possible that this theme of the eschatological demise of prophecy functioned secondarily[60] as a diatribe against prophets who were contemporary to the Deuteronomic redactor of II Zech in that this passage states that prophecy is limited and transitory. Also, when the overall eschatology of II Zech is taken into account, the chronological criterion relating to true prophecy is just one part of a theological view that could have easily served as a basis of rejecting some contemporary prophets as false. For example, if a contemporary prophet strove to rally the people of Yehud into an armed struggle against the Persians (a politically and militarily ridiculous message, given the strength of the Persian empire), this prophet would be judged false on the basis of Yahweh's eschatological plan for, according to II Zech, Yahweh will initiate the full restoration of Israel above all the nations, not humans. Therefore, although the chronological criterion given in Zech 13.2-6 primarily emphasizes the eschatological future, it also probably had some contemporary implications as well, especially within the overall theological view of II Zech.

Summary: The End of Prophecy in Deuteronomic Thought

Assuming that both Jer 23.34-40 and Zech 13.2-6 represent Deuteronomic thought, we can conclude the following concerning the 'end' of prophecy in Deuteronomic theology: True prophecy remained a current possibility but was expected to follow certain definite criteria. These criteria include strict adherence to monotheistic Yahwism,

---

60. What I have argued here as 'secondary' is generally understood as the primary function of Zech 13.2-6 by those who have not fully recognized the eschatological context of this passage. E.g. E. Meyers, 'Messianism in First and Second Zechariah', p. 15.

acceptable forms of intermediation, fulfilment, moral behavior, and the appropriate response to the divine will concerning weal or woe. Although the application of such stringent criteria may have meant that every contemporary prophet would be judged false,[61] Deuteronomic thought still allowed for the hypothetical possibility of a true 'prophet like Moses'. However, since Deuteronomic eschatology included a belief that all of the people would have direct knowledge of Yahweh's law in their 'heart', the task of the 'prophet like Moses'— that is, divine communication in relationship to an outward law— would become null and void. In this eschatological time ('on that day'), any one who would proclaim oneself as a prophet would be considered false and deserving of the punishment of death. Hence, only one criterion—that is, the chronological criterion which states that at the eschaton there will be no true prophets—would apply in the eschatological future.

Summary of Chapter 8: A Preliminary Sketch of Deuteronomic Theology in the Post-Exilic Period

The Deuteronomists understood that the destruction of Jerusalem and the Babylonian exile were just punishment for disobedient Israel, a punishment that would lead to Israel's purification and, eventually, its restoration.[62] They also understood that the return to Jerusalem would only occur with divine initiation; therefore, the Persian conquest of the Babylonians and their subsequent policy of returning exiled populations to their homelands were probably viewed as the result of Yahweh's initiative to restore Israel to its rightful place among the nations as Yahweh's chosen people (see 1 Kgs 8.46-50). With this theological understanding of political history, the Deuteronomic school initially supported the Persian effort to restore the Jerusalem temple cult.

However, as the pressure of unfulfilled expectations concerning the rebuilt temple mounted, some impulses to resist the Persian control of the Jerusalem administration arose. In this context, the Deuteronomsts were caught in their own theological bind. On the one hand, they understood that Yahweh worked through the Persians in the defeat of

61. See Carroll, *From Chaos to Covenant*, p. 194.
62. 2 Kgs 17.1-18; 25.1-21; Jer 32.26-35; 52.4-27; see also §§4, 18, 20, 25, ‡5, †12, ‡20, ‡21, †23, ‡25, ‡26.

the Babylonians and the rebuilding of the Jerusalem temple as a part of Yahweh's plan to re-establish fully Israel and the Jerusalem cult; therefore, resistance against the Persians was theologically problematic. On the other hand, the Persian-supported restoration and Persian-controlled adminstration of Jerusalem was far from a full restoration of Israel wherein Yahweh's chosen people would be set over the nations (Deut 28.1; Zech 12–14); therefore, some resistance of the Jerusalem authorities became theologically possible. Keeping in line with the Deuteronomic emphasis upon Yahweh's initiative, the Deuteronomists resolved this theological bind by partially withdrawing from (or being pushed out of) the messy realm of political compromises into the hope for the eschatological day of Yahweh, 'at the end of days' (Deut 4.30), when Yahweh would initiate the full restoration of Israel, thereby creating a new world order. Within this new order, Yahweh would circumcise their hearts (Deut 30.6) and write his new covenant on their hearts (Jer 31.31-34) so that every one would intimately and directly know God. This new relationship would abolish the need for any intermediary, including prophets (Jer 23.34-40; Zech 13.2-6) and priests (Zech 14.20-21).

Nevertheless, since the eschaton had not yet come, what were Yahweh's people to do? The Mosaic covenant continued to be valid; therefore, the Deuteronomists summoned the people to 'return' to Yahweh's way.[63] This message of 'return' was the very message of 'his servants, the prophets'.[64] However, since Israel did not heed the warning of the prophets, the people of Israel were taken into exile. After sufficient punishment in Babylonian exile, Yahweh caused the Persians to defeat the Babylonians and begin the restoration of Israel. This Persian-supported restoration led to the rededication of the Jerusalem temple and some political autonomy for the Jewish province of Yehud; however, the full restoration of Israel had not yet occurred. Therefore, just as those who followed Moses in the wilderness had to follow Yahweh's commandments in order to enter the promised land (Deut), and just as the people of Israel had to adhere to Yahweh's commandments in order to remain in the land after the conquest

63. Wolff ('Kerygma') discussed the theme of 'return' as exilic; however, this theme would be equally at home in the disillusionment of the post-exilic period following the rebuilding of the temple.

64. 2 Kgs 9.7; 17.13, 23; 21.10; 24.2; Jer 7.25*; 25.4*; 26.5*; 29.19*; 35.15*; 44.4*; see also Zech 1.6.

(Jdgs), the post-exilic community also had to 'return' to Yahweh to avert further divine punishment as they awaited Yahweh's initiative for a full restoration at the eschaton.

In relationship to this theme of 'returning' to Yahweh's way, the Deuteronomists reminded the people to beware of the false prophets who had led them astray in the past, and who in the present threatened to lead them astray. Who were the false prophets of II Zech's time, according to the Deuteronomists? Here, the biblical material provides us with few clues. However, when one surveys the criteria given in Deuteronomic literature for distinguishing true from false prophecy, it is difficult imagining any prophet passing the test within his or her own time. Given these stringent criteria, it is quite possible that, although the Deuteronomists theoretically allowed the possibility of true prophecy to continue, they nevertheless judged all prophets during the time of II Zech to be false and, therefore, deserving of death (Deut 13.6; 18.20; 1 Kgs 13.22, 24-25; Jer 14.15; 28.16-17; 29.21*, 32*; Zech 13.3).

Since it was improbable that any contemporary prophet could fulfil the Deuteronomic school's stringent criteria (especially the fulfilment criterion), where were the people supposed to find Yahweh's word? They were to turn to the interpretations of the prophets that were included in the Deuteronomic school's canon, most significantly those that were probably redacted by the Deuteronomic scribes (DtrH, Jer, Hos, Amos, Mic, Zech). The reinterpretation of earlier prophetic literature in II Zech (especially DtrH, Isa, Jer, Ezek) is an excellent example of how the Deuteronomists came to view 'true' prophecy— that is, true prophecy was increasingly that which was found within their prophetic canon and its authoritative interpretation.

CONCLUSION

Although II Zech is generally accepted as a redactional addition to
I Zech, solutions concerning the problem of the source and redaction
of II Zech differ greatly. This study addresses the problem of source
and redaction in II Zech from a somewhat different perspective than
previous studies. Whereas earlier studies emphasized the relationship
between the 'prophet' of II Zech (or 'prophets') and the other late
biblical 'prophets', this work emphasizes the relationship between the
'redactor' of II Zech and other redactional material in prophetic
literature, especially that in DtrH and Jer. This change in emphasis to
'redactor' rather than 'prophet' for the individual responsible for
II Zech is based upon the following two observations: (1) More than
any other prophetic literature, II Zech depends upon earlier biblical
literature so much so as to suggest that this individual may have been a
'redactor', who works with written texts, rather than a 'prophet', who
communicates directly with the divine. (2) The prosaic character of
II Zech (excluding Zech 9) perhaps suggests that this individual was
not a 'prophet', who generally proclaimed Yahweh's word in a more
poetic form, but a 'redactor', who made use of prophetic themes and
formulas within his or her prosaic reinterpretation of earlier literature.

Because this redactional process within prophetic literature is found
elsewhere in the Hebrew Bible (especially in Jer), the relationship of
the redactor of II Zech with other redactions was addressed considering the possibility that the redactor of II Zech belonged to the
Deuteronomic school.

Although much work has been done in the area of inner-biblical
exegesis in II Zech, the overall connection between II Zech and
Deuteronomic literature has not been previously studied, perhaps
because most scholars assumed the following: (1) The individual
responsible for II Zech is a 'prophet' rather than a 'redactor'. (2) Jer
is not Deuteronomic literature. (3) The Deuteronomic school ceased
in the exilic period. Most commentators have thus emphasized the

relationship between the 'prophet' of II Zech and the 'prophets' of the Latter Prophets but have not fully explored the possibility of Deuteronomic influence on II Zech. With these presuppositions rejected, the possibility of the Deuteronomic redaction of Zech appears more probable.

In Part I, I critiqued the widely held view that the Deuteronomic school ceased in the Babylonian exile, which assumes Noth's exilic date for DtrH. Noth's argument also influenced Hyatt's exilic date for the Deuteronomic redaction of Jer, which in turn has influenced numerous discussions of Jer. Noth's and Hyatt's arguments for these exilic dates are based upon the observation that the narrative in both DtrH and Jer ends with Jehoiachin's release during the Babylonian exile (2 Kgs 24.18–25.30; Jer 52), and they both assume that the narrative must have been redacted shortly after this event. After showing the inadequacy of this argument, text-critical and thematic evidence was given that suggests that the Deuteronomic redaction of these works continued into the post-exilic period.

The suggestion that the Deuteronomic school's redaction of DtrH and Jer continued into the postexilic period opens up the possibility that II Zech was also produced by a Deuteronomic redactor. In Part II, this possibility was explored by presenting evidence for the strong influence of Deuteronomic literature (DtrH and Jer) upon II Zech. This evidence is of three kinds: (1) II Zech contains distinctively Deuteronomic phraseology (Chapter 3), (2) II Zech was significantly influenced by several Deuteronomic passages in DtrH and Jer (Deut 13.2-6; 28; Jer 14.1–15.4; 23.1-8; 25.15-29, 34-38; 30–31) (Chapter 4), and (3) II Zech (except the poetry in Zech 9) evinces a high degree of Deuteronomic influence in its diction and imagery (Chapter 5). The strength of the parallels in vocabulary and themes suggests that II Zech (excluding Zech 9) is Deuteronomic prose similar to the redactional prose in Jer. Thus, with the addition of II Zech to I Zech, a Deuteronomic redactor brought Zech to its final canonical form (Chapter 6).

Chapter 7 explored the possible social setting of the Deuteronomic school in the post-exilic period. The Deuteronomists apparently returned to Jerusalem in the early post-exilic period with Persian authority to preserve the literature associated with the temple administration, probably coinciding with Zerubbabel's mission. This pattern, in which a native scribal group is commissioned by the Achaemenid administration to preserve their native religious texts, can be found elsewhere in the Achaemenid empire, including the contemporary mission of Udjahorresnet to Sais, Egypt. Within this official setting, the Deuteronomic school probably continued its scribal/redactional work on DtrH and Jer.

Although the Deuteronomic school returned to Yehud with Persian authority, conflict may have arisen later between the Jerusalem temple administration and the Deuteronomic school. This conflict probably arose because of a tension in the Deuteronomic understanding of history vis à vis Yahweh's use of foreign powers. The Deuteronomists understood that the destruction of Jerusalem and the Babylonian exile were Yahweh's punishment of disobedient Israel. The Persian conquest of Babylon was understood as Yahweh's punishment of the Babylonians; it opened the way for the restoration of Israel. The Persian-supported return of the exiles and the restoration of Jerusalem and Yehud was seen as the fulfilment of Yahweh's promise to restore Israel; therefore, Deuteronomic cooperation with the Persians was initially considered a fulfilment of Yahweh's will. However, the Persian-supported restoration of Jerusalem fell short of the Deuteronomic (and prophetic) vision of a full restoration of Israel, which would have included complete political autonomy and supremacy over the nations. Because the rededication of the Jerusalem temple did not lead to such a restoration, the Deuteronomists later became increasingly disenchanted with the Persian-controlled temple administration. This disenchantment was expressed in their increasingly eschatological understanding of history, which appears in II Zech but nevertheless draws upon earlier Deuteronomic thought. This Deuteronomic disenchantment may have been one element of the rationale for the imperial mission of Ezra, who was commissioned to go to Jerusalem and codify a (new) Jewish law—that is, this disenchantment may have contributed to some questioning of Persian authority. The possible conflict between the Deuteronomic school (and its canon) and Ezra (and his canon) may have led to the undercutting of the social support upon which the Deuteronomists had depended and, eventually, to their demise.

Chapter 8 presented a preliminary sketch of Deuteronomic thought in the post-exilic period, especially at the time of II Zech. Three theological themes were emphasized: eschatology, false prophecy, and the 'end' of prophecy. Within each of these themes passages in II Zech were compared with passages found in DtrH and Jer, showing the theological continuity among them. This sketch suggested that, as it became more disenchanted with its lot under the Achaemenid administration, the Deuteronomic school stressed more and more Yahweh's initiative as necessary for the full restoration of Israel. This emphasis possibly led to a more eschatological understanding of history (Zech 14), according to which at the eschaton Yahweh will directly initiate the full restoration of Israel. An important part of this full restoration would be a new order between Yahweh and the people, wherein the old covenant will be superceded and its functionaries—that is, the priests and prophets—will no longer be necessary (Jer 23.34-40; Zech 13.2-6; 14.20-21). In place of the old covenant, Yahweh will circumcise their hearts (Deut 30.6) and will write the 'new covenant' into their hearts (Jer 31.31-34), thereby making the new order permanent.

In summary: The prose in II Zech (10–14) was perhaps produced by a Deuteronomic scribe/redactor. I Zech may reflect a theological stance which was closely associated with that of the Deuteronomic school (DtrH and Jer) in the early post-exilic period—that is, the Persian-supported restoration was within Yahweh's plan for the future full restoration of Israel; therefore, cooperation was in obedience to Yahweh's will. However, after the rededication of the Jerusalem temple, the full restoration did not occur; Yehud and the Jerusalem temple administration remained under Persian control. Therefore, the Deuteronomists became increasingly disenchanted with the temple administration, as is evident in its increasingly eschatological outlook. Because of this later disenchantment, I Zech was reinterpreted in and by the addition of the more eschatological Deuteronomic prose in II Zech, which emphasized Yahweh's initiative in the full restoration of Israel.

BIBLIOGRAPHY

Achtemeier, E.R. *Nahum–Malachi*. IBC. Atlanta: John Knox, 1986.

Ackroyd, P.R. 'The Historical Literature'. In *The Hebrew Bible and its Modern Interpreters*, pp. 297-323. SBLBMI, 1. Ed. D.A. Knight and G.M. Tucker. Philadelphia: Fortress Press; Chico: Scholars Press, 1985.

—'The Jewish Community in Palestine in the Persian Period'. In *Cambridge History of Judaism*, pp. 130-61. Ed. W.D. Davies and L. Finkelstein. Cambridge: Cambridge University Press, 1984.

—'A Judgment Narrative between Kings and Chronicles? An Approach to Amos 7:9-17'. In *Canon and Authority: Essays in Old Testament Religion and Theology*, pp. 71-87. Ed. G.W. Coats and B.O. Long. Philadelphia: Fortress Press, 1977.

Amsler, Samuel. 'Amos, prophète de la onzième heure'. *TZ* 21 (1965), pp. 318-28.

Auld, A.G. *I & II Kings*. Philadelphia: Westminster Press, 1986.

—*Joshua, Moses and the Land: Tetrateuch–Pentateuch–Hexateuch in a Generation since 1938*. Edinburgh: T. & T. Clark, 1980.

—'Judges 1 and History: A Reconsideration'. *VT* 25 (1975), pp. 261-85.

—'The "Levitical Cities": Text and History'. *ZAW* 91 (1979), pp. 194-206.

—'Prophets through the Looking Glass: Between Writings and Moses'. *JSOT* 27 (1983), pp. 3-23.

—'Prophets through the Looking Glass: A Response to Robert Carroll and Hugh Williamson'. *JSOT* 27 (1983), pp. 41-44.

—'Textual and Literary Studies in the Book of Joshua'. *ZAW* 90 (1978), pp. 412-17.

Aune, D.E. *Prophecy in Early Christianity and the Ancient Mediterranean World*. Grand Rapids, MI: Eerdmans, 1983.

—'The Use of προφήτης in Josephus'. *JBL* 101 (1982), pp. 419-21.

Avi-Yonah, M. 'The Walls of Nehemiah'. *IEJ* 4 (1954), pp. 239-48.

Barthélemy, D. 'Trois niveaux d'analyse'. In *The Story of David and Goliath: Textual and Literary Criticism. Papers of a Joint Research Venture*, pp. 47-54. OBO, 73. Ed. D. Barthélmy *et al.*; Fribourg: Editions Universitaires Fribourg; Göttingen: Vandenhoeck & Ruprecht, 1986.

Barthélemy, D., D.W. Gooding, J. Lust and E. Tov, *The Story of David and Goliath: Textual and Literary Criticism. Papers of a Joint Research Venture*. OBO, 73. Fribourg: Editions Universitaires Fribourg; Göttingen: Vandenhoeck & Ruprecht, 1986.

Begg, C.T. '2 Kings 20:12-19 as an Element of the Deuteronomistic History'. *CBQ* 48 (1986), pp. 27-38.

—'A Bible Mystery: The Absence of Jeremiah in the Deuteronomistic History'. *IBS* 7 (1985), pp. 139-64.

—'The Death of Josiah in Chronicles: Another View'. *VT* 37 (1987), pp. 1-8.

—'The Significance of Jehoiachin's Release: A New Proposal'. *JSOT* 36 (1986), pp. 49-56.

Bic, M. *Das Buch Sacharja*. Berlin: Evangelische Verlagsanstalt, 1962.

Bickerman, E.J. 'The Babylonian Captivity'. In *Cambridge History of Judaism*, pp. 342-58. Ed. W.D. Davies and L. Finkelstein. Cambridge: Cambridge University Press, 1984.

Birch, B.C. *The Rise of Israelite Monarchy: The Growth and Development of 1 Samuel 7–15*. SBLDS, 27. Missoula, MT: Scholars Press, 1976.

Blenkinsopp, J. *A History of Prophecy in Israel: From the Settlement in the Land to the Hellenistic Period*. Philadelphia: Westminster Press, 1983.

—'Interpretation and the Tendency to Sectarians: An Aspect of Second Temple History'. In *Jewish and Christian Self-Definition*, II, pp. 1-26. Ed. E.P. Sanders. Philadelphia: Fortress Press, 1981.

—'The Mission of Udjahorresnet and Those of Ezra and Nehemiah'. *JBL* 106 (1987), pp. 409-21.

—*Prophecy and Canon*. Center for the Study of Judaism and Christianity in Antiquity, 3. Notre Dame, IN: University of Notre Dame Press, 1977.

—'The Sage, the Scribe, and Scribalism in the Chronicler's Work'. In *The Sage in Israel and the Ancient Near East*, pp. 307-15. Ed. J.G. Gammie and L.G. Perdue. Winona Lake, IN: Eisenbrauns, 1990.

—'Temple and Society in Achaemenid Judah'. In *Second Temple Studies*. I. *Persian Period*, pp. 22-53. JSOTSup, 117. Ed. P.R. Davies. Sheffield: JSOT Press, 1991.

Boecker, H.J. *Die Beurteilung der Anfänge des Königstums in den deuteronomischen Abschnitten des I. Samuelbuches: Ein Beitrag zum Problem des deuteronomistischen Geschichtswerkes*. WMANT, 31. Neukichen–Vluyn: Neukirchener Verlag, 1969.

Bogaert, P.-M. 'Les mécanismes redactionnels en Jér 10,1-16 (LXX et TM) et la signification des supplements'. In *Le livre de Jérémie: Le prophete et son milieu des oracles et leur transmission*, pp. 222-38. BETL, 54. Ed. P.-M. Bogaert. Leuven: Leuven University Press, 1981.

—'Les trois rédactions conservées et la forme originale de l'envoi du Cantique de Moïse (Dt 32,43)'. In *Das Deuteronomium: Entstellung, Gestalt und Botschaft*, pp. 329-40. BETL, 68. Ed. N. Lohfink. Leuven: Leuven University Press, 1985.

Böhmer, S. *Heimkehr und neuer Bund: Studien zu Jeremia 30–31*. GTA, 5. Göttingen: Vandenhoeck & Ruprecht, 1976.

Boling, R.G. 'In Those Days There was no King in Israel', in *A Light Unto My Path*, pp. 33-48. Ed. H. Bream, R. Heim and C. Moore. Philadelphia: Temple University Press, 1974.

Boring, M.E. *Sayings of the Risen Jesus: Christian Prophecy in the Synoptic Tradition*. Cambridge: Cambridge University Press, 1982.

Bracke, J.M. 'The Coherence and Theology of Jeremiah 30–31'. PhD dissertation, Union Theological Seminary in Virginia, 1983.

Brettler, M. 'Ideology, History and Theology in 2 Kings XVIII 7-23'. *VT* 39 (1989), pp. 268-82.

Bright, J. 'The Date of the Prose Sermons of Jeremiah'. In *A Prophet to the Nations: Essays in Jeremiah Studies*, pp. 193-212. Ed. L.G. Perdue and B.W. Kovacs. Winona Lake, IN: Eisenbrauns, 1984 (= *JBL* 70 [1951], pp. 15-35).

—*Jeremiah*. AB, 21. Garden City, NY: Doubleday, 1965.

Brueggemann, W. 'The Keryma of the Deuteronomistic Historian'. *Int* 22 (1968), pp. 387-402.

—'The Social Significance of Solomon as a Patron of Wisdom'. In *The Sage in Israel and the Ancient Near East*, pp. 117-32. Ed. J.G. Gammie and L.G. Perdue. Winona Lake, IN: Eisenbrauns, 1990.

Brunner, R. *Sacharja*. Zürcher Bibelkommentare. Zürich: Zwingli Verlag, 1960.

Buss, M. 'An Anthropological Perspective upon Prophetic Call Narratives'. *Semeia* 21 (1981), pp. 9-30.

Caquot, A. 'Breves remarques sur l' allegorie des pasteurs en Zacharie 11'. In *Mélanges bibliques et orientaux en l'honneur de M. Delcor*, pp. 45-55. AOAT, 215. Ed. A. Caquot, S. Légasse and M. Tardieu. Neukirchen–Vluyn: Neukirchener Verlag, 1985.

Carpenter, J.E. and G. Harford, *The Composition of the Hexateuch*. New York: Longmans, Green & Co., 1902.

Carroll, R.P. *From Chaos to Covenant: Prophecy in the Book of Jeremiah*. New York: Crossroad, 1981.

—*Jeremiah: A Commentary*. OTL. Philadelphia: Westminster Press, 1986.

—*When Prophecy Failed: Reactions and Responses to Failure in the Old Testament Prophetic Traditions*. London: SCM Press, 1979.

Cazelles, H. 'Jeremiah and Deuteronomy'. In *A Prophet to the Nations: Essays in Jeremiah Studies*, pp. 89-111. Ed. L.G. Perdue and B.W. Kovacs. Winona Lake, IN: Eisenbrauns, 1984 (= 'Jérémie et le Deutéronme'. *RSR* 38 [1951], pp. 5-36).

—'פדה'. *ThWAT*, VI, pp. 514-22.

Chary, T. *Aggée–Zacharie, Malachie*. SB. Paris: Librairie Lecoffre, 1969.

Childs, B.S. *Introduction to the Old Testament as Scripture*. Philadelphia: Fortress Press, 1979.

—*Isaiah and the Assyrian Crisis*. SBT, 3. London: SCM Press, 1967.

—'The Canonical Shape of the Prophetic Literature'. *Int* 32 (1978), pp. 46-55.

—'A Study of the Formula, "Until This Day"'. *JBL* 83 (1963), pp. 279-92.

Clements, R.E. *Isaiah and the Deliverance of Jerusalem: A Study in the Interpretation of Old Testament Prophecy*. JSOTSup, 13. Sheffield: JSOT Press, 1980.

—'The Isaiah Narrative of 2 Kings 20:12-19 and the Date of the Deuteronomic History'. In *Isac Leo Seeligmann Volume: Essays on the Bible and the Ancient World*, III, pp. 209-20. Ed. A. Rofé and Y. Zakovitch. Jerusalem: E. Rubinstein's Publishing House, 1983.

—*Jeremiah*. IBC. Atlanta: John Knox, 1988.

—'Patterns in the Prophetic Canon'. In *Canon and Authority: Essays in Old Testament Religion and Theology*, pp. 42-55. Ed. G.W. Coats and B.O. Long. Philadelphia: Fortress Press, 1977.

—*Prophecy and Tradition*. Atlanta: John Knox, 1975.

Coggins, R.J. *Haggai, Zechariah, Malachi*. Sheffield: JSOT Press, 1987.

Cohn, E.W. 'The History of Jerusalem's Benjamin Gate: A Case of Interrupted Continuity?' *PEQ* 118 (1986), pp. 138-43.

Colenso, J.W. *The Pentateuch and the Book of Joshua Critically Examined*. London: Longman, Roberts & Green, 1862–79.

Craigie, Peter C. *The Book of Deuternomy*. NICOT. Grand Rapids, MI: Eerdmans, 1976.

Crenshaw, J.L. 'Education in Ancient Israel'. *JBL* 104 (1985), pp. 601-15.

—*Prophetic Conflict: Its Effect upon Israelite Religion*. BZAW, 124. Berlin: de Gruyter, 1971.

—'The Sage in Proverbs'. In *The Sage in Israel and the Ancient Near East*, pp. 205-16. Ed. J.G. Gammie and L.G. Perdue. Winona Lake, IN: Eisenbrauns, 1990.

Cross, F.M. 'The Early History of the Apocalyptic Community at Qumran'. In *Canaanite Myth and Hebrew Epic: Essays in the History of the Religion of Israel*, pp. 326-46. Cambridge, MA: Harvard University Press, 1973.

—'The Evolution of a Theory of Local Texts. In *Qumran and the History of the Biblical Text*, pp. 306-20. Ed. F.M. Cross and S. Talmon. Cambridge, MA: Harvard University Press, 1975.

—'A Reconstruction of the Judean Restoration'. *JBL* 94 (1975), pp. 4-18.

—'The Themes of the Book of Kings and the Structure of the Deuteronomic History'. In *Canaanite Myth and Hebrew Epic: Essays in the History of the Religion of Israel*, pp. 274-89. Cambridge, MA: Harvard University Press, 1973.

Dearman, J.A. 'My Servants the Scribes: Composition and Context in Jeremiah 36'. *JBL* 109 (1990), pp. 403-21.

Delcor, M. 'Les allusions a Alexandre le Grand dans Zach 9.1-8'. *VT* 1 (1951), pp. 110-24.

—'Les sources du Deutéro-Zacharie et ses procédés d'emprunt. *RB* 59 (1952), pp. 385-411.

Dentan, R.C. 'Zechariah 9–14'. *IB*, VI, pp. 1089-1117.

Dick, M.B. 'Prophetic *Poiesis* and the Verbal Icon'. *CBQ* 46 (1984), pp. 226-46.

Dietrich, W. *David, Saul und die Propheten: Das Verhältnis von Religion und Politik nach den prophetischen Überlieferungen vom frühesten Königtum in Israel*. BWANT, 7.2. Stuttgart: W. Kohlhammer, 1987.

—*Prophetie und Geschichte: Eine redaktionsgeschichtliche Untersuchung zum deuternomistischen Geschichtswerk*. FRLANT, 108. Göttingen: Vandenhoeck & Ruprecht, 1972.

Dozeman, T.B. 'The Way of the Man of God from Judah: True and False Prophecy in the Pre-Deuteronomic Legend of 1 Kings 13'. *CBQ* 44 (1982), pp. 379-93.

Driver, S.R. *A Critical and Exegetical Commentary on Deuteronomy*. ICC. Edinburgh: T. & T. Clark, 1965.

Dumbrell, William J. '"In Those Days There was no King in Israel; Every Man Did What was Right in his own Eyes". The Purpose of the Book of Judges Reconsidered'. *JSOT* 25 (1983), pp. 23-33.

Elliger, Karl. *Das Buch der zwölf kleinen Propheten*. II. *Die Propheten Nahum, Habakuk, Zephanja, Haggai, Sacharja, Maleachi*. ATD, 25.II. Göttingen: Vandenhoeck & Ruprecht, 1951.

Even-Shoshan, A., ed. *A New Concordance of the Bible: Thesaurus of the Language of the Bible: Hebrew and Aramaic Roots, Words, Proper Names, Phrases, and Synonyms*. Jerusalem: Kiryat Sefer, 1985.

Finley, T.J. 'The Sheep Merchants of Zechariah 11'. *GTJ* 3 (1982), pp. 51-65.

Fishbane, M. *Biblical Interpretation in Ancient Israel*. Oxford: Oxford University Press, 1985.

Freedman, D.N. 'The Earliest Bible'. *Michigan Quarterly Review* 22 (1983), pp. 167-75.

—'The Formation of the Canon of the Old Testament'. In *Religion and Law: Biblical,*

Judaic and Islamic Perspectives, pp. 315-31. Ed. E.B. Firmage, B.G. Weiss and J.W. Welch. Winona Lake, IN: Eisenbrauns, 1990.

—'The Law and the Prophets'. In *Congress Volume, Bonn 1962*, pp. 250-65. Ed. J.A. Emerton *et al.* VTSup, 9. Leiden: Brill, 1963.

Friedman, R.E. 'From Egypt to Egypt: Dtr[1] and Dtr[2]'. In *Traditions in Transformation: Turning Points in Biblical Faith*, pp. 167-92. Ed. B. Halpern and J.D. Levenson. Winona Lake, IN: Eisenbrauns, 1981.

—*The Exile and Biblical Narrative: The Formation of the Deuteronomistic and Priestly Works*. HSM, 22. Chico, CA: Scholars Press, 1981.

Funck, B. 'Zur Burger-Tempel-Gemeinde in nachexilischen Juda'. *Klio* 59 (1977), pp. 491-96.

Gammie, J.G. and L.G. Perdue (eds.), *The Sage in Israel and the Ancient Near East*. Winona Lake, IN: Eisenbrauns, 1990.

Ginsberg, H.L. 'The Oldest Record of Hysteria with Physical Stigmata, Zech 13:2-6'. In *Studies in Bible and Ancient Near East*, pp. 23-27. Ed. Y. Avishur and J. Blau. Jerusalem: E. Rubinstein's Publishing House, 1978.

Gooding, D.W. 'An Approach to the Literary and Textual Problems in the David–Goliath Story'. In *The Story of David and Goliath: Textual and Literary Criticism: Papers of a Joint Research Venture*, pp. 55-86. OBO, 73. Ed. D. Barthélemy *et al.* Fribourg: Editions Universitaires Fribourg; Göttingen: Vandenhoeck & Ruprecht, 1986.

Görg, M. 'ישׁב'. *ThWAT*, III, pp. 1012-32.

Gosse, B. 'Jérémie xlv et la place du recueil d'oracles contre les nations dans le livre de Jérémie'. *VT* 40 (1990), pp. 145-51.

—'Le recueil d'oracles contre des nations du livre d'Amos et l'histoire deuteronomique'. *VT* 38 (1988), pp. 22-40.

Gottwald, N.K. *The Hebrew Bible: A Socio-Literary Introduction*. Philadelphia: Fortress Press, 1985.

Gray, J. *I and II Kings: A Commentary*. OTL. Philadelphia: Westminster Press, 1970.

Greenspahn, F.E. 'Why Prophecy Ceased'. *JBL* 108 (1989), pp. 37-49.

Greenspoon, L.J. *Textual Studies in the Book of Joshua*. HSM, 28. Chico, CA: Scholars Press, 1983.

Gundry, R.H. *The Use of the Old Testament in St Matthew's Gospel*. NovTSup, 18. Leiden: Brill, 1967.

Halpern, B. *The First Historians: The Hebrew Bible and History*. San Francisco: Harper & Row, 1988.

Hanson, P.D. *The Dawn of Apocalyptic: The Historical and Sociological Roots of Jewish Apocalyptic Eschatology*. Philadelphia: Fortress Press, 1979.

—'In Defiance of Death: Zechariah's Symbolic Universe'. In *Love and Death in the Ancient Near East*, pp. 173-79. Ed. J. Marks and R. Good. Guilford: Four Quarters, 1987.

—'Israelite Religion in the Early Postexilic Period'. In *Ancient Israelite Religion: Essays in Honor of Frank Moore Cross*, pp. 485-508. Ed. P.D. Miller, Jr, P.D. Hanson and S.D. McBride. Philadelphia: Fortress Press, 1987.

—'Zechariah 9 and the Recapitulation of an Ancient Ritual Pattern'. *JBL* 92 (1973), pp. 37-59.

Haran, M. 'On Diffusion of Literacy and Schools in Ancient Israel'. In *Congress Volume, Jerusalem 1986*. Ed. J.A. Emerton. VTSup, 40. Leiden: Brill, 1988.

Harris, R. 'The Female "Sage" in Mesopotamian Literature (with an Appendix on Egypt)'. In *The Sage in Israel and the Ancient Near East*, pp. 3-17. Ed. J.G. Gammie and L.G. Perdue. Winona Lake, IN: Eisenbrauns, 1990.

Hentzschel, G. *1 Könige*. Neue Echter Bibel. Würzburg: Echter Verlag, 1984.

Herrmann, S. *Jeremia: Der Prophet und das Buch*. ErFor, 271. Darmstadt: Wissenschaftliche Buchgesellschaft, 1990.

—*Prophetie und Wirklichkeit in der Epoche des babylonischen Exils*. Stuttgart: Calwer Verlag, 1967.

—*Die prophetischen Heilserwartungen im Alten Testament*. BWANT, 5.5. Stuttgart: Kohlhammer, 1965.

Heschel, A.J. *Prophetic Inspiration after the Prophets: Maimonides and Others*. Hoboken, NJ: Ktav, 1990.

Hill, A.E. 'Dating Second Zechariah: A Linguistic Reexamination'. *HAR* 6 (1982), pp. 105-34.

Hobbs, T.R. *2 Kings*. WBC, 13. Waco, TX: Word Books, 1985.

Hoffmann, H.-D. *Reform und Reformen: Untersuchungen zu einem Grundthema der deuteronomistischen Geschichtsschreibung*. ATANT, 66. Zürich: Theologischer Verlag, 1980.

Hoftijzer, J. 'Remarks concerning the Use of the Particle אח in Classical Hebrew'. *OTS* 14 (1965), pp. 1-99.

Hoglund, K.G. *Achaemenid Imperial Administration in Syria-Palestine and the Missions of Ezra and Nehemiah*. SBLDS, 125. Atlanta: Scholar Press, 1992.

Holladay, W.L. 'The Background of Jeremiah's Self-Understanding: Moses, Samuel, and Psalm 22'. In *A Prophet to the Nations: Essays in Jeremiah Studies*, pp. 313-24. Ed. L.G. Perdue and B.W. Kovacs. Winona Lake, IN: Eisenbrauns, 1984 (= *JBL* 83 [1964], pp. 153-64).

—'A Fresh Look at "Source B" and "Source C" in Jeremiah'. In *A Prophet to the Nations: Essays in Jeremiah Studies*, pp. 213-28. Ed. L.G. Perdue and B.W. Kovacs. Winona Lake, IN: Eisenbrauns, 1984 (= *VT* 25 [1975], pp. 394-412).

—*Jeremiah*. 2 vols. Hermeneia. Philadelphia: Fortress Press, 1986, 1989.

—'Prototype and Copies: A New Approach to the Poetry–Prose Problem in the Book of Jeremiah'. *JBL* 79 (1960), pp. 351-67.

Hyatt, J.P. 'The Book of Jeremiah'. *IB*, V, pp. 777-1142.

—'The Deuteronomic Edition of Jeremiah'. In *A Prophet to the Nations: Essays in Jeremiah Studies*, pp. 247-67. Ed. L.G. Perdue and B.W. Kovacs. Winona Lake, IN: Eisenbrauns, 1984 (= In *Vanderbilt Studies in the Humanities*, I, pp. 71-95. Ed. R.C. Beatty, J.P. Hyatt and M.K. Spears. Nashville: Vanderbilt University Press, 1951).

—'Jeremiah and Deuteronomy'. In *A Prophet to the Nations: Essays in Jeremiah Studies*, pp. 113-27. Ed. L.G. Perdue and B.W. Kovacs. Winona Lake, IN: Eisenbrauns, 1984 (= *JNES* 1 [1942], pp. 156-73).

Jacob, E. 'Principe canonique et formation de l'Ancien Testament'. In *Congress Volume: Edinburgh 1974*. Ed. A. Alonso Schokel *et al.* VTSup, 28. Leiden: Brill, 1975.

Jacobson, R. 'Absence, Authority, and the Text'. In *Glyph: Johns Hopkins Textual Studies*, III, pp. 137-47. Baltimore: Johns Hopkins University Press, 1978.

Jamieson-Drake, D.W. *Scribes and Schools in Monarchic Judah: A Socio-Archeological Approach*. JSOTSup, 109. Sheffield: JSOT Press, 1991.

Jansma, T. 'Inquiry into the Hebrew Text and the Ancient Versions of Zechariah ix–xiv'. In *Oudtestamentische Studiën*, pp. 1-142. DEEL, 7. Ed. P.A.H. de Boer. Leiden: Brill, 1950.

Janzen, J. Gerald. *Studies in the Text of Jeremiah*. HSM, 6. Cambridge, MA: Harvard University Press, 1973.

Jepsen, Alfred. 'בטח'. *TDOT*, II, pp. 88-94.

Jones, D.R. 'A Fresh Interpretation of Zechariah IX–XI'. *VT* 12 (1962), pp. 241-59.

—*Haggai, Zechariah, Malachi*. Torch Commentary. London: SCM Press, 1962.

Jones, G.H. *1 and 2 Kings*. 2 vols. NCB. Grand Rapids, MI: Eerdmans, 1984.

Junker, H. *Die zwölf kleinen Propheten*. II. *Nahum, Habbakuk, Sophonias, Aggäus, Zacharias, Malachias*. Bonn: Peter Hanstein Verlagsbuchhandlung, 1938.

Kellermann, U. 'Der Amosschluss als Stimme deuteronomistischer Heilshoffnung'. *EvT* 29 (1969), pp. 169-83.

Kenik, H.A. *Design for Kingship: The Deuteronomistic Narrative Technique in 1 Kings 3:4-15*. SBLDS, 69. Chico, CA: Scholars Press, 1983.

Kippenberg, H.G. *Religion und Klassenbildung im antiken Judäa: Eine religionssoziologische Studie vum Verhältnis von Tradition und gesellschaftliche Entwicklung*. Göttingen: Vandenhoeck & Ruprecht, 1978.

Kramer, S.N. 'The Sage in Sumerian Literature: A Composite Portrait'. In *The Sage in Israel and the Ancient Near East*, pp. 31-44. Ed. J.G. Gammie and L.G. Perdue. Winona Lake, IN: Eisenbrauns, 1990.

Kreissig, H. 'Eine beachtenswerte Theories zur Organisation altvorderorientalischer Tempel-gemeinden im Achämenidenreich. Zu J.P. Weinbergs "Burger-Tempel-Gemeinde" in Juda'. *Klio* 66 (1984), pp. 35-39.

Lacocque, A. 'Zacharie 9–14'. In *Commentaire de l'Ancien Testament*, XIc, pp. 127-216. Neuchâtel: Delachaux et Niestlé, 1981.

Lamarche, P. *Zacharie IX–XIV: Structure littéraire et messianisme*. Paris: Gabala, 1961.

Lemaire, A. 'The Sage in School and Temple'. In *The Sage in Israel and the Ancient Near East*, pp. 165-81. Ed. J.G. Gammie and L.G. Perdue. Winona Lake, IN: Eisenbrauns, 1990.

Lemke, W.E. 'The Synoptic Problem in the Chronicler's History'. *HTR* 58 (1965), pp. 349-63.

—'Way of Obedience: I Kings 13 and the Structure of the Deuteronomistic History'. In *Magnalia Dei: The Mighty Acts of God*, pp. 301-26. Ed. F.M. Cross. Garden City, NY: Doubleday, 1976.

Levenson, J.D. 'From Temple to Synagogue: 1 Kings 8', In *Traditions in Transformation: Turning Points in Biblical Faith*, pp. 143-63. Ed. B. Halpern. Winona Lake, IN: Eisenbrauns, 1981.

—'The Last Four Verses in Kings'. *JBL* 103 (1984), pp. 353-61.

Lloyd, A.B. 'The Inscription of Udjahorresnet: A Collaborater's Testament'. *JEA* 68 (1982), pp. 166-80.

Lohfink, N., ed. *Das Deuteronomium: Entstellung, Gestalt und Botschaft*. BETL, 68. Leuven: Leuven University Press, 1985.

Long, B.O. *1 Kings with an Introduction to Historical Literature*. FOTL, 9. Grand Rapids, MI: Eerdmans, 1984.

—'Social Dimensions of Prophetic Conflict'. *Semeia* 21 (1981), pp. 31-53.

Lust, J. '"Gathering and Return" in Jeremiah and Ezekiel'. In *Le livre de Jérémie: Le prophete et son milieu des oracles et leur transmission*, pp. 119-42. Ed. P.-M. Bogaert. BETL, 54. Leuven: Leuven University Press, 1981.

—'The Story of David and Goliath in Hebrew and Greek'. In *The Story of David and Goliath: Textual and Literary Criticism. Papers of a Joint Research Venture*, pp. 5-18. OBO, 73. Ed. D. Barthélmy *et al.* Fribourg: Editions Universitaires Fribourg; Göttingen: Vandenhoeck & Ruprecht, 1986 (= *Ephemerides theologicae lovanienses* 59 [1983], pp. 5-25).

Luyten, J. 'Primeval and Eschatological Overtones in the Song of Moses (Dt 32,1-43)'. In *Das Deuteronomium: Entstellung, Gestalt und Botschaft*, pp. 341-47. BETL, 68. Ed. N. Lohfink. Leuven: Leuven University Press, 1985.

Lys, D. 'Jeremie 28 et le probleme du faux prophete ou la circulation du sens dans le diagnostic prophetique'. *RHPR* 59 (1979), pp. 453-82.

Mack-Fisher, L.R. 'The Scribe (and Sage) in the Royal Court at Ugarit'. In *The Sage in Israel and the Ancient Near East*, pp. 109-15. Ed. J.G. Gammie and L.G. Perdue. Winona Lake, IN: Eisenbrauns, 1990.

—'A Survey and Reading Guide to the Didactic Literature of Ugarit: Prolegomenon to a Study on the Sage'. In *The Sage in Israel and the Ancient Near East*, pp. 67-80. Ed. J.G. Gammie and L.G. Perdue. Winona Lake, IN: Eisenbrauns, 1990.

Martin, J.D. *The Book of Judges*. CBC. Cambridge: Cambridge University Press, 1975.

Mason, R.A. 'Some Examples of Inner Biblical Exegesis in Zech. IX–XIV'. *Studia Evangelica* 7 (1982), pp. 343-54.

—*The Books of Haggai, Zechariah and Malachi*. Cambridge: Cambridge University Press, 1977.

—*Preaching the Tradition: Homily and Hermeneutics after the Exile*. Cambridge: Cambridge University Press, 1990.

—'The Prophets of the Restoration'. In *Israel's Prophetic Tradition*, pp. 137-54. Ed. R.J. Coggins, A. Phillips and M.A. Knibb. Cambridge: Cambridge University Press, 1982.

—'The Relation of Zech 9–14 to Proto-Zechariah'. *ZAW* 88 (1976), pp. 227-39.

—'The Use of Earlier Biblical Material in Zechariah 9–14: A Study in Inner Biblical Exegesis'. PhD dissertation, University of London, 1973.

May, H.G. 'Towards an Objective Approach to the Book of Jeremiah: The Biographer'. *JBL* 61 (1942), pp. 139-55.

Mayes, A.D.H. *Deuteronomy*. NCB. Grand Rapids, MI: Eerdmans, 1979.

—*The Story of Israel between Settlement and Exile: A Redactional Study of the Deuteronomistic History*. London: SCM Press, 1983.

McCarter, P.K. *I Samuel*. AB, 8. Garden City: Doubleday, 1980.

McKane, W. *A Critical and Exegetical Commentary on Jeremiah*, I. ICC. Edinburgh: T. & T. Clark, 1986.

—'משא in Jeremiah 23:33-40'. In *Prophecy: Essays Presented to George Fohrer on his Sixty-Fifth Birthday, 6 September 1980*, pp. 35-54. Ed. J.A. Emerton. Berlin: de Gruyter, 1980.

—'Relations between Poetry and Prose in the Book of Jeremiah with Special Refence to Jeremiah iii 6-11 and xii 14-17'. In *A Prophet to the Nations: Essays in Jeremiah Studies*, pp. 269-84. Ed. L.G. Perdue and B.W. Kovacs. Winona Lake, IN: Eisenbrauns, 1984 (= In *Congress Volume: Vienna 1980*, pp. 220-37. Ed. J.A. Emerton. VTSup, 32. Leiden: Brill, 1981).

McKenzie, Steven L. '1 Kings 8: A Sample Study into the Texts of Kings Used by the Chronicler and Translated by the Old Greek'. *BIOSCS* 19 (1986), pp. 15-34.

—*The Chronicler's Use of the Deuteronomistic History.* HSM, 33. Atlanta: Scholars Press, 1985.

—'The Prophetic History and the Redaction of Kings'. *HAR* 9 (1985), pp. 203-20.

Mendecki, N. 'Deuterojesajanischer und Ezechielischer Einfluss auf Sach 10.8-10'. *Kairos* 27 (1985), pp. 340-44.

—'Dtn 30,3-4—nachexilisch?', *BZ* 29 (1985), pp. 267-71.

Mettinger, T.N.D. *The Dethronement of Sabaoth: Studies in the Shem and Kabod Theologies.* ET F.H. Cryer. ConBOT, 18. Lund: CWK Gleerup, 1982.

Meyer, I. *Jeremia und die falschen Propheten.* Göttingen: Vandenhoeck & Ruprecht, 1977.

Meyer, L.V. 'Allegory concerning the Monarchy: Zech 11:4-17; 13:7-9'. In *Scripture in History and Theology*, pp. 225-40. Ed. A.L. Merrill and T.W. Overholt. PTMS, 17. Pittsburgh: The Pickwick Press, 1977.

Meyers, C.L. and E.M. Meyers. *Haggai–Zechariah 1–8.* AB, 25B. Garden City, NY: Doubleday, 1987.

Meyers, E.M. 'Messianism in First and Second Zechariah and the "End" of Biblical Prophecy'. In *Dwight Young Festschift.* Winona Lake, IN: Eisenbrauns, forthcoming.

—'The Persian Period and the Judean Restoration: From Zerubbabel to Nehemiah'. In *Ancient Israelite Religion: Essays in Honor of Frank Moore Cross*, pp. 509-21. Ed. P.D. Miller, Jr, P.D. Hanson and S.D. McBride. Philadelphia: Fortress Press, 1987.

—'The Use of *tôrâ* in Haggai 2:11 and the Role of the Prophet in the Restoration Community'. In *The Word of the Lord Shall Go Forth*, pp. 69-76. Ed. C.L. Meyers and M. O'Conner. Winona Lake, IN: Eisenbrauns, 1982.

Mitchell, H.G., J.M.P. Smith and J.A. Bewer. *Haggai, Zechariah, Malachi and Jonah.* ICC. Edinburgh: T. & T. Clark, 1912.

Montgomery, J.A. *The Book of Kings.* ICC. Edinburgh: T. & T. Clark, 1951.

Mottu, H. 'Jeremiah vs Hananiah: Ideology and Truth in Old Testament Prophecy'. *Radical Religion* 2 (1975), pp. 58-67.

Mowinckel, S. *Zur Komposition des Buches Jeremia.* Kristiania: Jacob Dybwad, 1914.

Nelson, R.D. *The Double Redaction of the Deuteronomistic History.* JSOTSup, 18. Sheffield: JSOT Press, 1981.

—*First and Second Kings.* IBC. Atlanta: John Knox, 1987.

Nicholson, E.W. *The Book of the Prophet Jeremiah, Chapters 1–25.* CBC. Cambridge: Cambridge University Press, 1973.

—*The Book of the Prophet Jeremiah, Chapters 26–52.* CBC. Cambridge: Cambridge University Press, 1975.

—*Deuteronomy and Tradition.* Philadelphia: Fortress Press, 1967.

—*Preaching to the Exiles: A Study of the Prose Tradition in the Book of Jeremiah.* New York: Schocken Books, 1970.

North, R. 'Prophecy to Apocalyptic via Zechariah'. In *Congress Volume, Uppsala 1971*, pp. 47-71. Ed. H. Nyberg *et al.* VTSup, 22. Leiden: Brill, 1972.

Noth, M. *The Deuteronomistic History.* JSOTSup, 15. Sheffield: JSOT Press, 1981.

—*Überlieferungsgeschichtliche Studien.* Tübingen: Niemeyer, 1943.

O'Conner, K.M. *The Confessions of Jeremiah: Their Interpretation and Role in Chapters 1–25*. SBLDS, 94. Atlanta: Scholars Press, 1988.

Orlinsky, H.M. 'The Kings–Isaiah Recensions of the Hezekiah Story'. *JQR* 30 (1939–40), pp. 33-49.

Otzen, B. *Studien über Deuterosacharja*. ATDan, 6. Copenhagen: Prostant apud Munksgaard, 1964.

Overholt, T.W. 'Commanding the Prophets: Amos and the Problem of Prophetic Authority'. *CBQ* 41 (1979), pp. 517-32.

—'The End of Prophecy: No Players without a Program'. *JSOT* 42 (1988), pp. 103-15.

—'The Ghost Dance of 1890 and the Nature of the Prophetic Process'. *Ethnohistory* 21 (1974), pp. 37-63.

—'Remarks on the Continuity of the Jeremiah Tradition'. *JBL* 91 (1972), pp. 457-62.

—*The Threat of Falsehood: A Study in the Theology of the Book of Jeremiah*. SBT 2.15. Naperville, IL: Allenson, 1970.

Perdue, L.G. 'Jeremiah in Modern Research: Approaches and Issues'. In *A Prophet to the Nations: Essays in Jeremiah Studies*, pp. 1-31. Ed. L.G. Perdue and B.W. Kovacs. Winona Lake, IN: Eisenbrauns, 1984.

Perdue, L.G. and B.W. Kovacs, eds. *A Prophet to the Nations: Essays in Jeremiah Studies*. Winona Lake, IN: Eisenbrauns, 1984.

Person, R.F., Jr. 'II Kings 24,18–25,30 and Jeremiah 52: A Text-Critical Case Study in the Redaction History of the Deuteronomistic History'. *ZAW* 105 (1993), pp. 174-205.

Petersen, D.L. *Haggai and Zechariah 1–8*. OTL. Philadelphia: Westminster Press, 1984.

—*Late Israelite Prophecy: Studies in Deutero-Prophetic Literature and in Chronicles*. SBLMS, 23. Missoula, MT: Scholars Press, 1977.

—'The Temple in Persian Period Prophetic Texts'. In *Second Temple Studies*. I. *Persian Period*, pp. 125-44. JSOTSup, 117. Ed. P.R. Davies. Sheffield: JSOT Press, 1991.

Phillips, A. *Deuteronomy*. CBC. Cambridge: Cambridge University Press, 1973.

Pierce, R.W. 'Literary Connectors and a Haggai/Zechariah/Malachi Corpus'. *JETS* 27 (1984): 277-88.

Plöger, O. *Theocracy and Eschatology*. Oxford: Blackwell, 1968.

Pohlmann, K.-F. *Studium zum Jeremiabuch: Ein Betrag zur Frage nach der Entstehung des Jeremiabuches*. FRLANT, 118. Göttingen: Vandenhoeck & Ruprecht, 1978.

Polzin, R. *Late Biblical Hebrew: Toward an Historical Typology of Biblical Hebrew Prose*. HSM, 12. Missoula, MT: Scholars Press, 1976.

—*Moses and the Deuteronomist*. New York: Seabury, 1980.

—*Samuel and the Deuteronomist: A Literary Study of the Deuteronomic History*. San Francisco: Harper & Row, 1989.

Portnoy, S.L. and D.L. Petersen. 'Biblical Texts and Statistical Analysis: Zechariah and Beyond'. *JBL* 103 (1984), pp. 11-21.

Puech, E. 'Les écoles dans l'Israël preexilique: données épigraphiques'. In *Congress Volume, Jerusalem 1986*. Ed. J.A. Emerton. VTSup, 40. Leiden: Brill, 1988.

Rad, G. von. 'The Deuteronomistic Theology of History in the Books of Kings' In *Studies in Deuteronomy*, pp. 74-91. ET D.M.G. Stalker. Chicago: Henry Regnery Company, 1953.

—*Deuteronomy: A Commentary*. OTL. Philadelphia: Westminster Press, 1966.
—'Deuteronomy's "Name" Theology and the Priestly Document's "Kabod" Theology'. In *Studies in Deuteronomy*, pp. 37-44. ET D.M.G. Stalker. Chicago: Henry Regnery Company, 1953.
—*Old Testament Theology*. I. *The Theology of Israel's Historical Traditions*. ET D.M.G. Stalker. New York: Harper & Row, 1962.
—'The Promised Land and Yahweh's Land in the Hexateuch'. In *The Problem of the Hexateuch and Other Essays*, pp. 79-93. ET E.W. Trueman Dicken. New York: McGraw–Hill, 1966.
—*Studies in Deuteronomy*. SBT, 9. London: SCM Press, 1953.
Radday, Y.T. and M.A. Pollatschek. 'Vocabulary Richness in Post-Exilic Prophetic Books'. *ZAW* 92 (1980), pp. 333-46.
Radday, Y.T. and D. Wickman. 'The Unity of Zechariah Examined in the Light of Statistical Linguistics'. *ZAW* 87 (1975), pp. 30-55.
Redditt, P.L. 'Israel's Shepherds: Hope and Pessimism in Zechariah 9–14'. *CBQ* 51 (1989), pp. 631-42.
Rehm, M. 'Die Hirtenallegorie Zach 11,4-14'. *BZ* 4 (1960), pp. 186-208.
Reid, S.B. 'The End of Prophecy in the Light of Contemporary Social Theory: A Draft'. In *SBL 1985 Seminar Papers*, pp. 515-23. Ed. K.H. Richards. Atlanta: Scholars Press, 1985.
Robinson, J. *The First Book of Kings*. CBC. Cambridge: Cambridge University Press, 1972.
Rofé, A. 'The Battle of David and Goliath: Folklore, Theology, Eschatology'. In *Judaic Perspectives on Ancient Israel*, pp. 117-51. Ed. J. Neusner, B.A. Levine and E.S. Frerichs. Philadelphia: Fortress Press, 1987.
—'Classes in the Prophetical Stories: Didactic Legenda and Parable'. In *Studies on Prophecy: A Collection of Twelve Papers*, pp. 143-64. VTSup, 26. Leiden: Brill, 1974.
—'The End of the Book of Joshua according to the Septuagint'. *Henoch* 4 (1982), pp. 17-32.
—'The History of the Cities of Refuge in Biblical Law'. In *Studies in Bible*, pp. 205-39. Ed. S. Japhet. ScrHier, 31. Jerusalem: Magnes, 1986.
—'Isaiah 66:1-4: Judean Sects in the Persian Period as Viewed by Trito-Isaiah'. In *Biblical and Related Studies Presented to Samuel Iwry*, pp. 205-17. Ed. A. Kort and S. Morschauser. Winona Lake, IN: Einsenbrauns, 1985.
—'Joshua 20: Historico-Literary Criticism Illustrated'. In *Empirical Models for Biblical Criticism*, pp. 131-47. Ed. J.H. Tigay. Philadelphia: University of Pennsylvania Press, 1985 (= In *Isac Leo Seeligmann Volume: Essays on the Bible and the Ancient World*, I, pp. 137-50 (in Hebrew). Ed. A. Rofé and Y. Zakovitch. Jerusalem: E. Rubinstein's Publishing House, 1983).
—'The Monotheistic Argumentation in Deuteronomy 4:32-40: Contents, Composition, and Text'. *VT* 35 (1985), pp. 434-45.
—'The Vineyard at Naboth: The Origin and Message of the Story'. *VT* 38 (1988), pp. 89-104.
Rose, M. *Deuteronomist und Jawist: Untersuchungen zu den Beruhrungspunkten beider Literaturwerke*. ATANT, 67. Zürich: Theologischer Verlag, 1981.
Rudolph, W. *Haggai—Sacharja 1–8—Sacharja 9–14—Maleachi*. KAT, XIII 4. Gütersloh: Gütersloh Verlagshaus Gerd Mohn, 1976.

Russell, J.R. 'The Sage in Ancient Iranian Literature'. In *The Sage in Israel and the Ancient Near East*, pp. 81-92. Ed. J.G. Gammie and L.G. Perdue, Winona Lake, IN: Eisenbrauns, 1990.

Saebø, M. *Sacharja 9–14, Untersuchungen von Text und Form*. WMANT, 34. Neukirchen: Neukirchener Verlag, 1969.

Sanders, J.A. 'Heremeneutics in True and False Prophecy'. In *Canon and Authority: Essays in Old Testament Religion and Theology*, pp. 21-41. Ed. G.W. Coats and B.O. Long. Philadelphia: Fortress Press, 1977.

Schenker, A. 'Nebukadnezzars Metamorphose vom Unterjocher zum Gottesknecht. Das Bild Nebukadnezzars und einige mit ihm zusammenhängende Unterschiede in den beiden Jeremia-Rezensionen'. *RB* 89 (1982), pp. 498-527.

Schmidt, W.H. 'Die deuteronomische Redaktion des Amosbuches: Zu den theologischen Unterschieden zwischen dem Prophetenwort und seinem Sammler'. *ZAW* 77 (1965), pp. 168-93.

Schneider, D.A. 'The Unity of the Book of the Twelve'. PhD dissertation, Yale University, 1979.

Shenkel, J.D. *Chronology and Recensional Development in the Greek Text of Kings*. HSM, 1. Cambridge, MA: Harvard University Press, 1968.

Simon, Uriel. '1 Kings 13: A Prophetic Sign—Denial and Persistence'. *HUCA* 47 (1976), pp. 81-117.

Sjöberg, Å.W. 'The Old Babylonian Edubba'. In *Sumeriological Studies in Honor of Thorkild Jacobsen on his Seventieth Birthday*, pp. 159-79. Ed. S. Lieberman. AS, 20. Chicago: University of Chicago Press, 1975.

Smelik, K.A.D. 'Distortion of Old Testament Prophecy: The Purpose of Isaiah xxxvi and xxxvii'. In *Crises and Perspectives: Studies in Ancient Near Eastern Polytheism, Biblical Theology, Palestinian Archaeology and Intertestamental Literature*, pp. 70-93. Ed. A.S. van der Woude. OTS, 24. Leiden: Brill, 1986.

Smend, R. *Die Entstehung des Alten Testaments*. Stuttgart: W. Kohlhammer, 1981.

—'Das Gesetz und die Völker. Ein Betrag zur deuteronomistischen Redaktionsgeschichte'. In *Probleme biblischer Theologie*, pp. 494-509. Ed. H.W. Wolff. Munich: Chr. Kaiser Verlag, 1971.

Smith, G.A. *Jerusalem: The Topography, Economics and History from the Earliest Times to AD 70*, I. New York: Ktav, 1972.

Smith, M. *Palestinian Parties and Politics that Shaped the Old Testament*. London: SCM Press, 1987.

Soggin, J.A. *Judges: A Commentary*. OTL. Philadelphia: Westminster Press, 1981.

Spieckermann, H. *Juda unter Assur in der Sargonidenzeit*. FRLANT, 129. Göttingen: Vandenhoeck & Ruprecht, 1982.

Stade, B. 'Deuterosacharja. Eine kritische Studie'. *ZAW* 1 (1881), pp. 1-96; 2 (1882), pp. 151-72, 275-309.

Steck, O.H. 'Theological Streams of Tradition'. In *Tradition and Theology in the Old Testament*, pp. 183-214. Ed. D.A. Knight. Philadelphia: Fortress Press, 1977.

Stern, E. 'The Persian Period and the Political and Social History of Palestine in the Persian Period'. In *The Cambridge History of Judaism*. I. *The Persian Period*, pp. 70-87. Ed. W.D. Davies and L. Finkelstein. Cambridge: Cambridge University Press, 1984.

Stoebe, H.J. 'Die Goliathperikope 1 Sam 17,1–18,5 und die Text-Form der Septuaginta'. *VT* 6 (1956), pp. 397-413.

Stulman, L. *The Prose Sermons of the Book of Jeremiah: A Redescription of the Correspondence with Deuteronomistic Literature in Light of Recent Text-Critical Research.* SBLDS, 83. Atlanta: Scholars Press, 1986.

Swanson, S.R. 'Zechariah 1–8 and the Deuteronomistic Stream of Tradition'. Paper Presented to the Annual Meeting of SBL, Chicago, 1988.

Sweet, R.F.G. 'The Sage in Mesopotamian Palace and Royal Courts'. In *The Sage in Israel and the Ancient Near East*, pp. 99-107. Ed. J.G. Gammie and L.G. Perdue. Winona Lake, IN: Eisenbrauns, 1990.

Tadmor, H. and M. Weinfeld, eds. *History, Historiography and Interpretation.* Jerusalem: Magnes, 1983.

Talmon, S. 'Case of Faulty Harmonization'. *VT* 5 (1955), pp. 206-208.

—'The Emergence of Jewish Sectarianism in the Early Second Temple Period'. In *Ancient Israelite Religion: Essays in Honor of Frank Moore Cross*, pp. 587-616. Ed. P.D. Miller, Jr, P.D. Hanson and S.D. McBride. Philadelphia: Fortress Press, 1987.

Thiel, W. *Die deuteronomische Redaktion von Jeremia 1–25.* WMANT, 41. Neukirchen: Neukirchener Verlag, 1973.

—*Die deuteronomische Redaktion von Jeremia 26–52.* WMANT, 52. Neukirchen: Neukirchener Verlag, 1981.

Torrey, C.C. *Ezra Studies.* Chicago: University of Chicago Press, 1910.

Tov, Emanuel. 'The Composition of I Samuel 16–18 in the Light of the Septuagint Version'. In *Empirical Models for Biblical Criticism*, pp. 97-130. Ed. J.H. Tigay. Philadelphia: University of Pennsylvania Press, 1985.

—'Exegetical Remarks on the Hebrew Vorlage of the LXX of Jeremiah 27'. *ZAW* 91 (1979), pp. 73-93.

—'The Growth of the Book of Joshua in the Light of the Evidence of the LXX Translation'. In *Studies in Bible*, pp. 321-39. Ed. S. Japhet. ScrHier, 31. Jerusalem: Magnes, 1986.

—'L'incidence de la critique textualle sur la critique littéraire dans le livre de Jérémie'. *RB* 79 (1972), pp. 189-99.

—'The Literary History of the Book of Jeremiah in the Light of its Textual History'. In *Empirical Models for Biblical Criticism*, pp. 211-37. Ed. J.H. Tigay. Philadelphia: University of Pennsylvania Press, 1985.

—'The Nature of the Difference between MT and LXX'. In *The Story of David and Goliath: Textual and Literary Criticism. Papers of a Joint Research Venture*, pp. 19-46. OBO, 73. Ed. D. Barthélmy *et al.* Fribourg: Editions Universitaires Fribourg; Göttingen: Vandenhoeck & Ruprecht, 1986.

—'Some Aspects of the Textual and Literary History of the Book of Jeremiah'. In *Le livre de Jérémie: le Prophete et son Milieu. Les Oracles et leur Transmission*, pp. 145-67. Edited P.M. Bogaert. BETL, 54. Leuven: Leuven University Press, 1981.

Trebolle, J.C. 'Redaction, Recension, and Midrash in the Books of Kings'. *BIOSCS* 15 (1982), pp. 12-35.

Ulrich, E.C. *The Qumran Text of Samuel and Josephus.* HSM, 19. Missoula, MT: Scholars Press, 1978.

Unterman, J. *From Repentance to Redemption: Jeremiah's Thought in Transition.* JSOTSup, 54. Sheffield: JSOT Press, 1987.

Van Seters, J. 'Histories and Historians of the Ancient Near East: The Israelites'. *Or* 50 (1981), pp. 137-85.

—*In Search of History: Historiography in the Ancient World and the Origins of Biblical History*. New Haven: Yale University Press, 1983.

Van Winkle, D.W. '1 Kings XIII: True and False Prophecy'. *VT* 39 (1989), pp. 31-43.

Vanoni, G. 'Beobachtungen zur deuteronomistischen Terminologie in 2 Kön 23,25–25,30'. In *Das Deuteronomium: Entstellung, Gestalt und Botschaft*, pp. 357-62. Ed. N. Lohfink. BETL, 68. Leuven: Leuven University Press, 1985.

Veijola, T. *Die ewige Dynastie: David und die Entstehung seiner Dynasties nach der deuteronomistischen Darstellung*. Helsinki: Academia Scientiarum Fennica, 1975.

Vries, S.J. de. *1 Kings*. WBC, 12. Waco, TX: Word Books, 1985.

—'David's Victory over the Philistine as Saga and Legend'. *JBL* 92 (1973), pp. 23-36.

—*Prophet against Prophet: The Role of the Micaiah Narrative (1 Kings 22) in the Development of Early Prophetic Tradition*. Grand Rapids, MI: Eerdmans, 1978.

—'The Three Comparisons in 1 Kings XXII 4b and its Parallel and 2 Kings III 7b'. *VT* 39 (1989), pp. 283-306.

—*Yesterday, Today and Tomorrow: Time and History in the Old Testament*. Grand Rapids, MI: Eerdmans, 1975.

Wallis, G. 'Pastor Bonus. Eine Betrachtung zu den Hirtenstücken des Deutero- und Tritosacharja-Buches'. *Kairos* 12 (1970), pp. 220-34.

Weinberg, J.P. 'Der *'am ha'ares* des 6.–4. Jh. v.u.Z.' *Klio* 56 (1974), pp. 325-35.

—'Das *beit abot* im 6.–4. Jh. v.u.Z.' *VT* 23 (1973), pp. 400-14.

—'Demographische Notizen zur Geschichte der nachexilischen Gemeinde in Juda'. *Klio* 54 (1972), pp. 45-59.

—'*netinim* und "Söhne der Sklaven Salomos" im 6.–4. Jh. v.u.Z.' *ZAW* 87 (1975), pp. 355-71.

—'Probleme des Sozialökonomischen Struktur Judas vom 6. Jahrhundert v.u.Z. bis 1. Jahrhundert u.Z.' *Jahrbuch für Wirtschaftsgeschichte* (1973.1), pp. 237-51.

—'Zentral- und Partikulargewalt im achämenidischen Reich'. *Klio* 59 (1977), pp. 25-43.

Weinfeld, M. *Deuteronomy and the Deuteronomic School*. Oxford: Clarendon Press, 1972.

Weippert, H. 'Die "deuteronomistischen" Beurteilungen der Könige von Israel und Juda und das Problem der Redaktion der Königsbücher'. *Bib* 53 (1972), pp. 301-39.

—*Die Prosareden des Jeremiasbuches*. BZAW, 132. Berlin: de Gruyter, 1973.

Wells, R.D., Jr. 'Indications of Late Reinterpretation of the Jeremianic Tradition of the LXX of Jer 21.1–23.8'. *ZAW* 96 (1984), pp. 405-20.

Westermann, C. *Prophetische Heilsworte im Alten Testament*. Göttingen: Vandenhoeck & Ruprecht, 1987.

Whitley, C.F. 'The Term Seventy Years Captivity'. *VT* 4 (1954), pp. 60-72.

Whybray, R.N. 'The Sage in the Israelite Royal Court'. In *The Sage in Israel and the Ancient Near East*, pp. 133-39. Ed. J.G. Gammie and L.G. Perdue. Winona Lake, IN: Eisenbrauns, 1990.

Williams, R.J. 'The Sage in Egyptian Literature'. In *The Sage in Israel and the Ancient Near East*, pp. 19-30. Ed. J.G. Gammie and L.G. Perdue. Winona Lake, IN: Eisenbrauns, 1990.

—'Scribal Training in Ancient Egypt'. *JAOS* 92 (1972), pp. 214-21.

Williamson, H.G.M. 'The Death of Josiah and the Continuing Development of the Deuteronomic History'. *VT* 32 (1982), pp. 242-48.

—*Ezra, Nehemiah*. WBC. Waco, TX: Word Books, 1985.

—'Reliving the Death of Josiah: A Reply to C.T. Begg'. *VT* 37 (1987), pp. 9-15.

Wilson, R.R. *Prophecy and Society in Ancient Israel*. Philadelphia: Fortress Press, 1980.

Winkle, R.E. 'Jeremiah's Seventy Years for Babylon: A Re-Assessment. Part I: The Scriptural Data'. *AUSS* 25 (1987), pp. 201-14.

—'Jeremiah's Seventy Years for Babylon: A Re-Assessment. Part II: The Historical Data'. *AUSS* 25 (1987), pp. 289-99.

Wolff, H.W. *Hosea*. ET G. Stansell. Hermeneia. Philadelphia: Fortress Press, 1974.

—*Joel and Amos*. ET W. Janzen, S.D. McBride, Jr and C.A. Muenchow. Hermeneia. Philaldelphia: Fortress Press, 1977.

—'The Kerygma of the Deuteronomic Historical Work'. ET F.C. Prussner. In *The Vitality of Old Testament Traditions*, pp. 83-100. Ed. W. Brueggemann and H.W. Wolff. Atlanta: John Knox, 1975 (= 'Das Kerygma des deuteronomistischen Geschichtswerks'. *ZAW* 73 [1961], pp. 171-86).

—*Micha*. BKAT, 14.4. Neukirchen–Vluyn: Neukirchener Verlag, 1982.

Woude, A.S. van der. 'Die Hirtenallegorie von Sacharja 11'. *JNSL* 12 (1984), pp. 139-49.

Würthwein, E. *Die Bücher der Könige: 1 Könige 1–16*. ATD, 11.1. Göttingen: Vandenhoeck & Ruprecht, 1977.

—*Die Bücher der Könige: 1 Könige 17–2 Könige 25*. ATD, 11.2. Göttingen: Vandenhoeck & Ruprecht, 1984.

—'Die Erzählung vom Gottesmann aus Juda in Bethel. Zur Komposition von 1 Kön 13'. In *Wort und Geschichte*, pp. 181-89. Ed. H. Gese and H.P. Rüger. AOAT, 18. Neukirchen–Vluyn: Neukirchener Verlag, 1973.

Zenger, E. 'Die deuteronomistische Interpretation der Rehabilitierung Jojachins'. *BZ* 12 (1968), pp. 16-30.

Ziegler, J., ed. *Ieremias, Baruch, Threni, Epistula Ieremias*. Septuaginta Vetus Testamentum Graecum Auctoritate Societatis Göttingensis, 15. Göttingen: Vandenhoeck & Ruprecht, 1957.

Zimmerli, W. *Ezekiel*, II. ET J.D. Martin. Hermeneia. Philadelphia: Fortress Press, 1983.

INDEXES

INDEX OF REFERENCES

NEW TESTAMENT

Note: Chapters 3–4 have not been included in the following index.

INDEX OF AUTHORS

JOURNAL FOR THE STUDY OF THE OLD TESTAMENT

Supplement Series